W9-AAK-845

It Happened to Me

Series Editor: Arlene Hirschfelder

Books in the It Happened to Me series are designed for inquisitive teens digging for answers about certain illnesses, social issues, or lifestyle interests. Whether you are deep into your teen years or just entering them, these books are gold mines of up-to-date information, riveting teen views, and great visuals to help you figure out stuff. Besides special boxes highlighting singular facts, each book is enhanced with the latest reading lists, websites, and an index. Perfect for browsing, they have loads of expert information by acclaimed writers to help parents, guardians, and librarians understand teen illness, tough situations, and lifestyle choices.

1. *Epilepsy: The Ultimate Teen Guide,* by Kathlyn Gay and Sean McGarrahan, 2002.
2. *Stress Relief: The Ultimate Teen Guide,* by Mark Powell, 2002.
3. *Learning Disabilities: The Ultimate Teen Guide,* by Penny Hutchins Paquette and Cheryl Gerson Tuttle, 2003.
4. *Making Sexual Decisions: The Ultimate Teen Guide,* by L. Kris Gowen, 2003.
5. *Asthma: The Ultimate Teen Guide,* by Penny Hutchins Paquette, 2003.
6. *Cultural Diversity—Conflicts and Challenges: The Ultimate Teen Guide,* by Kathlyn Gay, 2003.
7. *Diabetes: The Ultimate Teen Guide,* by Katherine J. Moran, 2004.
8. *When Will I Stop Hurting? Teens, Loss, and Grief: The Ultimate Teen Guide to Dealing with Grief,* by Ed Myers, 2004.
9. *Volunteering: The Ultimate Teen Guide,* by Kathlyn Gay, 2004.
10. *Organ Transplants—A Survival Guide for the Entire Family: The Ultimate Teen Guide,* by Tina P. Schwartz, 2005.

AUG 0 9 2012

Writing and Publishing

The Ultimate Teen Guide

Tina P. Schwartz

**Illustrated by
Conrad Locander**

It Happened to Me, No. 27

The Scarecrow Press, Inc.
Lanham • Toronto • Plymouth, UK
2010

Published by Scarecrow Press, Inc.
A wholly owned subsidiary of The Rowman & Littlefield Publishing Group, Inc.
4501 Forbes Boulevard, Suite 200, Lanham, Maryland 20706
http://www.scarecrowpress.com

Estover Road, Plymouth PL6 7PY, United Kingdom

British Library Cataloguing in Publication Information Available

Library of Congress Cataloging-in-Publication Data

Schwartz, Tina P., 1969–
   Writing and publishing : the ultimate teen guide / Tina P. Schwartz ; Illustrated by Conrad Locander.
      p. cm. — (It happened to me ; No. 27)
   Includes bibliographical references and index.
   ISBN 978-0-8108-5647-9 (hardcover : alk. paper) — ISBN 978-0-8108-6936-3 (ebook)
   1. Authorship—Juvenile literature. 2. Occupational training—United States—Juvenile literature.
   3. Vocational guidance—United States—Juvenile literature. I. Locander, Conrad. II. Title.
   PN159.S39 2010
      808'.02—dc22   2009026079

Printed in the United States of America

For my mother, Diane Purcell,
who believes in me always, no matter
what I attempt. Your support means
EVERYTHING to me.

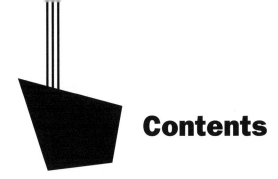

Contents

Acknowledgments

There are so many people to help bring a book to fruition. (To those whose names I've forgotten to include, my sincerest apologies!) I'd like to start with the patience of my family most of all. They had to be without me night after night while I camped out at my local Dunkin' Donuts to write this book. Many, many thanks go to my husband, Marc, and to my three wonderful children, Cameron, Heather, and Brandon.

Next, I'd like to thank my good friend Conrad Locander for his gorgeous artwork for this project. I love it, and I loved working together! You're the best, *Professor Whimsey*!

I would like to thank my other family members: Mom and Dad (Diane and Jim Purcell); my in-laws, Bob and Linda Schwartz; and many siblings with spouses, nieces, and nephews who continue to ask how the project is going.

It sounds funny, but I want to give sincere thanks to those late-night employees at the local Grayslake Dunkin' Donuts who kept my coffee mug full, even when all I had to offer was some linty change from the bottom of my purse. They always asked how it was going and listened sincerely, so thanks to the gang there, too!

Also, a huge thank you to my Ready Writers critique group—friends whose opinions, insights, and words of encouragement kept me going throughout this incredibly long project. They helped me through the yucky/boring phases of permissions, footnotes, and indexing (especially Lorijo Metz, Anne Courtright, and Roger Peck—thanks for your endless hours of help!) Without you all I'd surely go mad.

Acknowledgments

I'd like to thank all those who submitted works for the book (whether they made the final cut or not), along with those who granted interviews: Brent Runyon, Suzanne Firestone, Heidi Bee Roemer, Amy Palace, Stacy Chudwin, Eugene Fertelmeyer, Mary Wu, Sonya Kitchell, Jeni Stepanek (on behalf of Mattie Stepanek), Kevin Luthardt, Christopher Paolini, Farah Ahmedi, Shawn Wickersheim, Scott Bae, Boyd Herrin, and the many teens who gave their poetry and answered questionnaires for this book.

Last, but certainly not least, is my ever-patient editor, Arlene Hirschfelder, whose thumbprint on this book makes all the difference!

This book is one that I hope inspires many readers to continue their love of writing and reading. It is my pleasure to share with you my thoughts on the craft. Enjoy, and forge on!

Introduction

With so many choices and so many decisions to make, you probably wonder, "Where do I begin? Do I go to college or jump right into the workforce? If I go to college, should I start with a community college or go right to a big university? Do I declare a major right away, and if so, how do I choose from the hundreds of career paths I could take?"

Slow down! Although sometimes it seems like it, you do *not* need to have a master plan for your entire life figured out right this very minute! Like anything else, you do it with baby steps.

Take one thing you enjoy and are good at and start from there. For example, do you like to write? Did you know there are at least twenty vastly different careers just for writers? It's true! You can write novels, plays, TV or movie scripts, songs, stand-up comedy routines, press releases, and other public relations pieces. You could be an editor, a publisher, an advertising executive, a librarian, a journalist, or a teacher, just to name a few.

This book will show you how teens started off writing and "turned pro" while they were still young adults. Most people have traveled various paths to end up where they are. I was in public relations and media buying for years before becoming an author. Most, if not all, of my editors wear several "hats"— journalist, novelist, poet, and so on—in addition to editing.

Whether or not you know what you want to do, sometimes figuring out *how* to get started on a certain path can be the most daunting part. But you can really have fun if you know how. Glance through the table of contents; flip through pages to read sidebars filled with voices of various teens or biographies of your favorite authors. Everything you need to get started is right here in one book, *Writing and Publishing: The Ultimate Teen Guide.*

1 Reading

You might wonder why a book on writing starts out with reading. As any author will admit, one of the most important things you need to do each day is read. Read to find styles you like, and even styles you don't.

READING CAN BE A PROBLEM SOLVER FOR ALL WRITERS

Read to Learn Writing Skills

If you have a particularly hard time writing something—say, flashbacks, for example—you can try reading different styles from some of your favorite books. To help solve my own bout with the "flashback predicament," I began reading all the middle grade novels I could get my hands on, ones that used the diary format in particular. (Did you ever read Sharon Creech's *Absolutely Normal Chaos* or the two series, the Sisterhood of the Traveling Pants and the Princess Diaries? They all are crowd pleasers and for good reason. The characters are so honest and true, the reader feels like he or she *knows* them.) The more books you read that showcase a technique (such as flashback) you'd like to emulate, the more comfortable you'll feel using that technique in your own writing.

Another task writers have is choosing the point of view to write from. A story can be told in very different ways, depending on whose eyes the reader sees it through. By reading a book like Alex Sanchez's *Rainbow Boys*,[2] you can see an example of how to tackle this challenge. Sanchez uses three

I know how to read. What does that have to do with writing?

"If you don't have time to read, you don't have the time (or the tools) to write."
—Stephen King, *On Writing*[1]

1

⊚ ⊚ ⊚ ⊚ ⊚ ⊚ ⊚ ⊚ ⊚ ⊚ ⊚ ⊚ ⊚ ⊚

TEEN WRITER AMY PALACE DISCUSSES SOME OF HER FAVORITE READS[3]

What is your favorite book?
    The Puritans, by Jack Cavanaugh. It was one of the first books I read that was longer than 300 pages and it was a gripping novel that was completely unpredictable.

Who is your favorite author?
    T. S. Eliot is my favorite writer because I love his imagery, the deep concepts within his writing, the multi-level meanings, and his spectacular word choice.

What are some of the finest writing qualities you notice in certain authors?
    I love poetic detail and word images that authors paint in a reader's mind (such as John Updike in *The Centaur*). I also love embedded symbolism (like Ralph Ellison's references to vision and eyes in *The Invisible Man* as insights into a character's perspective on life), and I love when recurring themes within a story connect the seemingly unrelated events into a carefully manipulated web of ideas (like in Kurt Vonnegut's *Slaughterhouse Five*).[4]

different points of view in his novel. Although it may (or may not) take a while to catch on to whose perspective you are reading, by the end of a few chapters you will see that the three main characters' points of view are rotated. Each character is the narrator of a chapter; the narrator changes after *each* chapter. A writer must be quite advanced to pull off a three-person-point-of-view book, but Sanchez does it beautifully. It is a great way to present a story, once the reader catches on; but oftentimes you will lose some readers before they are willing to put in that extra effort to learn there are different points of view in the same story.

Let's say, during a writing dilemma, you can't find any books that suggest ways fix your problem. You need something more. Sometimes, you have no choice but to jump out of your isolation and find real, live, breathing people to help you out.

WORDS OF ADVICE FROM A GRANT WRITER

Grant writer Elizabeth Curtler says that reading helps you to be a better writer. She explains that you get new ideas from reading and seeing how words are used. Curtler believes the only way to learn how to write is to just do it! She also suggests asking people in your own life to read what you've written. For example, show it to someone at your church or synagogue, a local volunteer organization, or even a member of your family.[5]

Later on, in chapter 7, you'll read about how to find a mentor, a critique group, and/or a writing partner.

Read What You Can't Seem to Write

Another good thing to read is a genre you enjoy but cannot write. Say you love to read poetry but are not good at writing it. Read as much poetry as you can, and you'll begin to see different techniques and styles you can emulate.

AUDIO BOOKS CAN EASE YOU INTO THE HABIT

If you don't like to read—*Gasp! Do people still feel that way?*—try audio books. You can download them into your iPod or get books on tape or CD from your local library. Then turn them on and listen while you work out, walk to class, drive, or whenever you get a chance.

Okay, I'll admit, I tell people I'm not fond of reading . . . or at least I wasn't for a long time. They never believe it since I'm a writer. But as a child I didn't like to read because it came slow to me and I had to reread things often, as my mind would wander. (Have you ever read the same paragraph three times, and you still don't know what it says? It's the same concept.)

FINDING PODCASTS

If you're having a difficult time trying to decide what to read, check out podcasts or webcasts (under "Writing" at the iTunes store or on the Internet, and quite often for free) that feature authors and their books. In addition to discussing what their books are about, authors often go into their writing processes. There are many ways to find podcasts. Check out the following sites:

1. Barnes & Noble's "Meet the Writers" Podcasts.www .barnesandnoble.com/rss/mtw.xml (Copy this link into your web browser and then click on one of the links to get to the podcast site.)
2. Authors on Tour—Live! www.authorsontourlive.com (Link goes directly to the site.)
3. The Writer's Webcast. www.waukegan.org/RadioWaukegan/ default.asp#chrisA (Link goes directly to the site.)
4. Writers on Writing. feeds.feedburner.com/WritersonWritingPod cast(Copy this link into your web browser and then click on one of the links to get to the podcast site.)

THE MOVIE IS NEVER AS GOOD

Are you ever in the frame of mind where you don't feel like reading? I bet if you take a look at yourself, you'll see just how often you actually read. From flipping through magazines, to reading the jacket cover of a book in the store, to checking out articles online, you read several times a day and don't necessarily consider it "reading." But that's exactly what you are doing.

Perhaps you feel that reading is a chore. Or if you're a slow reader, you might feel like it's easier to watch a two-hour movie rather than investing a week or two of your time to read a book. However, if you've ever seen a movie made from a book you know that, most often, the book is better. Why? Because you are in the minds and hearts of the characters in a book, and the time it would take to include every detail, thought, and nuance would turn each movie into a miniseries!

While an actor might be outstanding with body language and facial expressions, he or she simply can't convey the *exact* thoughts of a character by a look alone. You need to *read* his or her thoughts. Don't forget, nothing can be as horrifying, sweet, or painful as the emotions conjured up by your own imagination.

Many times books adapted to movies are quite good; and many times they are not. Most often moviemakers must make several big changes in order to translate into a different medium. Entire subplots get cut from movie versions of book adaptations due to time restraints of the average ninety-minute movie.

For example, did you know that *The Wonderful Wizard of Oz* book by L. Frank Baum is only one title in an entire series of books about the Land of Oz?[6] And that in the book, Dorothy wore *diamond* slippers, not ruby? It's true! Grab yourself a copy at the library. The ruby-colored shoes in the movie made more of an impact than white diamonds would have. The era of black-and-white movies was over and a vibrant color such as red emphasized the distinctiveness of the shoes, while showcasing the new and exciting movie feature—Technicolor.

While films are a wonderful medium and highly glamorized by the stars that appear in them, they are an entirely different form of entertainment. You cannot compare movies to reading a story. For one thing, the director is interpreting the story himself. How a scene turns out may or may not have been the screenwriter's intent. For that matter, an actor can have another interpretation or delivery that adds an entirely different nuance or tone to a scene.

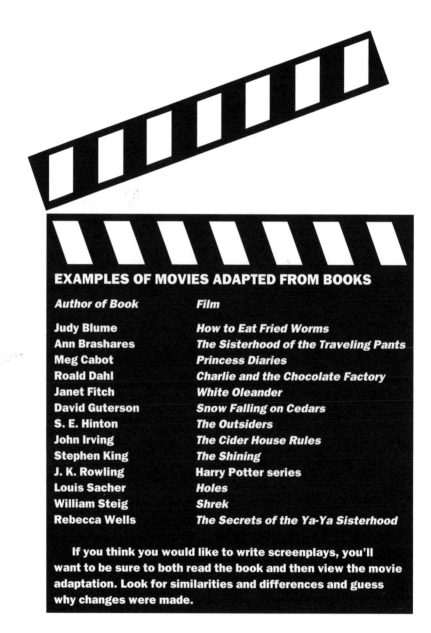

EXAMPLES OF MOVIES ADAPTED FROM BOOKS

Author of Book	Film
Judy Blume	How to Eat Fried Worms
Ann Brashares	The Sisterhood of the Traveling Pants
Meg Cabot	Princess Diaries
Roald Dahl	Charlie and the Chocolate Factory
Janet Fitch	White Oleander
David Guterson	Snow Falling on Cedars
S. E. Hinton	The Outsiders
John Irving	The Cider House Rules
Stephen King	The Shining
J. K. Rowling	Harry Potter series
Louis Sacher	Holes
William Steig	Shrek
Rebecca Wells	The Secrets of the Ya-Ya Sisterhood

If you think you would like to write screenplays, you'll want to be sure to both read the book and then view the movie adaptation. Look for similarities and differences and guess why changes were made.

The beautiful part of reading is that there is no limit to the stories or what can happen in the world that is created. For example, take the fantasy genre. Movies have come a long way over the years with special effects and computer-generated images, but they simply cannot compare to how far your imagination can take you when you see a scene in your mind. An example might be in *The Shining* by Stephen King.[7] The movie showed the main character, immortalized by Jack

Nicholson, going mad. However, it was hard to see exactly why. In the book, it is clear all along what this character thought, what he saw, what he heard that made him crazy. The horrors he experienced cannot be put into film the way a reader's imagination can play them out.

Another thing books can easily do is get readers inside a character's head. A character might be thinking something, and as a reader you can "hear" the person's thoughts. In movies, a narrator might have occasional voice-overs, but the actors tend not to play out inner thoughts of characters very often. If you've ever seen any of the movies in the sidebar on page 6, try reading the book and see which you like better.

MONKEY SEE, MONKEY DO

One secret to improving your writing in a specific genre is to find authors you like and, if possible, read all the books they've written. By doing this, you learn to appreciate their strong suits and perhaps even to emulate the qualities that fit you best.

If you write novels for middle grade, young adult, or adult readers and get stuck during the process, here's a tip to help you out. Find a new author and get hooked on him or her. Read all of his or her books, making note of styles that are prevalent in what you've read. Also pay close attention to how the writing style differs among various books by the same author.

Here are some great young adult authors to check out (in alphabetical order):

1. **Meg Cabot**
   The Princess Diaries (series)
   Teen Idol (New York: HarperCollins, 2004)

2. **Sharon Creech**
   The Wanderer (New York: HarperCollins, 2002)
   Absolutely Normal Chaos (Great Britain: Macmillan Children's Books, 1990)

3. **Patricia Reilly Giff**
   Pictures of Hollis Woods (New York: Dell Yearling, 2002)
   Lily's Crossing (New York: Dell Yearling, 1997)

4. Carolyn Mackler
The Earth, My Butt & Other Big Round Things (Cambridge, MA: Candlewick Press, 2003)

Love and Other Four-Letter Words (New York: Dell Laurel-Leaf, 2000)

5. Louis Sacher
There's a Boy in the Girls' Bathroom (New York: Dell Yearling, 1987)

Dogs Don't Tell Jokes (New York: Dell Yearling, 1991)

TO THE LIBRARY I GO

Dig around and find your old library card. Or go get a new card if yours expired back in fifth grade. Then start reading. Everything is free to check out at the library, so if you don't like a book return it. You haven't wasted a penny. If you love a book or an author, you can check it out again and again! Many libraries will also loan you new-release DVDs at no charge. You can get audio books and music from the library as well, without having to buy a whole CD just to listen to the two songs you like on it!

DIFFERENT MEDIUMS OF READING

Read a new genre you haven't tried before. Have you read any Clive Barker books? How about Danielle Steele? Romance and horror are both wonderfully intense types of stories. Below are ideas for different genres to read, with examples in each category. Perhaps it'll inspire you to choose something you hadn't thought of before.

Genre	*Example*
Autobiography	Ellen DeGeneres, *My Point . . . and I Do Have One* (New York: Bantam Books, 1995)
Biography	Maryann N. Weidt, *Oh, the Places He Went: A Story about Dr. Seuss—*

	Theodor Seuss Geisel (Minneapolis, MN: Carolrhoda Books, 1994)
Comic Book	Marvel Comics, *Superman* (DC Comics, 2008)
Fantasy/Magical Realism	Christopher Paolini, *Eragon* (New York: Alfred A. Knopf, 2002)
Historical Fiction	Dear America . . . (series by various authors) (New York: Scholastic)
Horror	Stephen King, *Pet Sematary* (Garden City, NY: Doubleday, 1983)
	R. L. Stein, *One Day at Horrorland* (New York: Scholastic, 2005)
How-To	Jason R. Rich, *Self-Publishing for Dummies* (Indianapolis, IN: Wiley, 2006)
Humor	Paul Reiser, *Couplehood* (New York: Bantam, 1995)
Mystery	Mark Haddon, *The Curious Incident of the Dog in the Night-Time* (New York: Doubleday, 2003)
Newspaper	*New York Times*; *Chicago Tribune*; *USA Today*
Nonfiction	Mitch Albom, *Tuesdays with Morrie: An Old Man, a Young Man, and Life's Greatest Lesson* (New York: Broadway, 2002)
Novel	Alice Sebold, *The Lovely Bones* (Boston: Little, Brown, 2002)
Periodical	*CosmoGirl!*; *TIME*; *People*
Play	William Shakespeare, *Romeo and Juliet* (New York: Washington Square Press, 1992)
Poetry	Shel Silverstein, *A Light in the Attic* (New York: HarperCollins, 1981)
Romance	Mari Mancusi, *Sk8er Boy* (New York: Smooch, 2005)
Science Fiction (Sci-Fi)	Star Trek (series by various authors)

| Self-Help | Stephen R. Covey, *The 7 Habits of Highly Effective People* (New York: Free Press, 1989) |
| | Barbara Mark and Trudy Griswold, *Angelspeake: A Guide—How to Talk with Your Angels* (New York: Simon & Schuster, 1995) |

FINDING LOVE

No, not *that* kind of love, silly! Once you find a *genre* you love, dig in and try writing something of your own. Think of it as an exercise in stretching your writing muscles. Do it just for fun! Just because you really like something doesn't mean you can do it, but you might find your niche that way. For example, I've always been a *huge* Stephen King fan but have yet to write anything in the "horror" category.

WHO WAS YOUR "FIRST"?

I can honestly say that the first author that made me *love* reading was S. E. Hinton. She was the first author who lured me to the library to check out every single book she'd written.

To this day, *The Outsiders* is my all-time favorite book, and S. E. Hinton remains my favorite author. It is the only book I've read over and over again. The fact that this tremendously honest portrayal of teenage boys in the 1960s, which remains a timeless story that still applies to today's youth, was written by a fifteen-year-old girl inspired me. Wow! I still can't believe it. How could she be in Ponyboy's head so well? Most schools have adapted this book into their curriculum, thus validating my belief in the strength of the story.

S. E. HINTON, AUTHOR

S. E. Hinton was first published at seventeen years old. Born in Tulsa, Oklahoma, in 1950, S. E. Hinton has always been a recluse, at least as far as the media is concerned. Rarely, if ever, granting interviews has been part of her mystery and intrigue.

When the twentieth anniversary edition of the movie of her first novel, *The Outsiders*, was released, she took time to speak with a reporter from the *New York Times*.

For those of you who aren't familiar with the author, "S. E." stands for Susan Eloise. When Hinton first published her novel, she started using her initials because being a female and a teen would have hindered her in the publishing world. After all, what could such a person know about boys in a gang? How could she so clearly know what was in their heads and hearts?

One of the reasons Hinton often wrote about boys was the belief that they would only read about other boys. Girls seemed to read about either gender, but for some reason, boys wouldn't.[8] (This is still somewhat true today.) Also, Hinton was a "tomboy" herself. Before the women's movement, if girls were put in some of the situations that the characters in her stories were placed in, it might not have been believable to her audience.

How Did She Get Published?

When her father was diagnosed with a brain tumor, S. E. Hinton was only fifteen years old. Writing became a form of escape. Hinton had a friend whose mother was a professional writer. After her friend showed her mother the manuscript, the mother gave Hinton the name of an agent to contact in New York. He liked her work and was able to sell it to the second publisher he submitted it to, Viking Press in New York City. That was an amazing feat, especially for an unknown, first-time author![9]

Viking bought the manuscript for a mere $1,000. By 2006, *The Outsiders* had sold more than fourteen million copies, four hundred thousand of them in 2004 alone!

Did It Take Long to Write Her Second Novel?

Unfortunately, the success of Hinton's first novel and the fact that she was so young and naïve to the business side of writing made the pressure to produce a second novel unbearable. When she was writing for her own enjoyment, it was fun. It was a pleasure. But when the press and fans began watching and waiting to see what she'd do next, it paralyzed her. Hinton couldn't write a follow-up story due to intense writer's block. Depression soon followed. Her boyfriend at the time, David—who she later married—made her write two pages a day "for fun." That's how she got out of her writing funk. If she didn't write her two pages, David wouldn't take her out for a date. It was as simple as that. How can a writer *not* be motivated by such "tough love"?

The book that came out of Hinton's "two-page-a-day" habit was *That Was Then, This Is Now.* It took all of three or four months to write, at the pace of two pages a day, every day. She got rolling with it, and never looked back.[11]

SAD MOTIVATION

S. E. Hinton was very close to her father, and when he died during her sophomore year in high school, she threw herself into her writing. Some suspect the loss of her dad might be part of the inspiration to have characters without parental figures.[10]

CHARACTER-DRIVEN TO THE CORE

In her books, Hinton tended to focus on characters above all else. Story was secondary, albeit tightly woven and wonderfully written. She created genuine characters and their own particular worlds, right down to their favorite color, food, and things of that nature. These details were often cut from her final manuscripts.

In a 2005 interview, Hinton admitted to being a character-driven author, explaining that plotting out story lines had been the hardest part of writing for her.[12] She said that she loved speaking as Ponyboy, since he was a lot like her. They shared many of the same values, including what was important to each of them in life, such as friendships. However, Hinton cites Tex McCormick (from the novel *Tex*) as the favorite (young) character she created. As he is the most childlike through the majority of the book, she appreciates that he then made the biggest steps in growing up and becoming an adult.

CHARACTER DRIVEN OR PLOT DRIVEN?

If you had to tell someone which type of reader you are, would you say you are character driven or plot driven? If you think

HINTON MOVIE TRIVIA

Since Hinton is my featured author for this chapter, I'd like to share a bit about how the success of her books allowed them to be adapted into movies. Here's a time-out for a fun quiz.

Q: What books by S. E. Hinton were adapted for the screen?

A: *Tex* (1982); *The Outsiders* (1983); *Rumble Fish* (1983); *That Was Then, This Is Now* (1985)[13]

Q: Which *one* of the four movies made from her novels did she *not* have an acting role in?

A: *That Was Then, This Is Now*

Q: What roles did Hinton play in the other three movies adapted from her books?

A: Mrs. Barnes in *Tex*, a nurse in *The Outsiders*, and a hooker on the strip in *Rumble Fish*.

Q: What two actors appeared in three of her four book adaptations on the big screen?

A: Matt Dillon played Dallas "Dally" Winston in *The Outsiders*, Tex McCormick in *Tex*, and Rusty James in *Rumble Fish*. Emelio Estevez played Keith "Two-Bit" Matthews in *The Outsiders*, Mark Jennings in *That Was Then, This Is Now*, and Johnny Collins in *Tex*.

back to some of your favorite books, is it the main character who makes you love and remember a story or simply the action? More often than not, it's a particular character. But some people just can't get enough of those action-packed series such as Lord of the Rings, Harry Potter, and similar tales.

Ms. Hinton wrote four complete drafts of *The Outsiders* over a period of eighteen months. She started with a forty-page

---

THE OUTSIDERS

The main character in *The Outsiders* is Ponyboy Curtis. He is a fifteen-year-old boy being raised by his two older brothers after their parents die in a car accident. Most of the kids in this book, along with most of Hinton's other books, are without any adult figures to tell them what to do. Kids have to figure things out on their own, but the forced independence is not portrayed as a good thing or a fun thing. Hinton's characters have hard lives, showing what it would be like without any adult role models.

Adolescence is a difficult time for anyone, whether he or she is rich or poor, has a big family or small, or has no family at all. But going through that transitional period without some guidance from an adult authority figure would make it unbelievably hard.

---

first draft. Then each time she went back, she'd add more details and thicken it up. The more the story was fleshed out, the more real the characters became. Hinton said she started writing because she'd read all of the horse books and cowboy books ever written. She wanted something more to read, about the things she was interested in. *The Outsiders* was written for her own entertainment. Since Hinton was an unpublished author, there weren't any pressures of deadlines, success, or expectations whatsoever.

THE BEGINNING OF REALISTIC TEEN LIT

Hinton's books were pioneering for the times. Books were not written as realistically back then. Most often they were upbeat with traditional "Hollywood endings" of "happily-ever-after." Hinton's novels showed the ugly side of life that Ponyboy, Dallas, Rusty-James, Bryon, and other now-famous characters dealt with. The fact that she wrote about death, violence, and prejudice was a huge deal that some celebrated and others ripped apart.[14]

CHAPTER 1 WRITING EXERCISE

Read a book in a genre, or category, you've never tried before. It could be nonfiction, such as a biography; a self-help book;

a how-to book; a romance novel; or historical fiction. Pick a book that you would normally never consider reading. While reading it, no matter how begrudgingly, pick out three positive aspects of the writing and one to three reasons why you didn't (or still don't) like the genre. Write a one-thousand-word story in this new genre.

NOTES

1. Stephen King, *On Writing: A Memoir of the Craft* (New York: Pocket Books, 2000), 142.

2. Alex Sanchez, *Rainbow Boys* (New York: Simon & Schuster, 2001).

3. Amy Palace, e-mail to author, January 2007.

4. Jack Cavanaugh, *The Puritans* (Colorado Springs: River Oak Publishing, 2005); John Updike, *The Centaur* (New York: Fawcett Crest, 1963); Ralph Ellison, *The Invisible Man* (New York: Random House, 1952); Kurt Vonnegut, *Slaughterhouse Five* (New York: Delacorte Press, 1969).

5. Diane Lyndsey Reeves, *Career Ideas for Kids Who Like Writing* (New York: Checkmark Books, 1998), 79.

6. Frank Baum, *The Wonderful Wizard of Oz* (New York: Signet Classics, 1984).

7. Stephen King, *The Shining* (Garden City, NY: Doubleday, 1977).

8. Dinitia Smith, "An Outsider, Out of the Shadows," *New York Times*, September 7, 2005, "The Arts" section, pp. E1, 7.

9. Smith, "An Outsider, Out of the Shadows," 7.

10. "Books," S. E. Hinton.com, www.sehinton.com (accessed June 2006).

11. "Books," S. E. Hinton.com.

12. falcon.jmu.edu/~ramseyil/hinton.htm (accessed June 19, 2006).

13. S. E. Hinton, *Tex* (New York: Dell, 1979); *The Outsiders* (New York: Puffin Books, 1967); *Rumble Fish* (New York: Delacorte Press, 1975); *That Was Then, This Is Now* (New York: Puffin Books, 1971).

14. Antoine Wilson, *S. E. Hinton* (New York: Rosen Publishing Group, 2003), 16.

2 Careers and Schooling

CAREERS IN WRITING: NOVEL WRITING IS *NOT* YOUR ONLY OPTION

If you like writing, there are a variety of careers you can choose. The career options are listed alphabetically, *not* in order of "best" to "worst" or by monetary compensation. This chapter offers a general overview of writing vocations and your choices depending on your strengths, personality, education, goals and interests. It will help you decide "what to do next": continue your education, get that résumé written, or compose and publish that story you've always wanted to write. (Note: Some careers, such as public relations, could have an entire chapter devoted to them. When that is the case, there will be a short explanation of the field, along with earning potential, and schooling recommended.)

ALWAYS A GOOD BACK-UP PLAN

Marketing courses are invaluable for almost *any* career choice you make. If you can market *yourself*, then you can place yourself in any career category you choose.

Q&A: FORMAL EDUCATION

What Relevant Classes Should I Take in High School and College?

This chapter discusses a wide variety of career choices you can make if you like to write; anything from advertising to editing, greeting card writing to song writing. Several of the writing careers listed include educational requirements, relevant courses, and related professional organizations.

What Extracurricular Activities and Classes Would Help Me Learn about the Craft *and* Look Good on a College Application and/or Résumé?

In high school and college, there are courses, classes, and clubs for creative writing, journalism, photojournalism, research, poetry, music, dance, acting, debate, school yearbook, and

When asked what high school, college, or extracurricular classes would be most helpful in developing and furthering one's talents and skills in the craft of writing, teens and young adults responded:

"I think there are some classes [that will help], but just know literature."

—Stefanie, age nineteen, Illinois (au pair from Germany)

"My school has something called forensics, which is like a debate team. You have to write strong arguments. That would help with a lot of writing careers or even law."

—C. G. S., age twenty

"There are music theory classes that would help music majors with writing . . . writing music."

—Stevie, age fifteen, Texas

school newspaper positions. Any of the creative arts can help make you a well-rounded individual who can create and inspire. You have to go outside your normal realm of thinking . . . go beyond that mind-set that writing is simply writing *novels*.

Classes—such as sociology, psychology, photography, art, directing, speech, computers, and political science—are excellent ways to develop new ways of contemplation that deviate from your normal thinking.

What Degrees Are Important (Bachelor's, Master's, Etc.)?

Many writing careers favor or require a college education and sometimes post-graduate work. And then others don't even require a GED (general equivalency diploma). A basic rule is to get at least a bachelor's degree. Its impact is almost what a high school degree was many years ago, the minimum requirement to get a job in a profession.

Does It Matter What College I Attend, If Any?

Depending on what career you choose, the exact school may or may not have a significant impact on your résumé. For example, if you'd like to be a journalist for the *New York Times*, going to Northwestern University in Evanston, Illinois, might provide more of an extra edge on a résumé than a community college would when you're vying for that all-important internship. However, if you wanted to be a stand-up comedian, college might simply be an elective. (Not to say that all comedians are uneducated; many have advanced degrees, especially those who are excellent political satirists like former *Saturday Night Live* (*SNL*) alumni Tina Fey, whose biography is featured in this chapter, or Dennis Miller.)

Noncredit Classes after High School

Before worrying about an advanced degree, consider taking a class at your community's park district or community college. You can take noncredit courses, often for low fees. You might even find a mentor in the form of an instructor or classmate.

People of all ages, with different writing experiences, career fields, and social and economic backgrounds enroll in community colleges. I think this is the best part of starting at this level, a nonthreatening "leisure" course for continuing education.

Your local high school may offer night courses that include writing classes. It's another economical way to get your feet wet and see if writing is something you want to pursue without making a huge monetary commitment.

PICKING THE RIGHT SCHOOL FOR YOU

With Literally Thousands of Colleges/Universities in the World, How Do I Even Begin to Choose One to Further My Writing?

Some universities in the United States and abroad are known for their outstanding programs in the arts, journalism, and communications. Depending on your budget, desired school location, choice of public or private institution, Ivy League aspirations, and a myriad of other considerations, you may feel overwhelmed before you even begin. Take it a tiny step at a time.

Step 1: When you begin to narrow down choices, it is often easier to start by what you'd rule *out*. For example, perhaps you want to go to an in-state school to keep costs down. That rules out all the out-of-state schools in the country, which typically run around $7,000 to $10,000 more per year than an in-state school (as of 2007).

Step 2: The next thing to do is rule out certain schools based on areas of study. Do you know what field of study you'd like to major in? Discard any school that doesn't offer a journalism program if you're interested in working for a newspaper, or dismiss any school without a music program, if you'd like to become a song writer. Remember, however, that around half of the college students who declare a major later change it, sometimes two or three times. So be sure to pick a college with a wide enough range of majors to accommodate this!

Step 3: Think of what *is* important to you . . . yes, *you*! Family pressure to attend someone's alma mater, for example, might weigh heavily on you, but you need to pick a school where you can be happy, inspired, and thriving. It's a huge time of growth. You will be on your own, perhaps for the first time, so it needs to be the right place for you.

WHAT WRITING CAREER INTERESTS YOU?

"Magazine editor."
—Natalie Bell, age fifteen, Arizona

"Literary agent or perhaps novelist."
—Feride, age twenty, Illinois

"Writing for magazines (like Dance Spirit magazine)."
—Meagan, age sixteen, Illinois

"Journalism, and I'd love to write poetry and short fiction, too!"
—Drew, age nineteen, Illinois

"I don't want to write as a career. I like to just write for myself."
—Stefanie, age nineteen, Illinois and Germany

"I'd like to write a book someday."
—Random, age fifteen, Illinois

"Sure, I think writing is a great way to express oneself. Maybe I'd go into journalism."
—Lindsey, age sixteen, Illinois

FREELANCE WRITER

One definition of freelancing is to work for yourself without being on staff or salaried with a specific company. Freelancers can work for several different employers without having permanent positions with any of them; they can be described as "independent contractors."

Freelance writers have jobs as varied as biographers, comedy writers, essayists, novelists, poets, and short story writers, with titles as different as author, copywriter, creative writer, playwright, screenwriter (film), scriptwriter (TV, stage), and technical writer. While "freelance" isn't a specific genre, it is a general term for a writer who goes from project to project independently. Freelancers don't work for one magazine, for example. They can work for various magazine publishers and write books simultaneously if they want. It is a great career choice if you get bored easily, are self-motivated, and don't necessarily want a nine-to-five day job. You work when and where you want.

Going to college is a big job. You'll work hard, learn lots, have fun, and mature. However, it is a huge investment of time and money that should not be taken lightly, whether you pay, earn scholarships, or have family members help foot the bill.

CAREERS IN WRITING

Advertiser

Do you *like* to watch TV commercials or look at billboards? (And not just during the Super Bowl!) Would you like to make mini-movies without having to live in Hollywood or Los Angeles? Then you might want to consider advertising.

Yes, advertisers are marketing people, strategists, and number crunchers, but just as important, they are writers. Do you like the challenge of transforming a refrigerator into something interesting or differentiating among various brands of diapers, soft drinks, or alcoholic beverages? How about producing a cool car ad where a sleek, German-designed automobile whips down the Autobahn at speeds over 100 mph? Sound like fun? Then agency life might be right for you.

Advertising agencies hire writers to perform tasks such as technical writing, business-to-business writing, and copywriting, to name a few. Often copywriters team with the art department for campaigns such as producing print ads for magazines and newspapers, outdoor advertising such as billboards or mobile ads on trucks, and broadcast spots shown on television and in movie theaters. Campaigns include various mediums combined to reach the biggest audience. Copywriters can write scripts for a TV ad or an ad you see before the previews at a movie theater. They also write the words on a billboard, or signage at a sporting event, or in magazine and newspaper ads.

Large companies often have their own "in-house" advertising department. The in-house part of a company serves only its own company's products and no other outside clients. In-house advertising copywriters, for example, would only write for their company, unlike freelance copywriters who could write advertisements for several clients.

RESPECTING OTHERS IN THE FIELD

At Columbia College in Chicago, Illinois, there was a class called Copywriter/Art Director Team. Students were paired up: one writer with one illustrator. Students would write almost an entire campaign (minus radio spots) consisting of a magazine/newspaper ad, a billboard, and a television spot. The class helped the artists and writers gain a healthy respect for each other and get a glimpse at what separate jobs entailed, including the process people go through to achieve their media goals.

INFO TO KNOW ABOUT BEING A COPYWRITER

Courses to Take

The top three classes recommended for advertising would be business, English, and speech classes; of course any creative writing classes would be helpful, too.

Minimum Education Level Required

Bachelor's degree

Professional Organizations for More Information

American Advertising Federation (www.AAF.org)
American Association of Advertising Agencies (www.aaaa.org)

Cartoonist

A cartoonist creates characters and draws for comics, political advertisements, greeting cards, television shows, and motion pictures or films, to name a few examples.

Not only does this job entail outstanding artistic skills, but the cartoonist must be a writer as well. Whether the image has words or not, the cartoonist will undoubtedly be conveying a story, either in one frame or an entire film. The point is that they are storytellers. A difficult part of cartooning is telling an entire tale or snapshot of a narrative in one frame or a small series of frames.

Illustrator and muralist Kevin Luthardt writes books that use few, if any, words. Yet the stories are clear and in-depth.

KEVIN LUTHARDT, MURALIST AND CHILDREN'S BOOK AUTHOR

Kevin Luthardt is the author and illustrator of six children's picture books: *Mine!* (2001), *Peep!* (2003), *Larabee!* (2004), *Hats!* (2004), *You're Weird!* (2005), and *Flying!* (2009). He illustrated two other picture books, *Zoom!* (2005) and *The Vowel Family: A Tale of Lost Letters* (2008).[1] A member of the Society of Children's Book Writers & Illustrators, Kevin is a muralist who uses art to teach and inspire students of all ages. He has spoken at more than 250 schools, libraries, and writing conferences.

Luthardt, born in June of 1973, grew up in Schaumburg, Illinois, a northwest suburb of Chicago. He says he grew up in a pretty simple, fun household as the middle kid with an older brother and younger sister. His mom is a registered nurse and his father a computer engineer; not the typical "artsy" family you might think of for such an expressive artist.[2]

Here are some Q&As from Luthardt's website, including some updated info that he sent me in an e-mail:[3]

Did you know you wanted to be an artist as a child?

Yes! I have been fanatical about drawing as far back as I can remember, admiring *Peanuts*, *Calvin and Hobbes*, plus Disney and Warner Brothers characters as well.

What were your favorite books growing up?

My favorite book as a child was *Mouse Soup*, by Arnold Lobel.[4] As I grew up I enjoyed Dr. Seuss books, Encyclopedia Brown series, and Agatha Christie mystery novels.

 INFO TO KNOW ABOUT BEING A CARTOONIST/ ARTISTIC STORYTELLER[5]

Courses to Take

A wide variety of art classes should be taken, including computer animation, as well as political science, history, and writing courses.

Minimum Education Level Required

Bachelor's degree

Professional Organizations for More Information

International Animated Film Society (www.asifa-hollywood.org)
National Cartoonists Society (www.reuben.org)
Society of Illustrators (www.societyillustrators.org)
Society of Children's Book Writers & Illustrators (www.scbwi.org)

Where do you get your ideas?

Personal experiences play a big role in generating ideas. I try to visit book stores and libraries about once a week to look at new books and illustrations. A lot of my inspiration comes from just sitting down with a pencil and paper and letting my mind wander.

What is your family like now?

I am married with a beautiful wife named Alicia and we have three sweet boys. We live in the Chicago area.

What advice would you give an aspiring artist or writer?

My advice is simple: Practice, practice, practice!!! The more you develop your skills as an artist or writer now, the stronger your work will be later. Work hard and remember you can also take writing and art classes outside of school. Read lots of books and look at lots of different artists' work. Most importantly, practice on your own.

Comedy Writer

Someone who specializes in comedy can write novels, sitcoms for television, and movies. There are comedians who do stand-up or who branch out into shows such as *SNL*, which requires high-volume writing on a daily basis. When you see a comedy special on HBO featuring someone like Chris Rock, you'd assume there is a team of writers working for him, and he

 INFO TO KNOW ABOUT BEING A COMEDY WRITER

Courses to Take

Helpful classes to take might include English, speech, theater, and dance.

Minimum Education Level Required

High school diploma

Professional Organizations for More Information

The Second City (www.secondcity.com)

memorizes the monologue and performs for an hour. Not so! Comedians write their own material. Though some may seem like the class clown types who are not into school or discipline, that isn't always the case. Sometimes, "creative types" might be perceived as silly, flighty, and even spacey; however, most just haven't found their niche yet. Once that energy is focused, they often skyrocket to success. Look at Adam Sandler. He worked his way up to *SNL*, then switched over to movies and started his own production company, Happy Madison. His company has turned out hits like *Click*, *Spanglish*, *Happy Gilmore*, and *Big Daddy*, to name a few. When you check credits, his name always appears on the "written by" line. So don't think of "funny types" as an undisciplined brood; they are some of the hardest working people in show biz.

TINA FEY, CLASS CLOWN GRADUATE

You may remember Tina Fey as Mrs. Norbury, the sometimes awkward but cool teacher of Lindsay Lohan in *Mean Girls*, but did you know she also wrote the screenplay? Fey has been a writer her whole life, and in 1999 she became the first female head writer on the long-running show *SNL*.[6] She is a bona fide triple-threat: writer, actress, comedian.

Unique Style of Her Own

Tina Fey's dry wit, somewhat smarty-pants style, matched by her signature no-nonsense glasses made her a perfect fit to share the *SNL* news desk with costar Jimmy Fallon. All the performers on *SNL* write material; they do their best to make up characters that will make it to the performance that airs on Saturday night. The competition is fierce, and successful characters have gone on to make television history and even hit the big screen.

She Makes Nerdy Cool

Tina Fey was born May 18, 1970, in Pennsylvania. She credits her mom for her dry wit, but her dad and brother, Peter, introduced her to classic comedy such as *Monty Python* and *SNL*.

In fact, she was too little to stay up late to watch *SNL*, so her brother would act out the skits for her the next day.

By middle school, Fey cracked jokes about school and became the class clown; by eighth grade, she wrote comedy reports for her classmates. She knew that comedy was going to be "her thing." She also had a quiet side, and was studious, pursuing activities such as drama, choir, the school newspaper, and the tennis team.

Fey started out as an English major at the University of Virginia, but quickly switched to drama. After graduation, she and a college friend headed to Chicago to study acting at Second City, a training center where many *SNL* actors and comedians she admired (such as Gilda Radner, John Belushi, and Dan Aykroyd) got their starts.

NO MEAN GIRL HERE

Rosalind Wiseman is the author of *Queen Bees and Wannabees: Helping Your Daughter Survive Cliques, Gossip, Boyfriends and Other Realities of Adolescence*.[7] The book, a national best-seller, was the inspiration for the film *Mean Girls*. Tina Fey bought the rights to write the screenplay and the rest is history.

A Healthy Addiction

At Second City, Fey became addicted to improvisation (or improv, where actors perform together without a script, making up skits as they go along, based on a theme or subject.) She explains it got her into the "writer" part of her brain, along with the actor part, all at the same time. It was the perfect combination.

After two years at Second City, Fey joined the touring group. In 1994, she was promoted to Second City's main stage in Chicago. She was in eight shows a week for more than two years, which she credits with helping her hone her skills as a writer *and* performer. Sharing some scripts with a friend of a friend at *SNL*, she was hired to work at the show and the rest is history.

Fey's writing and leadership is credited as one of the main reasons for *SNL*'s comeback. In 2002 the writing staff took home an Emmy (top prize for excellence in television) for the first time in years. She was one of only three female writers out of twenty-two staff writers. She created sketches to showcase some of her old Second City pals like Rachel Dratch and Amy Poehler (Poehler was also featured in the films *Mean Girls* and *Baby Mama*) to "up the female quota" on the show. For years, the men, including Mike Meyers, David Spade, Chris Farley, Adam Sandler, and Will Farrell to name a few, hogged the stage, winning most of the featured skits and becoming stars.

Fey left *SNL* in 2006 to pursue opportunities as head writer and performer on *30 Rock*, a comedy on NBC. She is a writer and performer not to be missed, so if you're the "class clown" like Fey that might not be a bad thing after all!

Editor

If asked, would you describe yourself as an avid reader? Would your local librarian describe you as a bookworm who constantly has a stack of items checked out from the library?

OBJECTIVITY NEEDED

Writers of any kind have a great opportunity to express their feelings and beliefs. That is not always a good thing, especially for nonfiction writing. (Granted, political commentators who are being *paid* to voice their opinions are exceptions.) However, for any other nonfiction writing, you must remain the objective observer, simply reporting the facts. The brutal truth is that your opinion doesn't matter, and it's often inappropriate to include it in any kind of factual article. Your primary goal is to report the facts in a clear, concise, interesting, and well-written way, allowing readers to form their own opinions after reviewing the information you've given them.

Arlene Hirschfelder and Tina Schwartz speak at a seminar for non-fiction writers on the author–editor relationship and how it develops.

Do you find yourself with a "wish list" of books you'd like to read this year, or do you subscribe to several magazines and/or newspapers? If any of this makes you smile and nod, then you might be the right type of person to be an editor.

Not only are some editors great writers, but they are most often such well-read people that they can instantly come up with several ideas, articles, and resources to enhance even the most solid manuscripts. Take the series editor for It Happened to Me (which you are now reading) for example. The editor sent me somewhere around thirty articles on organ transplants while I was writing another book in this series. Granted, it is a hot topic covered in the daily news. But she clipped every newspaper and magazine article she came across and sent it on to me.

Another important talent editors have is the ability to read a manuscript with an objective eye. If a writer gets overly emotional or opinionated about a particular point he or she wants to make, the editor has to reel the author in. That's why a relationship with your own editor is so important. He or she has to be comfortable enough to ask you, "Are you *sure* you'd like to share that particular experience?" or perhaps, "You're foisting your beliefs on readers. Simply relay the facts so they can draw their own conclusions." *Ouch!* I hate to admit it, but I've been told that by my own editor, and it is embarrassing. The bottom line is that an editor sees ways to make your material better. You need to trust in his or her vision and in the teamwork that is involved with making a book, article, or story the best it can be.

The Voice in my Head

One of the favorite things I still hear in my head is my editor's voice saying, "Have you thought of maybe . . . ," which is her polite way of trying to redirect me. Sometimes she tries to have me consider another perspective than the one I've taken, which inevitably results in a new and often better take on a situation. What's more, some of her suggestions have ended up sparking fresh ideas for entirely new chapters.

That is the most important word I can think of to describe an outstanding editor: *spark*! While not all author-editor relationships are close, ideally you should feel open enough to discuss, even debate, any issue.

Editors spend probably twelve hours a day reading, by my estimate. And that's just for their job! Many read for enjoyment, too, if time permits.

An editor must possess the ability to see mistakes, find inconsistencies, and maintain the overall tone of a piece. Have you ever worked on your school's newspaper or yearbook staff? Both are excellent places to start honing your skills.

Various Editorial Jobs

"Editor" is a sizeable generalization covering things such as magazines, books, and newspapers. It also covers other forms of media, such as film, television, and radio. Anything that requires a script will need editing. The Info to Know section on the next page contains information regarding school requirements, professional organizations, and websites for more information.[8]

INFO TO KNOW ABOUT BEING AN EDITOR[9]

Courses to Take

English, journalism, speech, and creative writing

Minimum Education Level Required

Bachelor's degree

Professional Organizations for More Information

National Newspaper Association (www.nna.org)
Magazine Publishers of America (www.magazine.org)

Niche Writer

If you have a specific expertise or interest in a subject, you can parlay it into something saleable. You need to find a niche, or specialized market, where you can showcase your talents. If, for example, you are a runner, you could write several articles that focus on different angles of the sport. Some refer to this as "slicing and dicing" where you use one event, subject, or idea to create several different articles to sell. In the sport of running, one article might be about marathons. Another might cover charity events—say a cancer marathon or some other fund-raiser. And yet another might be an "exercise with baby" or "getting into shape after childbirth" article featuring the latest in high-tech/high-impact three-wheeled strollers for runners with kids.

Another niche might be dancing. Say you are a volunteer at a local boys or girls club, and you teach hip-hop classes twice a week. You could write an article from the perspective of volunteering; another perspective might be about interning at a dance studio over the summer if you were a dance major in college. You could write an article from the angle of technical expertise, explaining all of the steps and how to do them, or deal with the history of hip-hop. Again, there are so many different ways you can position yourself as an expert. It depends on how you look at it. As a writer, it is all about perspective, through whose eyes you are telling a story, not to mention your specific reading audience.

The possibilities are endless, so look at your life and see what motivates you, what you are passionate about. What is *your* niche? It's a great place to start and find motivation.

Writer for High Interest/Low Reading Level

Hi/Lo books deal with age and reading level. It is an abbreviation for high interest/low reading level. For *Motocross Freestyle*, a nonfiction book on the extreme sport of motocross, one of the specifics (or specs) the editor dictated was that the audience is second to ninth graders.[10] The book must appeal to a second grader and a freshman in high school, and both students must be able to read it without feeling spoken down to or confused by the technical language. Really, now, if you were talking to a seven-year-old and a fourteen-year-old, don't you think your language might be a tad different between the two you're addressing? That is a challenge for any writer.

Ghostwriter

The term *ghost* does *not* refer to the horror genre or any supernatural activities. It simply means that although an author's name is on the cover of a book, technically it may have been written by someone else, most likely a professional writer. Many celebrities have written books or memoirs, for example. Some have actually *written* the books alone, but others rely on a ghostwriter. They may have come up with the concept and ideas they want conveyed, but when it comes to the actual text in the book, a professional *writer* is called in to do the work. A celebrity name will surely sell *many* more books than a relatively unknown author.

Why Would I Want to Be a Ghostwriter? Aren't Ghostwriters Usually Established or Even Successful Writers Already?

If you ghostwrite a celebrity book, the sales on it could be amazing, even if it isn't one of the most successful celebrity books. When you have your first book published as an unknown author, the chances of having a shot at a best-sellers' list is exponentially harder. But having a celebrity name associated with your book could get it amazing publicity.

Does a Ghostwriter Get Royalties, or Just a Set Fee, Like on a Work-for-Hire Assignment?

Author Jenna Glatzer answered a similar question on an online writing site by saying, "I have typically charged a $5,000 flat rate to ghostwrite a book proposal. Then we've negotiated the price for the book itself after a publisher has made an offer. Normally, it's a nice advance and a small percentage of the royalties for me. In cases where they don't want to do any royalties, I charge a higher flat rate."[11]

Another author named Janis writes,

> We do a lot of ghostwriting and have charged different rates depending whether the book will be self-published or published by a publishing house. Axel [writing partner] has an MFA in creative writing and taught at the college level, which gives him the credentials to charge $100 to $150 per hour. We have the additional advantage in that we are represented by a renowned agent. If the book is going to be self-published, you want to get an hourly rate only because the prospect of royalties will be bleak. You also want to get money upfront.
>
> If the book is going to be published by a publishing company, you want to do a combination of hourly and royalties. We are currently ghostwriting a memoir for someone

 INFO TO KNOW ABOUT BEING A GHOSTWRITER

Courses to Take

English, journalism, and creative writing are the top three courses to take for this kind of job.

Minimum Education Level Required

Bachelor's degree

Professional Organizations for More Information

Society of Children's Book Writers & Illustrators (www.scbwi.org)
Authors Guild (www.authorsguild.org)

who is pretty famous and our agent has agreed to represent it since the person has a huge existing platform. We are charging a $10,000 advance to get the proposal done, which will be deducted from the advance once it's picked up by a publisher. We are then getting one-third of the royalties. There are a lot of different options and price points. Hope this helps.[12]

Children's Book Author

Writing for children is a broad category that can be broken down into age groups, fiction or nonfiction, and a variety of formats such as novels, picture books, and magazine articles. It is an important segment of the freelance market and a freelance career to consider.

It is a common perception, most notably among celebrities, that writing for children is an easy gig. The world of children's book writing is not only competitive but can be downright discouraging! With rejection a constant part of freelancing, it's important to keep on writing. As many authors advise, you should *practice, practice, practice.* Don't just write one manuscript and spend years sending it out, without something new in the works. Continuing to write will keep you active in your craft, not to mention occupied so you don't obsess about when you'll hear back about your submissions.

Grant Writer

What Are Grant Writers and What Do They Do?

The simplest description of duties would be soliciting scholarships or endowments from a person, organization, or a corporation for one's clients.[13] To be more specific, these writers ask for money in a dignified and professional manner. The best ones are successful at soliciting prospective donors to give large sums of money to various charities and nonprofit organizations.

How Do Grant Writers Convince Large Corporations, Foundations, Wealthy Individuals, and Even the Government to Share Their Money?

They are expert writers, pure and simple. Equally important, they know their stuff! Much research goes into writing a proposal to a foundation or a company. To prove that any money given will be money well spent, grant writers have to build compelling arguments. But before they can even write a proposal on the "cause" the grant will support, the actual people/corporations being targeted for soliciting these grants must be carefully selected.

Is Money the Bottom Line?

No. When choosing the place to ask for grant money, the writer must find a perfect match between the benefactor and the client. The writer cannot simply check out Forbes' Top 100 money-making companies and start there. The grant writer must have an angle, a tie-in that makes sense for the company to actually take the time to *listen* to (or read) a pitch, let alone respond positively. Some grant writers resubmit proposals quarterly. The people being targeted by the grant writer are very, *very* busy executives who are constantly inundated with proposals and "junk mail." It can be difficult to make sure your query doesn't slip through the cracks of a highly sought-after benefactor.

Once the proper organizations are targeted, grant writers must learn everything they can about them. Grant writers must research what causes potential benefactors already support, what donations have been given in the past and to whom, and what the companies beliefs are. Ideally, an obvious target (and simple example) might be a college alumnus who went on to start a successful business. Say he was a science major in school, and your job (as grant writer) is to get funds to build a new science facility at his alma mater. This would have a personal tie-in for that person. Perhaps he remembers the old labs and how they seemed run-down even when *he* went to school there, and how nice it would have been to have more state-of-the-art equipment to work with. He might go one step further to think about how much it would benefit the future students (and possible future employee recruits). And he will know firsthand that recent graduates from that university or college will have studied in the best possible facilities available.

One of the most difficult tasks in convincing a potential benefactor to part with funds is writing a compelling argument as to why he should donate to that *specific* cause. As a grant writer you must be able to create the strongest argument in the least amount of words. It must be clear and concise, yet compelling, with a vivid enough picture that the person you are soliciting will sit up and take notice. That person has to *want* to hear what you have to say, and more importantly, be willing to reach for the checkbook!

Is Grant Writing a Major in College?

No, there aren't entire areas of study designed to teach grant writing. However, there are classes to take that will teach you the ins and outs of grant writing, from research to writing pitches. Some major areas of study that people who go into grant writing typically choose are public relations, political science, and even nonprofit administration.

 INFO TO KNOW ABOUT BEING A GRANT WRITER[19]

What Does a Grant Writer Do?

Nonprofit organizations need to find outside sources of money (or grants) to run their general operations. That's why they need to hire professionals to do the task successfully and why there is an entire career dedicated to the craft.

Courses to Take

Communications, business, English, math/economics, and management

Minimum Education Level Required

Bachelor's degree

Professional Organizations for More Information

American Association of Fundraising Counsel (www.aafrc.org)
Association of Fundraising Professionals (www.afpnet.org)

Last, and quite possibly most important, grant writers need to be able to network and build lasting relationships. They have to earn an executive or philanthropist's trust, not only for the cause and organization for which they are working, but in their own vision and sincerity.

Greeting Card Writer

Could this be a full-time freelance gig, writing greeting cards? Absolutely! Have you ever found yourself almost *stuck* in the greeting card aisle at the store because you think, "Okay, I'll just read *one* more!" Then you are laughing out loud and looking around?

Truthfully, who *hasn't* done that? It may sound impossible, but you could have an entire career writing greeting cards. It's true! It is a multibillion-dollar-a-year industry. Of course, many writers do it part time for steady income. But, as all writers know, acceptance doesn't come easy. Until you really study the market, the various companies, and what they're looking for, the rejections will be there in the beginning. Don't be discouraged. If you want a fun and challenging job (after all, it is difficult to find just the right words for those awkward and difficult situations like grief, divorce, or declining health, for example), this one is hard to beat!

There is an excellent eleven-page detailed article titled "How to Get Paid Writing Simple Greeting Cards."[15] The article advises that humor is probably the best-selling ingredient in making a sale to card companies—assuming the occasion is appropriate, of course. Today's greeting card publishers are looking for fresh new ideas, versus the corny or cliché sentiments that have been done over and over for the last several decades. Many companies seem to be searching for crazy, goofy, laugh-out-loud, risqué, sassy, crude, and even tactless and improper humor.

How to Submit to a Greeting Card Company[16]

Most companies have their own specific submission guidelines, as do traditional book or magazine publishers.

(Your cover letter for greeting card submissions needn't be any longer than three sentences. See chapter 8 on cover letters.) You can find a list of greeting card publishers in many of the writer's market guides, or you could write to

Artist and Writer's Market
The Greeting Card Association
1356 New York Ave. NW, Suite 615
Washington, DC 20005

(Be sure to include a size #10 business, self-addressed, stamped envelope with your request.)

MOVIE FEATURING AN ASPIRING GREETING CARD WRITER[17]

In 2002, Adam Sandler starred in the remake of the 1936 classic *Mr. Deeds Goes to Town*, which starred Gary Cooper. The new version, simply titled *Mr. Deeds*, portrays the main character, Longfellow Deeds, as a simple man who owns a small-town pizzeria and constantly submits ideas to greeting card publishers. There is an entire wall of his rejected submissions. With each new idea, he reads it to the restaurant's patrons in an "open-mike" type of atmosphere.

Finally, at the end of the film, one card he has written from his own personal experiences, with a particularly funny poem, is finally accepted. *That* is a prime example of how perseverance, along with humor, pays off in the greeting card industry!

INFO TO KNOW ABOUT BEING A GREETING CARD WRITER[18]

Courses to Take

Art, computer science, creative writing, poetry

Minimum Education Level Required

High school diploma, but advanced training is a plus

Professional Organizations for More Information

Greeting Card Association (www.greetingcard.org)
Hallmark Cards, Inc. (www.hallmark.com)
Writer's Digest Books (www.writersdigest.com)

Short but Sweet

Remember some general rules when submitting to greeting card companies:

- Each card should be typed on a separate 8½ x 11 inch sheet of paper or even a 3 x 5 inch index card. There should be writing on only one side of each submission page, including your name, address, and phone number in the upper left-hand corner, with the message or verse in the center of the page.

- Most companies will allow between five and fifteen separate card ideas for each submission. If unsure about a particular company's rule, don't send more than ten.

- Artwork is the same as for other manuscripts; unless you are an artist yourself, do *not* submit art.

- Novelty ideas are great moneymakers. Companies are quite open to concepts for buttons, mugs, key rings, computer mouse pads, and magnets that can tie in with the cards you write. If you can create a character that can then be expanded upon (example: the "Maxine" character on t-shirts and mugs started out on greeting cards), it makes potential for earnings that much greater.

Potential Earnings

Substantial earnings can be made in the multibillion dollar industry of greeting cards. On average, companies pay from $25 to $150 for each freelance idea or verse they buy. It has been reported that some companies pay as much as $500 for a single idea or verse. To gauge your success, you should know that a writer who sells two to three ideas out of a batch of ten to fifteen submissions is doing quite well. In fact, it isn't out of the realm of possibility for an editor to buy most or all of the ideas in a single submission![19] It's up to *you* to come up with the most fresh, funny, innovative ideas if you want to make top dollar in this often overlooked field.

Indexer

There are people who read through lengthy texts to make a list of words and phrases, usually organized alphabetically, which help people find specific information in a book. That list is what is known as an "index." The index must include references to all the important information in a text. Professionals who read through texts and form such lists in

 INFO TO KNOW ABOUT BEING AN INDEXER[20]

Courses to Take

English, computer science, history, social sciences

Minimum Education Level Required

Bachelor's degree in English or library science (plus, most indexers have one or more advanced degrees as well)

Professional Organizations for More Information

American Society of Indexers (www.asindexing.org)
Correspondence Study Program: Graduate School, United States Department of Agriculture (USDA) (www.grad.usda.gov)

books are known as "indexers." It is a real job, and if you really love to read, this might be the job you're looking for—especially for the detail-oriented types.

Journalist

Journalism is a type of writing like no other. It is quite arguably the most stressful writing choice in terms of quick turn-around and impossible deadlines. However, many journalists thrive on quick assignments, making that aspect of the job quite thrilling. Deadlines are fast and fierce and of the utmost importance. Journalism requires great attention to detail, accuracy, and tremendous follow-up skills. You must be persistent to find the stories and get great quotes. Another must-have skill would be the ability to do research, research, research!

 INFO TO KNOW ABOUT BEING A COLUMNIST (ONE FORM OF JOURNALISM)[21]

Job Description

Write opinions for newspapers and magazines.

Courses to Take

English, journalism, communications, economics, psychology

Minimum Education Level Required

Bachelor's degree

Professional Organizations for More Information

Society of Professional Journalists (www.spj.org)
American Society of Journalists and Authors (www.asja.org)
National Association of Broadcasters (www.nab.org)

Due to human nature, one task that can be most difficult for journalists is remaining objective. They cannot let personal bias interfere with how they report the facts or influence what subjects they decide to cover. They have to be confident in their decision making, often having little time to decide if something is newsworthy or not.

There is another dilemma that plagues journalists. It is the hot topic of *ethics*, for which entire books are written. How do you decide if the public's right to know certain information is greater than the subject's right to privacy? What do you do if information you have might incite public hysteria? A perfect example is a national story about how the Qur'an (Islamic bible) was handled improperly, which appeared on the Internet in May 2005. The article reported on rumors of the Qur'an being put in a toilet; rumors which, when read, caused riots and angry protests from Afghanistan to Gaza to Indonesia.[22] People were killed in the violence. The question is, should a story of that nature ever have been reported?

MAGAZINES FOR TEENS BY TEENS

Some magazines for teens require submissions from teens only. One example is a publication called *Teen Ink*. It is a magazine that was started in 1989 and was then called *The 21st Century* to acknowledge belonging to today's generation. Now that it *is* the twenty-first century, the name seemed outdated, according to the website. All writers who submit must be between the ages of thirteen and eighteen years old. Go to the website www.teenink.com, and click on "How to Submit" to check out the guidelines.

Teen Ink now has a book series that compiles the best pieces that have been published in the magazine over the years. There are six books available nationwide.

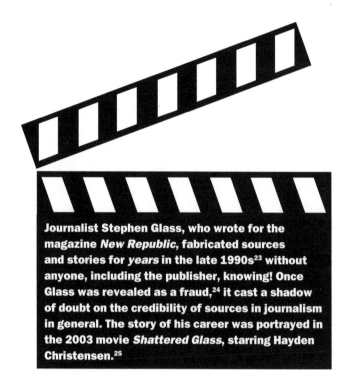

Journalist Stephen Glass, who wrote for the magazine *New Republic*, fabricated sources and stories for *years* in the late 1990s[23] without anyone, including the publisher, knowing! Once Glass was revealed as a fraud,[24] it cast a shadow of doubt on the credibility of sources in journalism in general. The story of his career was portrayed in the 2003 movie *Shattered Glass*, starring Hayden Christensen.[25]

Novelist

It takes a certain amount of skill, lots of practice and determination, knowledge about the genre, and a bit of pure talent to create a great novel. Age does not come into the equation, however. Check out the sidebars in chapter 4 to be inspired by young adult authors who were published at your age, and even younger. Use it to give yourself that extra encouragement or incentive to believe that *you* can do it!

Stephen King was published in his teen years and created his own magazine during high school. However, in it he told of mischievous events, without changing any names or details, ultimately getting himself in trouble; but still, it was read and enjoyed by his peers! His book *On Writing: A Memoir of the Craft* includes wonderful stories of his youth, along with amazing advice on how to do the actual writing.[26]

INFO TO KNOW ABOUT BEING A NOVELIST

Courses to Take

English, creative writing, history, social sciences

Minimum Education Level Required

Bachelor's degree in English helpful but not required

Professional Organizations for More Information

For Writers (www.forwriters.com)
The Horror Writers Association (HWA) (www.horror.org)
The National Writers Association (www.nationalwriters.com)
Writers' Digest—has 101 top sites for writers (www
.writersdigest.com/101sites/2007_index.asp)

Playwright

If dialogue is your strong suit, then being a playwright might be for you. Since the entire script is made up of stage direction and dialogue, it makes sense to choose that genre.

Can you tell an entire story from beginning to end, whether it is a one-day story or a ten-year tale, within ninety pages of dialogue, give or take? One typed page equals one minute on stage, on average. If you write a one-and-a-half-hour play, it amounts to approximately ninety pages.

While still in high school, Eugene Fertelmeyer won a contest in which the prize was to have his play produced by a professional director. When I sat down to speak with the young playwright, he had this to say about the experience and writing in general.

PLAYWRITING: WRITE WHAT YOU RARELY GET TO READ

Scenario: One day out of the blue, Doug McDade, director of a local theater company, called a children's book author and asked her to write a children's play. She said she'd love to, but had never written in the genre before. The director didn't care. He said it was for the company's readers' theater, which means the actors don't memorize their lines. They read the lines, since it is a "work in progress." Readers' theater shows an audience how a writer's process works, while showing the author spots that work well and areas that need help.

It sounded easy enough to the writer. Doug then asked, "What's the name of the play?" The press release had to go out the next day, and the show would be performed in eight short weeks!

Okay, once the shock wore off, the author wondered how she *always* got involved in things of this nature . . . things way over her head. With hard work and determination, the cliché of "What doesn't kill you makes you stronger" took over, and she did it. She came up with a concept in the moment as requested and wrote the play. That's how *The Great Tooth Fairy Mystery* was born. That new playwright was me.

I can't even describe how cool it is to see something go from an idea in my mind to being a real play with actors on stage! I literally had to think of an idea right there on the phone for the director and turn it in under a two-month deadline. I'll confess I was in the middle of writing this book, so it cut out a good chunk of my deadline time. But sometimes you have to follow your gut instinct and grab an opportunity when it arises, no matter how inconvenient. Lesson learned: *Step out of your comfort zone and amazing ideas will grow. Take a leap of faith and believe in yourself more than anyone else ever could.*

Interview 1 with Playwright Eugene Fertelmeyer: August 2004[27]

What is the typical length (if you have one) of the plays you write?

My shortest play is ten minutes. My longest play is one hour. On average, my writing runs approximately one minute per written page. But television, for example, is different. It averages five pages per minute.

Eugene Fertelmeyer—teen playwright

Have you submitted any work to publishers, and if so, do you use market guides to research where to send your manuscripts?

No, I don't use market guides. I go online to find contests to submit to.

I heard you won a contest you entered during a Young Playwrights Festival while still in high school. Congratulations. Can you tell me a bit about that experience?

Sure. I wrote a play, and the grand prize was to have it produced and performed for a one-week run. It was produced in Hollywood and was directed by Jon Shear (the writer/ director of the film *Urbania*). Noah Wiley, of television's *ER* fame, was the artistic director of the Blank Theatre Company, so that was cool.

I'll say! That'll be a hard act to follow, winning such a prestigious award. Who has inspired you or given you guidance that you'd like to publicly thank?

Mr. Johnson (retired) was my mentor and playwriting teacher at Stevenson High School (Lincolnshire, Illinois), and he had several plays produced at Steppenwolf.

I know your high school is one of the most competitive in the country. Within your class, were others competing for contests writing plays that you know of, if so, did any of them win?

Yes. All three of the girls I went to school with who entered contests won. Megan (Lake Forest College), Jenna (University of Illinois), and Philippa (New York University) are all attending college in the fall, and each won a contest as well.

Do you plan on declaring a major right away as a college freshman or will you go in "undeclared"?

I plan on getting a bachelor of arts in theater, with a performance emphasis, and a minor in musical theater.

You've got a great start on a career path I'm sure you'll succeed at. Thanks for taking the time to chat with us. I'm excited to follow up with you next year!

Interview 2 with Playwright Eugene Fertelmeyer: December 2006[28]

When we spoke last, you were about to enter college. Where are you going to school now? What year are you in?

I'm at school at the college I was planning to attend when we last spoke, Marymount Manhattan College in New York. I'm halfway through my sophomore year now.

You planned on majoring in performance theater and minoring in music theater. Now that you're halfway done with your sophomore year of college, is that still your plan?

Yes that is, in fact, my major and minor, and it has been an amazing time so far!

Have you saved time to write in your busy college life, or has it taken a back seat to term papers and other studies?

Interestingly enough, I have still kept writing plays. It has slowed due to my writing for other areas of life (though not necessarily academic) such as songwriting. But I do have a couple plays in progress that I hope to finish in the next few weeks.

Have you entered any theatrical or writing contests lately? Any successes to share?

Not much in terms of contests. Right now, my main focus is more toward my performing in regard to seeking out opportunities and the like. Well, successes . . . I don't know if it's relevant, but I am working as a writer now. More on that in a minute. . . .

So far, are there any courses in college you would recommend to those interested in the arts, specifically? Are there any courses, in your opinion, you'd avoid if you had to do it all over again?

Everyone should take a dance class. I've been dancing for about eight years now, and it is unbelievable useful in all aspects of life. Don't be scared. Do it! My biggest piece of advice in terms of college course selection would be to be honest with yourself. Don't be afraid of trying a class and dropping it in the first week because you're worried you might hurt a professor's feelings—you're paying for school; time is, in fact, money at this point.

What extracurriculars have you become involved in through your college life?

Ask anyone who lives in New York City—it's an extra-curricular activity all its own!

Now that you're older, is there any advice you can give to a writer just starting out?

Look. Listen. Write. You are enough. Don't ever think you're trying to be better than anyone else. There is something you can do that nobody in the world has ever done before—don't try to figure it out, just know it's there.

What upcoming projects can we look for from you? Anything you'd like to "plug" here?

Right now, I am the head writer and co-executive producer for a talk show that (if all goes well) will be going national in the coming year. The show is called *The EDGE with Jake Sasseville*; look for it on TV next year [circa 2007]—as

INFO TO KNOW ABOUT BEING A PLAYWRIGHT

Courses to Take

English, creative writing, script writing, acting, movement classes

Minimum Education Level Required

Bachelor's degree in English helpful but not required

Professional Organizations for More Information

International Centre Women Playwrights (www. womenplaywrights.org)
PlayScripts, Inc. (www.playscripts.com)
Playwrights Platform (www.playwrightsplatform.org)

negotiations are currently in progress. I can't tell you which network it will be on, but hopefully all will soon be definite.

Thanks for taking the time to catch us up on your progress, Eugene. I wish you every continued success.

Songwriter

The music industry has catapulted young singers, songwriters, and musicians to superstardom. These artists are writing and performing what their fans want to hear. Basically teens and young adults want to listen to someone their own age. Who better to understand the daily grind of the difficult transition years than a peer?

There are obvious sensations like boy bands In Sync and Backstreet Boys, all the way back to The Beatles, as well as teen queen rivals (who were teens when they broke on the scene) including Britney Spears, Christina Aguilera, Jessica Simpson, Hilary Duff, and Lindsay Lohan. Profiled later this chapter is a young, successful musician who writes her own material and gained fame as a teen.

INFO TO KNOW ABOUT BEING A SONGWRITER

Courses to Take

English, creative writing, music theory, poetry, speech

Minimum Education Level Required

High school diploma

Professional Organizations for More Information

American Society of Composers, Authors and Publishers
(www.ascap.com)
Songwriters' Guild of America (www.songwritersguild.com)

Publicist

What Does a Publicist Do?

A publicist is a master at getting a foot in the doors of the people who can promote your work the most efficiently. The best ones can give a full pitch in a matter of thirty to sixty seconds. Your publicist will be your own personal cheerleader who will sing your praises to the masses; more specifically, to the editors, media, book reviewers, and so on. They will take care of all your PR (public relations) needs, right down to creating an image for you, if that's your desire.

To put it in the most general of terms, a publicity department is a team of executives, writers, artists, and researchers. They work together to provide information

INFO TO KNOW ABOUT BEING A PUBLICIST[29]

Job Description

Get as much media coverage on a client as possible in order to promote him or her and the client's work.

Courses to Take

English, journalism, business, communications

Minimum Education Level Required

Bachelor's degree

Professional Organizations for More Information

International Association of Business Communicators
(www.iabc.com)
Public Relations Society of America (www.prsa.org)

to the public about their client's goals, accomplishments, and future plans or projects. The publicist's main responsibility is to form solid relationship with media contacts in radio, television, newspapers, and magazines on behalf of his or her client(s). If being a publicist interests you, then check out the sidebar above for the facts you'll want to know.

A WRITER'S PAY: TRADITIONAL CONTRACT VS. WORK FOR HIRE

Whatever you choose to write, if working as a freelancer, as opposed to for one specific company, writers can get paid in a variety of ways. Some magazine publishers that don't offer fees publish a work and provide a writer with several copies of the issue in which the work appears. Other publishers may give an advance plus royalties. Then there are contracts called "work for hire." Can you guess what this might mean? With work for hire, publishers might farm out their assignments to freelance writers rather than use an in-house, or on-staff, writer. When authors do work for hire, they get flat fees, nothing more. If a

Why I Write

It's not for you.
It's not for them.
I write until
The feelings end.
To let them out and
Set them free.
Writing gets them
Out of me.
Anger, sadness,
Or pure joy,
Writing helps to
Fill the void.
My private thoughts
Can be in code.
Sometimes they're flushed
Down the commode!
It doesn't matter.
One thing I know:
"Just keep writing.
Don't wreck the flow!"
Revision's where you
Spin the gold.
And lead your story
To unfold.
It twists and turns,
And intertwines;
Round two, and now,
I'm feeling fine.
I'm in the zone
Of writing now.
It's getting good,
Hey, holy cow!
How did this come
Out of my brain?
Get it published,
Is that insane?
If nothing else,
I've said my piece.
Emotions spent . . .
Can finally sleep!

—C. G. S., age twenty

book only sells two copies, the money agreed upon still goes to the writer. Similarly, if a book sells twenty thousand copies, the writer doesn't get any extra money or a cut of the profit, either. He or she gets the agreed upon fee.

So why would anyone want to do work-for-hire writing? Well, speaking from personal experience, I'd say that it can be a quick turnaround, usually a few weeks or less, and an author can get a pretty decent chunk of money, anywhere from say, $200 to $2,000, depending on the length and technical aspects of the book. If an author is assigned an entire *series* of books, say, an eleven-book series on the planets (now that Pluto has been downgraded to a star, and two new planets have been added) there will be a *huge* demand for information for the school and library market. For the sake of this example, say an author receives $300 per book, times the eleven books; he or she would make $3,300 in a few short weeks. Not bad for a writer! It also makes a nice addition to a writer's résumé.

SOME CHALLENGES OF CHOOSING A CAREER AS A WRITER

Isolated and, at Times, Lonely

Writing is a solitary job with no one to talk to on a day-to-day basis. Unless, of course, you are part of a writing team, you will most likely do the bulk of your writing all alone. I spend most of my writing time at my kitchen table, upstairs in our office, down in the basement, or at whatever local coffee shop lets me stay the latest. Regardless of where I write, I am most often by myself. Libraries are great too, but many close by 9:00 p.m., and if you're a nighttime writer, you're barely getting started by that time!

Loneliness is a reason some people simply can't continue in the field. Other than the obvious need for self-motivation, it's hard being alone all the time when you really need to get down to business.

No Monetary Safety Net

Freelance writers get paid for what they write. They don't get "sick days" like a regular nine-to-five job provides. They don't have paid vacations or even a set forty-hour workweek. Sure, they can decide to run off to the Bahamas or somewhere fun if they have the money and aren't scheduled for interviews, public relations, or speaking engagements. However, if writers are not writing, they aren't making money.

Of course, once you have some books under your belt, you will get royalties. But you only get them once or twice a year. Occasionally, you'll find a publisher that gives quarterly royalty checks, but it tends to be the exception, not the rule as far as payments are concerned.

When you're just starting out and have no royalties coming in, you might work for two years without being paid. So you either need another job to pay the bills or you need to have saved up a huge sum of money to support yourself for a year or so to finish a writing project. You could also be married with a spouse who earns enough income for you to focus solely on getting your writing career up and started.

How and When Do I Get Paid for a Book?

Upon signing a contract, you will usually get the first half of whatever advance (if any) you have negotiated. Then you have a deadline to write the book, say, for example, one year, for a nonfiction book. There is usually a year of content editing, line editing, typesetting, and public relations. So now your second year has gone by without seeing a dime past the initial advance. Once an author completes all other tasks like footnoting and indexing, and the completed manuscript is accepted, most publishers pay the second half of the advance.

Paid upon Publication

"Paid upon publication" refers to someone who gets a manuscript accepted for publication, but he/she will not be paid until the article or story runs. This can take years sometimes. For example, an author may have sold a story to *Sports Illustrated Kids*, but it won't run for eighteen months. The writer won't get paid until the article has physically "gone to press." This makes it difficult to earn a living if you have to wait months, often *years*, to see any money for your writing.

Discipline

If you are not a motivated self-starter, you cannot expect to be a successful freelance writer. You have no one to keep you on task but yourself. If you have an assignment, and you wait until the last minute to do it, chances are you won't hit the deadline. It is not an option to blow deadlines. Granted, sometimes there is some leeway, like for a book with a deadline a year away. But for journalism, or "work for hire" books with a quick turnaround, comedy routines for stand-up performances or television shows, or scripts for TV or film, the deadlines are firm. One day late and your contract will be null and void!

You need to have a tremendous work ethic and self-discipline to keep a work schedule (and stick to it) and hit all deadlines, plus the follow-up work that is less than glamorous, such as marketing your books once they hit the shelves. You need to approach local papers, any organizations or groups you are in (such as a sorority, a social club, a trade journal), and find *any* kind of hook you can to promote your work. If there is any duplication on the part of your publisher, then great! It will stick in the minds of those approached by both the author and the publisher that much more (but this will be a rare problem, I assure you). Keep in touch, and develop a relationship with your publicity department to make sure you're not simply duplicating its work.

Many writers hate the follow-up that is part of publication. A writer might not want to do his or her index, or call the local papers, or write a press release if the publisher doesn't provide it, or call local schools to do an author visit to show off his or her latest work, or a myriad of other tasks that can seem so daunting or even *blah*. When authors are done with books, they're ready to move on to the next ones. But they *must* have the discipline to follow through with projects from the very beginning planning stages of pitching work to potential editors/publishers, all the way through helping their publishers promote the work. If it means finding out how to get on a local podcast, so be it. Get it done!

Feast or Famine

While this isn't true for everyone, many authors say they get work in batches; it's like the expression "feast or famine," meaning there's either too much work all at once or not a single thing going on. It's somewhat cyclical as well. For example, during the winter holidays and in the summer, the publishing industry seems to slow down to a snail's pace.

Frustration

Not only do writers have to deal with a lot of rejection— sometimes years pass before making a sale—but when they do finally succeed, the pay is often slow to come. If you write a magazine article, you wait for it to be published before getting paid. It might get published in two months or two years, but a majority of the time a writer is "paid on publication" *not* "paid on delivery" (delivery of manuscript). And, as mentioned earlier, for book writing, it is common practice for an author to get half of an advance upon signing a contract, then the other half after the manuscript is approved.

High Pressure

The pressure starts with "Will I ever get published?" Next, you start working your way up that career ladder to score your dream job as associate reporter for the *Chicago Tribune* or whatever local paper is the biggest in your town. Then you're pressured by deadlines. If you've gone the route of writing books, not only is there pressure to come up with a book on time, but also one that nets respectable sales.

Baring Your Soul

Are you an introvert? Are you painfully shy or at the very least . . . extremely private? Yet, the words may just flow out of you. Depending on your personality, baring your soul to hundreds, possibly even millions of people, may be daunting or liberating. Pro or con, you decide! Even nonfiction writers reveal their *voices*—their "fingerprints"—in what they write. You should be able to differentiate between authors by their tone, verbiage, pacing, and a variety of different writing traits. (See chapter 4 for more on voice.)

PERSONAL WEBSITE: AN ABSOLUTE MUST

A website is a tool every business needs; it's especially important for a writer and his or her career. It is a must if you're going to promote your work accurately. A person can literally set up a website in one night. It may be minimal at first, but with time it will expand and grow as your résumé does. It doesn't matter what your website is for, whether for business or just fun. You can employ a freelance web designer to give it that extra punch.

A writer-friend of mine made her website on her iMac laptop (G4 Powerbook). With the use of the iLife:iWeb program, she got her site up and running in days. Check it out! (Go to www.lorijometz.com.)

My friend isn't a web designer, or an artist, or an illustrator by any means. She is a writer and sticks solely to that particular medium. Yet on her own trusty little computer, she set up a spectacularly professional website. That's something anyone can do with a little research and a lot of imagination! For more examples of writers' websites, you can go to www.scbwi-illinois .org/Speakers.html.

All in a Day's Work

The evening I made my website (*singular* . . . I made it in *one* night) was the first night of a three-day author visit to a grade school in Anthem, Arizona. My site has evolved into a much

more detailed resource since that first week, of course, but at least I had a site to refer kids, parents, and teachers to when they asked for further information.

In 2004, I created my own website with the help of a company called 2-Tier Software. It is amazingly affordable. I set up my entire site, but the company hosts it for me. Still in business as of 2008, the company has simple and user-friendly templates on its website that customers plug their own information into. It can upload photos, too.

If you decide to pursue writing as a profession, it's invaluable to refer people to a website so they can contact you directly to order books, link to your publishers, and set

---

BLOGS

Have your heard the term *blog*? Sure you have! Do you know what it means? Though the term *blog* has not been formally added to the dictionary, it is commonly known as a noun, more specifically, a contraction for *web log*.

A blog is a web page that someone hosts, similar to a website, but it usually has some sort of theme and central topic of discussion. Others are often encouraged to comment and/or participate in current discussions on the blog. Blogs tend to be like online personal journals and often contain sarcastic and/or highly editorialized commentaries of the hosts' views.

There is a blog directory to search for topics or names called Blogflux Directory, at dir.blogflux.com. If you Google "teen blogs," you will get some of the following hits. (FYI: 5,290,000 hits came up in 0.22 seconds on June 4, 2008.)

www.journals.student.com/
www.teenvogue.com/teamvogue/blogs/intern
dir.blogflux.com/cat/teen.html
www.libsuccess.org/index.php?title=Blogs_for_Teens
www.yalibrarian.com/
www.beloblog.com/KHOU_teentalk/

---

up "author visits." (FYI: author visits and teaching/editing are what make up a majority of many writers' incomes.) A frequently asked questions, or FAQ, section is convenient if someone wants to interview an author, but doesn't have time to set something up or if the author is unavailable. A site can also include a calendar of events page, which lists a schedule of appearances, should someone want to meet the author in person.

A STARTING POINT

There is a wealth of information on anything you could hope to learn just by surfing the Internet, not to mention spending the day at the library. The point is to see what's out there and keep your options open. We've barely scratched the surface in this chapter about career options. Start with one of the job descriptions in this chapter and continue on with your own specific research. Remember, you'll be in a career for a long time (if you love it) so *really* look into all the details you can find. Last, have *fun*!

CHAPTER 2 RESEARCH EXERCISE

Pick three careers you'd consider looking into further and research them more deeply. Next, decide if the schooling necessary for such a job is in line with what you had planned for your future.

You can also Google a career choice, but be sure to add "+ continuing education" or a similar tag to find where you can learn/train to do that career.

NOTES

1. Books written and illustrated by Kevin Luthardt: *Mine!* (New York: Antheneum, 2001), *Peep!* (Atlanta, GA: Peachtree Publishers, 2003), *Larabee!* (Atlanta, GA: Peachtree Publishers, 2004), *Hats!* (Morton Grove, IL: Albert Whitman, 2004), *You're Weird!* (New York: Dial Books, 2005), and *Flying!* (Atlanta, GA: Peachtree Publishers, 2009). Books illustrated by Luthardt: *Zoom!* (Atlanta, GA: Peachtree Publishers, 2005) and *The Vowel Family: A Tale of Lost Letters* (Minneapolis, MN: Carolrhoda Picture Books, 2008).

2. "Kevin Luthardt," Society of Children's Books Writers & Illustrators—Illinois Chapter, www.scbwi-illinois.org/Luthardt.html (accessed December 5, 2006).

3. "About Kevin," Kevin Luthardt.com, www.kevinluthardt.com/about.html (accessed December 20, 2006); Kevin Luthardt, e-mail to author, December 1, 2008.

4. Arnold Lobel, *Mouse Soup* (New York: HarperCollins, 1977).

5. *Career Discovery Encyclopedia*, 5th ed. (New York: Ferguson, 2003), 1:30, www.fergpubco.com.

6. "Tina Fey Biography," Notable Biographies, www.notablebiographies.com (click on "Ca-Ge" then "Tina Fey Biography" (accessed May 24, 2006).

7. Rosalind Wiseman, *Queen Bees and Wannabees: Helping Your Daughter Survive Cliques, Gossip, Boyfriends and Other Realities of Adolescence* (New York: Crown, 2002).

8. *Career Discovery Encyclopedia*, 2:162; 3:116; 5:48, 157.

9. *Career Discovery Encyclopedia*, 8:122.

10. *Motorcross Freestyle* (Mankato, MN: Capstone Press, 2004).

11. "About the Author," Jenna Glatzer.com, www.jennaglatzer .com/about-jenna.htm (accessed November 7, 2006).

12. "Ghost Writers on Commission?" Yahoo! Answers, answers .yahoo.com/question/index?qid=20060705081117AAPKcDy (accessed November 7, 2006).

13. Diane Lindsey Reeves, *Career Ideas for Kids Who Like Writing* (New York: Checkmark Books, 1998), 77.

14. *Career Discovery Encyclopedia*, 4:36.

15. "How to Get Paid Writing Simple Greeting Cards," HowtoAdvice.com, www.howtoadvice.com/GreetingCards (accessed December 18, 2007).

16. *Career Discovery Encyclopedia*, 4:36.

17. *Mr. Deeds* (Columbia Picture Corp./Happy Madison Productions/New Line Cinema/Out of the Blue Entertainment, 2002).

18. *Career Discovery Encyclopedia*, 4:42.

19. "How to Get Paid Writing Simple Greeting Cards."

20. *Career Discovery Encyclopedia*, 4:42.

21. *Career Discovery Encyclopedia*, 2:86.

22. "Riots Spread over Alleged Gitmo Qur'an Desecration," Jihad Watch, May 14, 2005, www.jihadwatch.org/archives/006165.php (accessed January 10, 2007).

23. Rick McGinnis, "A Tissue of Lies," www.rickmcginnis.com/ articles/Glassindex.htm (accessed April 3, 2008).

24. Rebecca Leung, "Stephen Glass: I Lied for Esteem," CBS News.com, August 17, 2003, www.cbsnews.com/stories/2003/05/07/ 60minutes/main552819.shtml (accessed April 3, 2008).

25. "*Shattered Glass*," The Internet Movie Database, www.imdb .com/title/tt0323944/ (accessed August 26, 2006).

26. Stephen King, *On Writing: A Memoir of the Craft* (New York: Pocket Books, 2000).

27. Eugene Fertelmeyer, interview with author, August 2004.

28. Eugene Fertelmeyer, interview with author, December 2006.

29. *Career Discovery Encyclopedia*, 2:86.

Beginner Basics

THE BUSINESS SIDE OF THE JOB

Before you get down to the matter of cover letters, query letters, formatting your manuscript according to submission guidelines, and more, you'll need to review how you work and set up some steady writing habits. After all, honing your craft is something you should work at every day, right?

NEVER TOO YOUNG TO START

There is no specific age limit required to be a writer. A "beginning writer" might be as young as three years old or as

Big sister Lyndsay Bassett, age 6, writes poems for her litle sister Lily, age 3, in 2006.

old as ninety-three. The following is a poem written by a six-year-old up-and-coming author.

For My Sister

I am big and
you are small;
But don't you worry,
'cause you'll grow tall.
You like one show;
and I like another.
But it doesn't matter
'cause we have each other.
I am me
and you are you.
We're especially made
in a package of two!

—Lyndsey Bassett, age six, Hainesville, Illinois

SET UP YOUR WRITING SPACE/HOME OFFICE

As with any task you do, workspace is of the utmost importance. When you are writing, organization is key. How

AN INTERESTING CONCEPT (BY DON CROWTHER)[1]

Is there magic in the number 48? Does this number hold any significance in your future success? Crowther suggests that it does. In a presentation, Don told the audience that forty-eight minutes is the magic number. Here's how it works: Set a timer for forty-eight minutes. Close out all distractions and work continuously for forty-eight minutes. When the timer goes off, get up and stretch, get a drink, and use the restroom in the following twelve minutes. Repeat such breaks as necessary.

Don reports that this technique repeated four times a day allowed him to write a two-hundred-page book in just two weeks. The ability to focus on one task for forty-eight minutes straight was the key. Some who have tested Don's idea say it works well. It eliminates the distractions that have a way of derailing even the best-laid plans. Taking a short twelve-minute break once an hour is refreshing but not enough to get you off track.

So the question comes up, if this solution works well, how can you use it in planning your daily schedule and applying it to future goals? Can you successfully write a blog post in forty-eight minutes? Can you write a book chapter in that time? After one writer tried the process, he reported that it was a challenge to sit in one place that long. But when he did, his productivity soared. He said he found it best to simply keep writing, not worry about mistakes, and get everything on paper. Once the major points were made, he was able to go back and make his edits and corrections.

If you find yourself getting distracted while working on your projects, try this simple technique. It might be just the trick!

can you market your work properly without a productive workspace? Take your writing seriously. If you went into business, say, as an owner of a record store, and everything was in random piles everywhere, with no rhyme or reason or organizational way to find what customers wanted, what would they think? They'd probably think, *This place is a joke; it's not a* real *store!*

That's just how you'll come off if you send in submissions on notebook paper ripped out of your spiral notebook, written in purple-sparkled ink from your "lucky pen." If you want to be taken seriously, then take yourself seriously. Your writing can be fun, humorous, or whimsical, but the way you present it to publishers should not be.

Before getting to the specifics of what exactly you need, do your best to start with a clean, clutter-free surface, in a part of the house where people won't be tempted to disturb you. If you are on a deadline and have stacks of articles, books, and other information everywhere, you won't want to scoop up your piles of information, only to waste a bunch of time re-sorting it all. You will need a place that is off-limits others, so if you make a bit of a mess it's fine. (This is assuming it isn't in the kitchen or living room, for example, where your family might want to entertain.)

Here are some suggestions for the basic equipment you will need to become a writer:

1. **Desk, lamp, small space heater, fan (last two optional, depending on where you write).**

2. **Desktop computer, laptop computer, or preferably both (since it's convenient to have a back-up computer if yours crashes; also, it's nice to be able to be portable and write in various locations).**

3. **Power strip.**

4. **Printer, preferably color (but not essential). The faster the output is, the better. When trying to beat the last FedEx pick-up, you don't want to be waiting to reprint your three-hundred-page manuscript.**

   One type of printer is the all-in-one, which gives you a printer, scanner, copier, and fax all in one unit, and it can be purchased for approximately $150, in 2008. (You'll find it to be a wise investment!)

5. **Phone line and fax line.**

6. **Office supplies: pencils, pens (various colors), highlighters, markers, colored pencils, erasers, pencil sharpener, stapler, staple-pull, scotch tape, packing tape, binders, binder clips, paper clips (of various sizes), file folders, pendaflex folders (hanging folders for inside a drawer with side-rails; they expand to fit several file folders at a time), accordion files, stacker trays (in/out/pending boxes), notebooks and/or legal pads, Post-it**

notes, "flag" stickies to mark pages, 3 × 5 inch and/or 4 × 6 inch index cards, garbage can *and* recycling box (you'll go through more paper than you can imagine), shredder if you feel it necessary, envelopes (from regular letter sized—Number 10 business to 11 × 14 inch), and stamps—*lots and lots of stamps*!

You will also need the following resources:

1. Internet access: Most writers interviewed say they prefer DSL, as it seems to be the quickest and most reliable, although more expensive option. Otherwise, you can still use dial-up Internet service.

2. General reference shelf: collegiate dictionary, thesaurus, and encyclopedias (either in CD-ROM, printed books, and/or on-line version); subscriptions to newspapers such as the *New York Times*, *Chicago Tribune*, *Los Angeles Times*, *Wall Street Journal*, *USA Today*; and magazines such as *Time*, *Newsweek*, *Forbes*, *National Geographic*, and other print sources. The following list (arranged alphabetically by author, not preference) will help build your own collection on your desk. You'll have others you'll want to add, but this is a great start:

   ◎ Tami D. Cowden, Caro LaFever, Sue Viders, *The Complete Writer's Guide to Heroes & Heroines: Sixteen Master Archetypes* (Hollywood, CA: Lone Eagle, 2000).

   ◎ Greg Daugherty, *You Can Write for Magazines* (Cincinnati, OH: Writer's Digest Books, 1999).

   ◎ James Cross Giblin, *Writing Books for Young People*, new expanded ed. (Boston: The Writer, Inc., 1995).

   ◎ Vincent F. Hopper, Cedric Gale, Ronald C. Foote, and Benjamin W. Griffith, eds., *Essentials of English*, 5th ed. (Hauppauge, NY: Barron's Educational Series, 2000).

   ◎ Kelly James-Enger, *Six Figure Freelancing: The Writer's Guide to Making More Money* (New York: Random House Reference, 2005).

   ◎ Stephen King, *On Writing: A Memoir of the Craft* (New York: Pocket Books, 2001).

   ◎ Viki King, *How to Write a Movie in 21 Days*: *The Inner Movie Method* (New York: Perennial, 1992).

◎ Marni McNiff, ed., *Book Markets for Children's Writers 2006* (West Redding, CT: Writer's Institute Publications, 2007).

◎ William Strunk Jr. and E. B. White, *The Elements of Style*, 4th ed. (Needham Heights, MA: Allyn & Bacon, 1999).

MAKE A PLAN BEFORE TAKING ACTION

Once you find a little chunk of space in the house that you can call your own, or at least "your office," get out a sheet of paper to take inventory. Write (or fold) a line down the middle of the page, dividing the right side from the left side. On the left, list all the things you'll need from the previous lists (supplies, reference materials, furniture) and any other things you can think of that you'll need to succeed.

On the right side of your paper, check off what you've already got. The next step is to go to a store, or online to www .staples.com, www.officemax.com, or www.penny-wise. com, for example, and fill in the costs of each of the things on your list. Having this information will help you to prioritize what you need to have. *Some* kind of typewriter, computer, or laptop—even if it's from a garage sale or an old typewriter from the Salvation Army—is essential. You'll need something that you can type on instead of writing a proposal freehand.

Once you've put your list in order of importance *and* cost, you can tweak the list to get the most urgently needed supplies.

Daily Schedule

Whether you write at the same time, the same day(s) each week, or at various times on different days whenever you have a moment, you'll figure out your own method of how to get your writing done.

If, for example, you're going off to college soon, and know you'll take a full load of classes, have a part-time job, join a club or rush a fraternity or sorority, plus e-mail your boyfriend or girlfriend any spare minute you get, your writing (for pleasure, not school) might fall by the wayside. It doesn't need to be that way.

The pages you write will add up if you set a schedule as simple as using one of the following ideas:

- Write for fifteen minutes while eating breakfast.
- Write for twenty to thirty minutes before bed instead of watching TV or reading e-mails.
- Write for twenty minutes before or after studying to relax and clear your mind.

Any of these efforts might work for you. Many people don't write every day, and in a way, yes, e-mailing counts as *some* sort of writing. Start small and write in fifteen-minute blocks, while waiting for a bus, for example, or when you're waiting for a class to begin—any little snippets of time that can be filled are great. All you need is a legal pad or notebook and a pen. You can travel light; no need to have a laptop every time you leave your home.

Inspiration That Knows No Excuses

Renowned children's book author Christopher Paul Curtis landed top honors for his first *and* second novels. *The Watsons Go to Birmingham—1963*, published in 1995, was a Newbery honor book and winner of the Coretta Scott King Award; while *Bud, Not Buddy*, published in 1999, won both the Newbery Medal and the Coretta Scott King Award.[2]

While working in a car factory in Detroit, Michigan, Chris took turns installing car doors with a partner. He'd install one, and the other guy would install the next. The cars kept coming down the assembly line, and the two young men would get the doors on the car one after another for hours on end, all day long.

One day, Chris decided he'd like to be able to just sit for a half hour at a time. He suggested to his partner that each guy do eight to ten doors while the other one rested. Then they would switch places, and the other would get a half hour to relax. The partner thought it might be hard to keep up with the line with only one guy, but agreed to try it for a half hour at a time. Once they got used to it, it was a great system for both of the men.

Chris would write on and off by the half hour for eight or more hours a day. That's how his first published novel was written. He was an hourly factory worker in Detroit, Michigan! A true success story of finding time when you don't think you have *any* to spare![3]

Leave a Message with My Secretary

Why is it when you are a freelance writer, people assume you can chat when they call during the day? Most conversations start with something along the lines of, "Hey, how's it going? What are you doing?"

Even if you reply, "I'm working on a new article" or "I'm working on the book," or something referring to your writing, people's response the majority of the time is "Oh yeah? Cool," then they go on as if it was a leisure activity and not your job. Has this ever happened to you? I suppose if I were to play the devil's advocate, I could excuse it by saying perhaps they figure if you are answering your phone, you have the time to talk; otherwise, you'd let your voice mail pick it up. It's not like you have a conventional job with a secretary to whom you can say, "Hold my calls please. I can't be interrupted."

Having said that, I suppose that leaves it up to you to take the lead and either

1. do not answer the phone during a set writing time;

2. use Caller I.D. to screen calls and only answer the emergency ones (*however, stopping to check out who is calling or listen as someone leaves a message can be more of an interruption than just letting the machine pick up your calls*); or

3. set up regular hours each day and let your friends and family know that you are unavailable during that time (*however, you must stick by it if they are to really understand and abide by your rules!*).

Avoid Distractions

At age nineteen, when asked his opinion about the hardest part of writing a novel, author Christopher Paolini said, "persistence and discipline." He went on to say, "It's far too easy to get distracted from your work or tire of it and find a simpler project. The true sign of a professional writer is that he or she can and does write every day, even without feeling inspired. Writing is not a gift from the gods . . . Writing is a craft, and, like any craft, you must practice, practice, practice to hone your skills."[4]

Finally, when asked what advice he would give to aspiring writers of any age, Paolini said, three simple things:

1. **Write about what excites and moves you the most, otherwise your enthusiasm will never sustain you through an entire novel.**

2. **Be persistent and disciplined, otherwise someone more determined will take your place.**

3. **Be humble enough to accept editorial criticism and learn all you can about your craft.[5]**

Sage advice for a writer of any age!

SOMETHING'S GOT TO GIVE: TIME WASTERS YOU CAN ELIMINATE

While working on a big writing project, I was bogged down with personal obligations such as moving and the imminent arrival of a new baby. Time was such an important commodity that something had to give. I'm sure you can think of tons of responsibilities that take up your time, such as studying, a part-time job, family obligations, and perhaps a boyfriend or girlfriend.

People often say they want to get published but are frustrated because they don't have time to write. Cop-out? Perhaps. Does that sound harsh? Sure, but if you were forced to write down every single thing you do in a day, no doubt you could find an extra fifteen minutes if you had to. Time spent on the Internet surfing the Web, or talking on the phone, or some other activity could simply be shortened or even eliminated.

A quick and easy way to find more writing time without giving up everyday life necessities like eating and sleeping, is to give up one of America's most popular time wasters—television. Those few minutes you intend to watch while eating a snack or a meal can easily turn into a few hours, while inspiration to get things down on paper just dwindles away to nothing.

FRIGHTENING RECOLLECTION

To this day, famous teen author S. E. Hinton says she doesn't like TV. She admits that she disliked it dating back to the time she was a teen. She would be writing or reading, and sometimes her mother dragged her by the hair into the family room to watch television, telling her to act like a part of the family.[6]

Taking It One Day at a Time

Especially when writing, try to keep up your no-television resolve, no matter how tempting it might be to turn it on. For me, watching television became like an addiction. I would start by checking the scores of sports games and eventually slide back to my habit of having the TV on in the background all day. Hating the silence, I was addicted to the soothing white noise television provided.

Giving up television gives you two gifts: (1) the ability to complete tasks more quickly instead of stopping what you're *supposed* to be doing to watch something on the tube; and (2) more time to read.

Get into Your Own Groove

For my first book, I was able to find my own specific "work time," from 10:00 p.m. until 2:00 a.m., and stick to it religiously. Although I'd feel tired most of the day, at ten o'clock at night, my mind would literally "turn on" and I was alert and ready to go. It was almost a Pavlovian response!

Schedule Your Time Like a Nine-to-Fiver!

I've read about different rituals or styles, where some writers pick a certain amount of time they will write each day, say four to eight hours. Then they spend a certain amount of allotted time editing, working on pitches, and checking in and answering e-mails.

These writers stick to their schedule, and the tasks that need to get done each day are certain to be finished. It might sound rigid, but in a field like freelance writing that requires self-motivation, you've got to be sure the work gets done.

Like anything that becomes a habit, exercise for example, one of the only ways to stick to it is to be consistent. Lots of people I interviewed said they found it easiest to stick to a certain time of day. Depending on your schedule, you can start

---

IN THE ZONE!

"I've heard that the actual act of creating involves some different brain waves more similar to those we experience as we're falling asleep. So, it's only natural to feel a little 'foggy' when you come out of a creative endeavor such as writing or painting. I always tell people that if they call me when I'm 'in the zone' and I tell them I'm drawing or writing or designing, no matter how much like a conversation it might seem, I will NOT remember most or all of anything they tell me because it's like I'm sleepwalking. Maybe that's why people think artists are just spacey!"

—Gail Green, artist and author.[7]

out writing for one hour every Friday, Saturday, and Sunday evening from 6:00 p.m. to 7:00 p.m. before you go to a job or out with friends or your significant other. Family and friends will eventually know not to plan on seeing you until 7:30 p.m. or later on weekends, and they will start to work around your schedule. You will need to carefully examine your daily life and see if there is one chunk of time that is always available. Build around that time and create a writing schedule.

Early Bird Catches the Worm

Another idea that has worked for writers is to wake up one to two hours earlier than normal, every single day (or at least on "writing days"). Once the body adapts to the new schedule, it could make waking up easier and even inspire you to get excited about your writing time before hopping in the shower or going to work out. A note of caution: It is easy to get on a roll while writing and lose all track of time. Make sure you aren't late for school or work!

Added Bonus

If you try the early morning writing routine, you might gain the added benefit of jump-starting your mind first thing in the morning. Often, people feel more awake and can concentrate better throughout the day when they start the morning with a

writing session. The same is true for early morning workout sessions. You might think it would tire a person out for the day, but more often than not, the opposite is true. Your endorphins start pumping and you're revved up to go.

There's something to be said for writing first thing in the morning while you're fresh, alert, and rested. Not to mention the fact that if you write early in the morning, you don't have the hassles of phone interruptions, siblings bugging you, parental interruptions, friends IMing you, or a million other distractions.

When teen and twenty-something "creative types" such as writers, artists, and musicians were asked, "*What, if any, rituals do you perform to settle down when it's time to get to work?*" they responded with the following answers:

"First I crack all my knuckles to warm up my fingers and sit real still and get comfortable. It's hard to work if you're uncomfortable . . . it's distracting."

—Stevie Powers, age eighteen

"To settle down, it helps me to make lists of everything I need to get done personally. Once I put it in chronological order and get one or two things checked off, I feel calm enough to work."

—Juli Powers, approx. age twenty-five

"It sounds weird, but when writing one specific novel, I always play a certain CD I like. Then if I hear one of the songs from it on the radio, I have an immediate urge to write. It's kind of cool!"

—Shawn Wickersheim, approx. age nineteen

You must examine your own life, list of responsibilities, obligations, and your own body rhythms. If you are a night owl who hits the snooze button three to five times before dragging yourself out of bed in the morning, then waking up an hour earlier each day will not do it for you. There are no set answers except to do what's best for you.

Ten Minutes—Maximum!

When reading over questionnaires for this book, I was pleased to learn that I'm not the only person addicted to sudoku! Many participants confessed to playing a few games of solitaire, sudoku, or text twist, and many others meditate to wind down and settle into their various tasks. (The important thing, all agreed, was to set a time limit of about ten minutes or less. Otherwise, you might end up wasting a half hour and get tired before getting anything done, which completely defeats the purpose.)

DON'T GET CAUGHT IN THE TIME-WASTER TRAP!

E-mail is a *huge* time waster, most writers will agree. Time flies by and before you know it, you've lost your urge to write. You should try hard to limit checking your e-mail; scan for notes from editors, publishers you've queried, and any urgent notes from family or friends. Otherwise, get in and get out. It's way too easy to get sucked in to reading jokes, responding to silly questionnaires, and so on!

Similarly, surfing the Web can send you off on so many different tangents that you depart from the original reason you were doing research. It is another tool that requires much discipline on the part of the user!

As with any discipline where you have to concentrate, you need a "clean slate," so to speak. That is how I think of my mind after I sit down, do a few little rituals, and settle in to write for the day. It leaves me open to all the new research I find and takes me on tangents that often develop into new chapters right before my eyes.

Set Page Goals

Some writers write a certain amount of pages each day. An author friend of mine sets his daily writing to ten pages. When he hits ten pages—be it 5:30 a.m., 8:00 a.m., or even 2:00 p.m.—he's done. Some days it might take two hours, while other days it takes six or seven hours. It just depends on what he's writing and if he's motivated, distracted, or whatever else might be going on around him.

BEGINNER INFO TO GET YOU STARTED

It might seem like the easiest lesson in this book, and in fact, it is. The first things you should know as a writer are what counts as a submission envelope, what *SASE* means, and how to fill out each of them.

SASE and SAE

The acronyms stand for self-addressed stamped envelope and self-addressed envelope, respectively. One requires postage, and one does not. However, some publishers are doing away with them by simply saying, "Don't bother sending a SASE/SAE. If we want to offer a contract, we'll contact you. Otherwise, if you don't hear from us, assume you've been rejected." (Note: In 2006, I saw one publisher's guidelines that read, "Without a SASE, the entire submission will be tossed out immediately" so be sure to follow the specific guidelines for each publisher.)

Harsh, right? Well, that's the reality of being a freelance writer these days. On the bright side, it is not completely the norm—yet. My writer friends and I get so excited sharing our rejection letters. We consider them milestones, triumphs even! And if you are lucky enough to get a handwritten note on the usual form-letter rejection, offering encouragement to submit to that editor again, you've hit the jackpot!

In the competitive business of writing, you need to celebrate handwritten rejection letters. If you are at all good with numbers, then you know that based on the law of averages, each rejection brings you one step closer to a sale.

I was so excited when I got my first rejection slip. It felt like I was finally initiated into the secret club of writers. After all, people like Stephen King experienced the same thing I had, as he mentions in his book titled *On Writing*.[8] (This book is one of the most valuable books on my "writer's shelf" of resources. I recommend buying your own copy.)

Technical Nitty-Gritty

To mail your manuscript to a publisher, you should always use a 9 × 12 inch envelope or larger. If your manuscript is lengthy, you can put a rubber band around it (but do not bind it) and place it in a box. Manuscripts should never be folded, no matter what the length, as it looks unprofessional.

In center of the envelope, put the contact name and title on the first line. On the second line write the name of the publishing house and on the third and fourth lines, its address. I always go to the company's website to double-check submission editors or find the specific person who is to receive unsolicited manuscripts. Then I call the office to verify the person's title and the spelling of his or her name, along with the current mailing address and zip code. Sure, it's an extra step, but a small one to ensure you don't make a bad first impression. Nothing is worse than screwing up the person's name when you're trying so hard to impress. Worse yet would be putting Mr. for a Ms. or vice-versa for a non–gender specific name such as Chris or Pat. *Always* check and recheck your facts, even when doing something as simple as addressing your envelope for a submission!

Last, when addressing your SASE, fill in your *own* address for both the return address *and* the mailing address. This way, the publisher can return your manuscript with or without a note if they reject it. Include the title of the piece and the publisher it was sent to in parentheses on the first line after your name, in the return address. That way, if you're circulating several manuscripts to several different publishers you won't get confused as to which manuscript is being returned and by whom, not to mention any responses received back.

CHAPTER 3 WRITING EXERCISE

Go back and review Don Crowther's "An Interesting Concept" from earlier in this chapter and try to do the forty-eight-minute exercise. See if you can write an entire short story in the time given. Take your twelve-minute break, then go back and revise.

NOTES

1. Don Crowther, "The Power of 48 Minutes," Success Begins Today, successbeginstoday.org/wordpress/2006/09/the-power-of-48-minutes/ (accessed September 21, 2006).

2. Christopher Paul Curtis, *The Watsons Go to Birmingham—1963* (New York: Delacorte Press, 1995), and *Bud, Not Buddy* (New York: Random House Children's Books, 1999).

3. Christopher Paul Curtis speaking at conference for the Society of Children's Book Writers & Illustrators (SCBWI) in New York, 2001, and again for SCBWI in Los Angeles, 2005

4. "Author Profile: Christopher Paolini," Teenreads.com, www.teenreads.com/authors/au-paolini-christopher.asp (accessed April 15, 2007).

5. "Author Profile: Christopher Paolini."

6. *Chicago Tribune*, Parade section, December 10, 2006, p. 8.

7. Gail Green, e-mail to author, March 2006.

8. Stephen King, *On Writing: A Memoir of the Craft* (New York: Pocket Books, 2001).

4 Fiction Basics

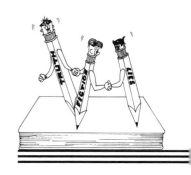

WHAT DO YOU LIKE TO WRITE?

Don't answer too quickly. Deciding what you like to write might be difficult to pinpoint if you're just starting out. Have you always liked writing, or is it a new interest? How long have you written? Have you kept a diary/journal since childhood? Or are you an investigator of sorts, surfing the Web to find any and all information about various topics that interest you before you write a fantastic article?

Before you pick a topic, you should decide on a fiction genre. Next, you must pick an audience. Will you be writing for children or adults, professional markets, or another audience that inspires you? For each piece you write, you'll have to narrow it down to a specific group. Using writing for children as an example, you'll choose your readership by picking categories such as toddlers, early readers, grade school age, middle school, teens, and young adult. And within those categories, you can get even *more* specific, such as "athletes twenty-five to fifty-four" or "women eighteen to twenty-five."

Once you've decided who you will be writing for, you will need to make even more decisions. Did you realize how much planning was involved in writing before you even put pen to paper? If you take the time to do these tasks in an organized way, things fall into place quickly. That's true even if you're writing a poem or fantasy novel. People often think that only nonfiction writers have to be orderly and systematic. Not true. Of course, that is my personal (and professional) opinion. However, proper planning will leave you open to let the words flow out of you.

TWO BASIC ELEMENTS OF FICTION

Genre

The word *genre* can be defined as a specific category of literature marked by a particular style, form, or content. Some examples of fiction genres are action-adventure, crime, mystery or detective, humor, romance, horror, thriller, Western, fantasy, science fiction (or sci-fi), and historical fiction.

If you think you'd like to write children's books, one way to narrow this category down is by types of books, beginning with what you prefer. Some examples are picture books, board books, concept books, easy readers, middle grade novels, teen fiction, and so on. Don't be afraid to get out of your comfort zone and try a new genre that you haven't written in before.

Audience

There are many ways to describe your audience. One way would be to literally describe it with facts such as age and gender. Not only are the demographics of the audience important to know, but the arena in which you are writing is important as well. Will you be writing an article, or a short novella, or a long book? *Why does this matter?* You might wonder. Let's explore.

How you talk to your audience will depend on its age and, at times, gender. For example, when writing for boys eight to ten years old, you will use different expressions and language than you would for a book for girls thirteen to eighteen years old. You'll be able to use slang, themes, subject matter, and scenarios more appropriate for the age, not to mention gender.

Let's say you're writing a story for a teen girls' magazine where the main character is buying her first bra. Obviously, the language, expressions, and topic will be vastly different than if you are writing a story for younger boys. A short story for boys might have a character involved in the Boy Scouts of America, and the language would have less "teen speak" due to the younger audience.

When you write a story for a young audience, it needs to be streamlined and get right to the point. With limited attention spans, there isn't much time to set up and explain an in-depth story line. Get in there with an engaging "hook," and keep the plot simple.

That is completely different from a book in which you'll have many pages to expand on characterization, back story, set up, and plotting. Magazine stories usually range from 250–2,000 words. Needless to say, each word much be chosen carefully.

When writing for young children, you must remember to end with a feeling of *hope*. The characters might be in an awful situation, face many hardships, and deal with seemingly insurmountable problems. But all stories, no matter how bleak, should end with an aura of hopefulness! That is a common rule when writing for a younger audience.

When writing for adults, there are important elements to consider as well. Starting with plotting and the ability to make more complex and intertwining story lines, an adult audience can be challenging and exciting to write for. Other than the differences in vocabulary and content, the adult audience allows for more graphic avenues and mature themes.

Writing for teens or young adults positions you in the middle, with an audience between children and adults. While there is room for broader subjects than writing for children, there are still certain lines that are not often crossed. Some may argue that lines have been crossed in certain books like those mentioned in chapter 9, "Emotional and Gritty Realism." A certain amount of sex and violence is tolerated in young adult books, considering the works that have been published, but keep in mind that teen readers are not full-fledged adults yet. With that in mind, temper your subject matter. And remember to keep that shred of hopefulness in the overall message or tone of the story.

BASIC TIP: SHOW, DON'T TELL

Always remember to use all five senses when possible. How does your character's room smell? What does the paint color or lighting (or lack thereof) make her feel when she's in her room? Is it her safe haven or more of a jail when she's in trouble? Example 1—*telling*:

My room is pink, wall-to-wall, with thick matching curtains. There are no mirrors and just a mattress on the floor, a bean bag chair, CD player, and two huge windows. The sun makes the room really hot.

This example gives some basic information, but the reader doesn't get a chance to see the character's personality or what she might be like. It is dry and uninteresting and not much of a page-turner.

Example 2—*showing*:

My room has two huge windows I can look out onto the lake to see people ice fishing. I can close the thick curtains to make it dark as a cave, so I can sleep soundly. My room is so warm and cozy in the afternoon when the sun spills in, I just lie on my beanbag in the corner and read. I have a CD player next to my bed, if I want to just veg out. And I *love* pink. It's my favorite color, so I painted the walls and ceiling a warm, rosy pink. FYI, there are no mirrors anywhere. Why bother?

What have you learned about this character in the second example? Even though she didn't say it specifically, we know she's a minimalist, having mentioned nothing but a bean bag chair and a CD player. She may need the darkness to sleep, but the big windows let her observe what's going on around her if she's in the mood. She may be a bit shy or introverted—more of a "watcher" than a participant. The pink is a warm and soothing (and girlie) color, making her a bit feminine. And last, the detail of mentioning no mirrors gives us a subtle clue that she's either self-conscious or doesn't want to deal with her looks. All in all, the second example comes off as a confession to the reader about what the character is all about. This will make for a much more interesting book, since you are right there with the character, experiencing things *together*. As the reader, you aren't hearing a report like a court stenographer reading back what was said word-for-word. You are experiencing what is going on through a character's eyes.

RECOMMENDED BOOKS EVERY FICTION WRITER SHOULD GET

There is an outstanding book on creating believable characters, and more importantly, the ways different types of characters interact with each other. *The Complete Writer's Guide to Heroes & Heroines: Sixteen Master Archetypes*, by Tami D. Cowden, Caro LaFever, and Sue Viders, is a must have for any fiction writer.[1]

The book gives a detailed description of the strengths and flaws of sixteen archetypes and how each type relates to the other archetypes. Then the book cross-references the archetypes as friends, enemies, and romantic pairings. For example, the "Spunky Kid" is described as wholesome and refreshing, cooperative, a team player who is reliable and dependable and keeps all commitments, among other things. Some of her flaws include the fact that she can slide into the martyr role, is unassertive in her love life, and unaware that she undermines herself. Regarding love life, the Spunky Kid can be paired with the "Bad Boy," an example being the movie *Grease* with the archetypes played by Olivia Newton John and John Travolta.

When writing believable characters, you can double-check how they would interact and see if the relationships ring true. An example that comes to mind is a manuscript I read for a middle grade novel. There were two girls that started out as best friends. They met in kindergarten and were like sisters up until seventh grade when all the conflict between them starts. However, after reviewing the manuscript a few times, I discovered that the girls were both the "Boss." Since I was having a lot of problems critiquing situations the girls would get into, I turned to this book for help. After reading just a few chapters, I discovered that two Bosses would not be best friends! A best friend pairing usually has a contrast such as a Boss and a "Nurturer." The protagonist's and antagonist's strongest personality traits would have to *complement* each other, not clash.

LESSONS IN WRITING FICTION

Do some preliminary homework. It all starts with an idea. I found a great list called "TIPS on getting ideas" that goes like this:

- Read.
- Ask questions.
- Learn something new.
- Listen to what people say.
- Watch the world around you.
- Think of how to improve things.
- Invent an imaginary world.
- Remember details.
- Keep a journal.
- Doodle.
- And don't forget to brainstorm![2]

Start at the Beginning

How do you start writing a novel? Well, some start at the beginning, with an introduction. Author Jan Chappuis has written *Six-Trait Mini-Lessons*.[3] In the lessons, she suggests a

variety of openings. Here are her starter ideas, followed by my examples in parentheses:

- ⊚ *Open with a question* ("Have you ever fallen in love?" she asked her big sister.)
- ⊚ *Open with an announcement* ("I'm dropping out of college, and nothing you can say will make me go back!" Jen shouted at Mom and Dad).
- ⊚ *Open with a bold and challenging statement* ("If you touch one hair on my daughter's head, it'll be the last breath you draw!" Cynthia threatened).
- ⊚ *Open with a quotation from somebody* ("There is one scene in that movie that will make you want to hurl. . . . I swear!" my best friend said when I told her we should rent *Van Wilder*).
- ⊚ *Open with a personal experience* (Megan felt like crying, she was so scared when she was wheeled into surgery to get her tonsils out. But she told her parents, "It's no big deal." She wanted to be strong for them, since they looked worried, too).
- ⊚ *Open with how you felt* (My heart was racing. Sweat ran down my face and I tasted the saltiness of it on my lips. How could I have predicted what would happen when I woke up at 2:30 a.m.?)

These are some ideas to get your mind working and put the ball in motion. Once you try one or two of these "starters," you'll be surprised at how fast your thoughts will take off and get you going on a variety of topics!

Character Basics

When you first dream up a character, you don't need to know every little nuance, phobia, and past embarrassment of the person. Start with the basics. A blank page with a blinking cursor can be intimidating. But if you start with simple traits like the ones listed below, the ball will start rolling, and pretty soon you'll have a snowball effect, with ideas spewing out of you.

young or old

neat or sloppy

silly or serious

nice or mean

tall or short

Capricorn or Gemini

ugly or cute

outgoing or shy[4]

You can make a list that goes on and on. After you've got a brief idea about your character, you can fill in more specific details. One of the most important things about your characters is their names. Do they go by a nickname? Are they more formal? Do their names fit them, or is it ironic that they were given names that would ultimately be the complete opposite of what and whom they turned out to be?

WORDS OF WISDOM FROM A PRO

S. E. Hinton talks about an interesting transformation that takes place in the beginning of a book. When interviewed, she mentions how she'd start to think about her narrator when beginning to write, but then just switch to *being* him. This is one of the fun things she enjoys about being a writer. Her favorite character to "become" as narrator was Ponyboy Curtis.[5]

STEPHEN KING, AUTHOR PUBLISHED AS A TEEN[6]

Stephen King was born in Portland, Maine, in 1947. In high school, he got in trouble for a parody "school newspaper" he created and was bold (or stupid, as he himself admitted) enough to sign his real name to. That little stunt got him in a world of trouble. Still, it showcased his talents when he was a teen!

King's first professional sale came at age twenty, in 1967, when he sold a short story titled "The Glass Floor" to *Startling Mystery Stories*. He continued to sell stories to men's magazines, which years later appeared in his anthologies, such as the *Night Shift* collection.

A HEARTFELT PLEA

A man walks alone in the depths of his own mental consciousness, as he battles the everyday struggles of difficult decisions, confusing choices and unexpected consequences.

"Today will be different. Today will be better than the days before," he tells himself over and over again, only to be blindsided by the merciless onslaught of this cold, cynical world.

He wonders to himself, "Where is the light?" as he looks hopelessly down the long, dark tunnel that is his life.

He throws his fist-clenched hands into the air while he screams into vast open sky and pleads to anyone listening to show him that there is hope, that there is meaning, even in his painful and meaningless life.

His heart cries out for something or someone to hear its woes. But there is no one around him, for he is alone.

He has nowhere to go. He is lost. He is confused.

He does not see the truth that is waiting for him, the truth that yearns to set him free. He has lost his way and has been blinded by the darkness of his own mind.

So who, then, will set him free?

So who then will open his eyes so that he can see what he is meant to see?

—Scott Bae, early twenties, Northbrook, Illinois

Stephen's life rolled along; he married, taught high school English classes, and wrote in the evenings and on the weekends. In 1973, six years after his first professional sale, he sold his first novel, *Carrie*.[7] His new editor told him that a major paperback sale would give him enough income to become a full-time writer and retire from teaching. The rest, as they say, is history. King's illustrious career has included over forty books and two hundred short stories. He and his wife Tabitha provide scholarships for local high school students and contribute to many other local and national charities. Stephen King, many feel, can be likened to the gold standard for writing.

Setting

Setting is where a story takes place, but it should tell when it takes place, too. However, it is not as simple as saying "Chicago,

WRITERS CONNECTING WITH READERS

Before getting to the basics of writing fiction, let's look at what one might consider "great writing." Oftentimes, the simplest explanation of a truly great piece of writing is, when you, the reader, are privy to a glimpse into the creator's heart and soul; when the essence of the writer's spirit and vision is captured in a way that readers feel connected. Ultimately, one of a writer's goals is to make a reader think, "Wow! That's exactly how *I* feel. I didn't know other people felt this way, too. Maybe I'm not totally alone after all."

Illinois." Sure, you can start with a place, but it may need to be more exact. Other times, you may want it to be less exact. Your character might live on the north side of the city in Lincoln Park, not far from the zoo. The entire story might take place early morning before the sun comes up, on a freezing February morning. Or it might take place over a ten-year span, traveling through trade school, a few romances, marriage, two children, an unforeseen illness, and then divorce. Who knows where you will go within the time frame of your story. What's more, will it be set in the present, a period piece set in the 1860s, or sometime in the golden age of disco, the 1970s? Maybe it's a futuristic story set in the year 2602? You need a time frame that is clear so the audience knows what to expect. For example, if you have flying cars in your story, it had better be set in the future.

Setting can also be as simple as the bedroom of the main character. You'll still need to know about the bedroom, as it could become almost a character itself. The main character may always be there, reading, or on the Internet, or sleeping a ton, or too depressed to get out and face the world, or bedridden with an illness—who knows? Well, actually *you* do. That's what makes being the author so much fun! You have power to create the entire world of the characters. (You'll still need to give your audience a time frame—what part of the day or month or year.)

How to Explain Your Story's Setting

Setting is entirely up to you, the author, as well as how you reveal it to your audience. You can categorize it using three separate types of descriptions. More specifically, let's call them "Vague," "More Specific," and "Exact" setting descriptions. Here is an example of each:

> *Vague*: my basement last night
>
> *More Specific*: early one winter morning at Prairieview Elementary [no date or town given]
>
> *Exact*: Just past midnight on December 25, 1985, in the small Midwestern town of Deerfield, Illinois, in the United States . . .

As shown above, various descriptions are acceptable. However, the tone of your story will be noticeably different, simply by how you decide to set it up.

Outlining: Mapping Your Course

Now that you've come up with characters, setting, and time frame, you're ready to get to your outline. Outlining is the end-all-be-all way to guarantee you succeed at writing. *Why?* you wonder. Think of it as a map. If you're taking a road trip to visit colleges around the country, but you've never been to them, how will you get to your destination? It's not enough to know that Harvard is in Cambridge, Massachusetts. You'll need to know what highways to take to get there, where and when to stop for gas and food, and once there, where to find the dean's office. You can't just drive there from some small town in the Midwest and hope to get to the school without a map.

Writing is the *exact* same concept! Your outline will be your driving directions. You might get from point A to point B without them, but it would take substantially more time, not to mention more frustration. Why do that to yourself? Just make a map!

Outlining Fiction

For nonfiction, you can't live without outlining. However, some argue it is equally important for fiction, especially novel writing. Your outline need not be set in stone. It can be one that changes, evolves, and most importantly, grows!

If, for example, you're in the middle of writing a novel and stuck at chapter 12 of a seventeen chapter novel, unsure of where you are headed or even how to get back on track, have no fear. You'll get out of there!

It's not too late—*drum roll please*—to create an outline this very minute! Start with an outline as simple as five points to help you organize your thoughts and ideas. For example,

    I. **Teen doesn't want to go to college.**

    II. **Parents force the issue, stating they are dropping her off at the university, only two hours from home, at the end of the week.**

    III. **Main character runs away, unaware that eleven-year-old sister has followed her with a backpack of her own.**

    IV. **As main character starts to board cross-country train, catches glimpse of sister out of corner of eye and stops.**

    V. **Finds out stepfather has been hitting their mother and has to decide how to protect sister and convince mother to leave as well.**

Are you beginning to understand how to get your story rolling? Make a quick outline to get down a beginning, middle, and end. Then add one or two subplots and look for ways to add lots of tension to enrich the story.

As a writer of fiction, you should outline quickly then go back again and again, twenty times if necessary, and thicken it up (in other words, add to each point of your outline) each

Here's a layout for how to start your outline with a three-part design:

   I. **Plot: beginning, middle, end (what is the story about; what *happens?*)**
   II. **Problem: some dilemma for the main character to overcome and grow from. Without this, what's the point of writing the story? Usually, there *is* no story without a problem.**
   III. **Solution: how the main character gets *himself or herself* out of the jam without someone else swooping in to "save the day." After the protagonist (or lead character) gets out of trouble, get him or her in *even more trouble*! Repeat *as often as necessary* for the personal growth your character is to experience within your story.**

time you read through it. Before you know it, chunks of text will become story lines, then different scenes and chapters. And all of a sudden, you'll look down at the bottom of your screen to see you've hit page 200 and wonder how you got to the final chapter so fast. (Of course, some writers like to write the outline first, and *then* go for the climatic scene to get it out of the way. Go for the kill, then fill in all the extraneous details like back story, setting, and so on afterward.)

HELEN OYEYEMI, EIGHTEEN-YEAR-OLD NOVELIST[8]

Helen Oyeyemi was born in Nigeria on December 10, 1984, and moved to London with her family when she was four years old. She has described herself as a literary, smart, smart-mouthed child with an imaginary friend named Chimmy.

Oyeyemi confessed to know despair and to seek an authentic self when she felt like an outsider after moving to England. At age fifteen, she attempted suicide. She says that she and other classmates of color didn't realize that they could be the characters in stories people wrote. Since she had never read black writers with black characters, all the characters in Oyeymi's own stories were white. She didn't get the best grades for stories she had written for school. Even she admitted that something was missing from her writing.

A THRILL OF A JOB . . . WRITING IS

An exciting part of writing is getting to do vastly different projects, often at the same time. It's like when you have multiple assignments for your classes in school. It can help the freshness of one project by being able to set it aside for a bit then return to it after working on a totally different subject. If you get stuck on one thing, turn to another and come back to the first one later with a new perspective. That's one way to avoid the ever-talked-about "writer's block." Some people have too many ideas and stories to work on at one time. If that's the case for you, list all your projects/ideas and place them in order of importance. One tip: if you work this way, try to make the projects opposites of some sort. For example, do a history report one day, then a science lab write-up another day. Or work on a speech or oral report one day, then a book report another day.

Opposite Views from Two Different Writers

Stacy Chudwin and Eugene Fertelmeyer are teens who have been friends since high school. In 2006, while both were in college and pursuing writing, we sat down for a chat. We discussed how each works at his and her writing craft; Stacy is a published novelist and Eugene a playwright.

"I always work on at least two projects at a time. I have to, so if I'm not in the mood to work on a particular manuscript or am stuck on a project, I work on the other," says Eugene.

"No. Never, ever! I cannot work on more than one thing at a time. It is too confusing and would completely wreck my flow. I need to immerse myself in the world I'm creating," says Stacy.[9]

Thankfully, she survived adolescence, and in order to avoid studying for finals (she says), she began writing a story, not knowing it would grow into a novel.

Oyeyemi's first published novel, *The Icarus Girl* (2006), was an instant hit in England, garnering reviews that called her "extraordinary" in the *London Sunday Telegraph* and "astonishing" in the *Financial Times*.[10]

In contrast to the self-proclaimed, sassy-mouthed child she started out as, a soft-spoken twenty-one-year-old Helen Oyeyemi describes her novel writing as obsessive; she writes at her parent's computer on weekends, after school, and in the middle of the night. She compares it to being in love. After the first twenty pages were written, she sent it to an agent she randomly picked from an agent directory. She was the youngest writer ever signed by Alexandra Pringle, the editor in chief at Bloomsbury in the United Kingdom. Bloomsbury insisted that her talent, not her age, was what got her published.

In 2007, while at Cambridge University, Helen Oyeyemi studied political science as well as social science. When discussing writing her novel, she said it wasn't scary since she didn't think it *was* a novel until the end. It was something she was doing for fun. That completely took the pressure off of her. She said it was like writing a story that kept getting longer and longer.

GET INSPIRED! FICTION AUTHORS PUBLISHED IN THEIR TEENS[11]

Amelia Atwater-Rhodes (fourteen years old), *In the Forests of the Night* (New York: Dell Laurel-Leaf, 1999).

Isabelle Carmody (fifteen years old), *Obernewtyn* (New York: Random House, 1987).

Maureen Daly (seventeen years old), *Seventeenth Summer* (New York: Simon & Schuster, 1942).

Walter Farley (fifteen years old), *Black Stallion* (New York: Random House, 1941).

Miles Franklin (sixteen years old), *My Brilliant Career* (New York: HarperCollins, 1901).

Kimberly Fuller (sixteen years old), *Home* (New York: Tom Doherty Associates, 1997).

Robert Geile (eighteen years old), Noah Barrow, and Richard Tanne, eds. *On Our Way : A Collection of Short Stories by Young American Filmmakers* (Lincoln, NE: iUniverse, 2004).

S. E. Hinton (sixteen years old), *Outsiders* (New York: Viking Press, 1967).

Gordon Korman (sixteen years old), *This Can't Be Happening at McDonald Hall* (Ontario: Scholastic, 1978).

Benjamin Lebert (sixteen years old), *Crazy* (New York: Alfred A. Knopf, 2000).

Megan McNeil Libby (sixteen years old), *Postcards from France* (New York: HarperTorch, 1997).

Christopher Paolini (nineteen years old), *Eragon* (New York: Alfred A. Knopf, 2002).

Dav Pilkey (nineteen years old), *World War Won* (Frederick, MD: Landmark Editions, 1987).

Mary Shelley (nineteen years old), *Frankenstein* (New York: Simon & Schuster, 2004).

CALLING ALL YOUNG AUTHORS[12]

The Institute of Children's Literature prints two market guides a year, one for the magazine market and one for the book market. The following are websites of magazine publishers that accept submissions from young authors.

The Apprentice Writer (www.susqu.edu/writers; click "high school students"). Magazine accepts fiction, essays, plays, photographs, and artwork.

The Claremont Review (www.theclaremontreview.ca). Magazine features poetry, short stories, short plays, artwork, and author interviews. It prefers work that reveals something about the human condition.

Teen Ink (www.teenink.com). Magazine accepts fiction and nonfiction from teen authors.

In *The Icarus Girl*, the main character has an imaginary friend named TillyTilly who soon gets her in trouble. It was experience with her own imaginary friend, Chimmy, that was the springboard to inspire her novel, which was primarily fictional.

Oyeyemi also wrote two plays that were staged while she was at Cambridge and published by Methuen. They came out in the United States in September 2005. In 2008, she was working on a second novel about Afro-Cuban mythology.

Stating that it's good to have another career to fall back on, not to mention a subject that intrigues her, Oyeyemi continued studying political science. She said that she will continue to try to improve her writing as time goes on.

STACY CHUDWIN, TEEN AUTHOR

In 2006, Stacy Chudwin of Lincolnshire, Illinois, was a sophomore at Duke University, where she studied English and marketing. Her first novel, *Sands of the Desert*, was published in 2003 by Publish America, Inc., when she was sixteen years old.[13] Since 2007, Stacy has been looking for a publisher for her second novel, a historical fiction piece. She plans to continue reading and writing and encourages other teens to do the same.

Stacy Chudwin—teen novelist, 2006.

Interview with Stacy Chudwin[14]

I met Stacy in 2005 when she was finishing high school and promoting her first novel, *Sands of the Desert*. Two years later, I caught up with Stacy to see what she had learned from the college experience and to see whether her goals had changed after becoming a young, published, and award-winning teen author.

Let's start with your family life. Who is at home, and what if any aspect of your family has influenced your writing?

I have an older brother who goes to Penn State University and lives with my parents. My mother has multiple sclerosis (MS). Seeing her go from being an athletic, active mother to one who can't even walk has deeply influenced the way I feel about others' misfortunes. I am grateful that I still have such a wonderful, supportive mother, even if she can't do a lot of the things she used to do. I think her MS has taught me to be more compassionate toward others. I chose to donate 20 percent of my profits from *Sands of the Desert* to the National Multiple Sclerosis Society, and I intend to do the same if my next novel is published.

How old were you when you started writing?

I began reading right after I turned four, and before I could even pick up the pen to write, I would create stories in my head and play them out with plastic figures. Once I could write, I would sometimes take books down off the shelves and copy them onto a piece of paper so I could tell my mom I had "written" a book. She would say, "No, honey, that's plagiarism."

As your first book gets more attention, and you are viewed as more of a young adult than simply a teen, what do you plan to do next in your budding career? What is your declared major in college?

I am majoring in English with a certificate in markets and management and a minor in linguistics. My plan is to continue writing and spend a summer in New York working for a literary agency to gain a better understanding of the business side of writing. I have completed writing a second novel and plan to do some short story writing while I am in college.

I chose English because it is without question my greatest intellectual passion. I love reading and dissecting literature. I believe that the best way to become a better writer is to read great canonical works and unpack what it is that makes them great. I chose to complement English with marketing because the two go well together. Both involve creativity and communication skills, and there is a great deal of marketing involved in the writing industry. English covers the craft, and marketing covers the business of writing.

Did you find novel writing to be a bit easier the second time around?

No! If anything, it was more difficult. My biggest goal for myself is to have each successive novel I write grow more complex, more thought provoking, and in general, better written than the one before it. I want to challenge myself to outdo myself every time I write. The one thing that helped was knowing I had it in me to see a novel through to completion.

Do you have a mentor?

I never really had one specific mentor, and I am still looking for one. I think a mentor is crucial to improving your work and being honest with yourself. I have had many English teachers who have been very helpful at crucial points in my life. A few that stand out in my mind are Ann Bates (second grade), Anne Browne (eighth grade), and Betsy Verhoeven (freshman year of college). These three were especially encouraging and went the extra mile to support me and my writing, and for that, I am very grateful.

Are you a mentor for anyone else?

I would definitely like to think of myself as one. One of the most rewarding aspects of being a teen author is that I am in the position to serve as an example to other young writers. I hope that my story in general could help inspire other teens to put their dreams into action and to not be afraid to take chances. People who never thought they could publish a book see that it is possible with lots of hard work and a little bit of luck. I love to critique other people's work and give them advice about the publishing industry, because I know how much such advice has helped me in the past.

When the eighth graders at my old junior high read *Sands of the Desert*, I got to come in twice to speak to the classes about the novel and about writing in general. After I did this, a few of the students emailed me with stories they began after hearing me speak. It was wonderful to know I had made a small difference in their lives, and I intend on speaking to a lot more of the local schools.

Any special project you've done that you'd like to plug here?

I recently finished writing a historical fiction novel titled *The Will* and am currently searching for an agent. I envision the audience as young adult/college age.

The Will tells the story of Melisenda Du Pres, a young woman living in France at the end of the nineteenth century. For all her wealth and social ranking, Melisenda finds herself tangled in a life of abuse from her piggish husband, bullying from the other aristocrats, and depression at the routine her life follows day after day. She is nearly driven to take her own life, but she is stopped by a surprising and timely twist of fate: her mother has left her a fortune in her will. Here's the catch, though: the money is hidden somewhere in the world, and Melisenda must embark on a quest to find it.

With a travel adventure story like *Around the World in Eighty Days* and a quirky, introspective heroine like *Pride and Prejudice*, *The Will* is more than just a story of a journey across the globe. It is the story of Melisenda's struggle to overcome her abuse and become the young woman she has always known she could be. This novel shows that we must constantly push ourselves to explore new regions, both in the outside world, and within ourselves.

After you graduate, what would be your ideal job/company to work for?

I wish I knew! Ideally, I would want writing to be my only job, but that may not be realistic. I want to have a job that excites me and gives me lots of interesting experiences to write about . . . anything that can give me grist for the mill. I have no idea what that is yet, but I would love if it involved traveling.

Thank you so much for your time. You've got a full load ahead of you with grand plans and an amazing future! Best wishes on your upcoming successes.

Point of View

The overall tone of a story can be very different depending on its point of view. With first-person point of view, readers are privy to the innermost thoughts and feelings of characters, since they tell their thoughts themselves. There is no "self-censorship" going on—people think what they think without necessarily being politically correct or even kind for that matter. It's an extremely honest way to see all aspects of an individual. However, a first-person narrator's interpretations of what someone else says or does can be incorrect, but we, as readers, get to see how the character feels about how a situation is played out. We see how they internalize feelings. A secondary character might mean to say one thing, but the lead of your story can take it the wrong way, in turn often causing some sort of conflict. Miscommunications between characters add conflicts, which move stories along.

With third-person limited point of view, the story is told through a narrator who knows only the thoughts and feelings of one character. It doesn't have all of the information such as other characters' thoughts or feelings, only that of the one, usually the main, character. Other characters are presented as seen or perceived by the narrator.

With third-person omniscient point of view, the story is again told by a narrator, but this time the narrator knows what all the characters are thinking or feeling.

GREAT MINDS THINK ALIKE

Have you ever noticed that movies seem to be made in pairs and come out around the same time? Look at movies over the last ten years—*Volcano* and *Dante's Peake*; *Antz* and *A Bug's Life*; *United 93* and *World Trade Center*; *Madagascar* and *The Wild*. You get the point? It is often said that good ideas float. What this means is that if there is a good idea out there, you probably aren't the only one thinking it. Sure you might be the only one to act on it, but oftentimes, similar ideas are written about at the same time.

People get their writing copyrighted because they fear their work might be "stolen" by another writer or even a publisher. In reality, that's not necessary. An idea is legally your own once that idea is written (or typed) on paper. Even if someone else writes about the same subject, your "voice" is what will separate your writing from another person's work.

The best way to explain point of view is to think of a movie camera and what it sees. It can pull back to show the audience a bigger picture of everything going on or zoom in to a particular scene in a more intimate manner.

A difficult task to perform is switching between points of view in a story. Those who can do it well are rare. One author particularly good at this technique is Alex Sanchez, author of the Rainbow series featured in chapter 9, "Emotional and Gritty Realism."

Voice

What Is It?

A writing term that you will hear over and over again is *voice*. It is what every great author strives to achieve. Your voice is like your own personal fingerprint on your writing. It's more than literally what your voice sounds like, although that is part of it. A character might have a stutter, speak in a slow drawl, use slang, be judgmental, have a wry sense of humor, write in pedantic ways—being showy about his or her

---

EXAMPLE OF A SPECIFIC VOICE

"Tommy, you dolt, how can someone with straight A's be such an idiot?" Jack asked.

"Shut up. I t-t-t-told you m-m-my mom threw away our notes! I w-w-w-wrote down everything we t-t-t-talked about after lab."

"I don't believe you. You have your baseball cards, your Pokémon cards, and your football cards organized and sectioned by type, name, and all that crap. Why would you mess up our homework? This is a group project, and now I'm screwed!" Jack said, face reddening with each word he spat out.

"Y-y-y-you always do this, Jack! You m-m-m-make me do all the work, then get pissed when *y-y-y-you* have to do some of the work y-y-y-yourself. Gimme a b-b-b-b-b-break," Tommy said, exasperated.

knowledge or overly concerned with minute details. These are just a few examples of how to show personality through voice.

How Do I Find Mine?

When you do all the prep work before beginning a story, you will know your characters intimately. You may imagine their favorite colors, foods, and pastimes. Perhaps you'll figure out any phobias, superstitions, likes and dislikes. You will become one with them through the process; therefore your voice should come through nicely. Details like dialect, social class, and intelligence—or lack there of—are all ways of creating a genuine voice of a three-dimensional character.

The Intimacies of a Diary

In some writers' opinions, the diary format is the best way to display your voice, because you can share the deep, dark feelings of a character. Diaries are confessional. When writing fiction, you can have your protagonist share his or her thoughts without holding back feelings, even if he or she has selfish or even "politically incorrect" thoughts.

A character can be nasty, selfish, lusting, or even boastful without self-censorship. The truth comes out much more naturally. Things a person might never have the courage to say to someone else, she can confess to her diary. This will add an aura of truth to your storytelling.

When writing in your own diary, it's best not to self-censor. Get your raw feelings and emotions down on paper. This can help you recapture the feelings you were experiencing while writing, and help you to remember them more vividly when revisiting what you wrote.

THE END OR JUST THE BEGINNING?

Now that you've finally finished your first draft, full of holes, misspellings, grammatical errors, and so on, it's time to get to one of the hardest, yet most important jobs of your writing career: *revising*.

Revise

You will go through *many* revisions before you reach your final draft—*many* revisions, even if you're doing something as seemingly simple as a five-hundred-word short story. Even Steven King rewrites! You'll revise things, such as taking out "really," "very," "etc.," and other nondescriptive words wherever possible. You'll make sure all your tenses match correctly. You'll change adjectives if you've used the same one too often in dialogue, for example. You may change a chunk of text or an event to an entirely different chapter. Who knows?

There will be so many changes that you'll probably have to walk away from your manuscript for a day or two at a time throughout the revision process, just to clear your head. After you look at the same thing over and over again, it begins to lose its meaning, like if you say the same word fifty times in a row. Say "fork" fifty-five times and see what happens. Does it even make sense? Is that really the word we use for an eating utensil? That's an illustration of how your manuscript might look after working on revisions too long without a break.

Self-editing is another way to talk about revising. An author goes through his or her manuscript again to fix all the technical errors that might have been missed, not to mention tightening up the text, rewriting areas, and eliminating inconsistencies. There will be misspellings (because we *know* spell check doesn't know the difference between *to*, *two*, and *too* and other such homophones.) You'll forget that *you're* (you are) dad's name is not Jim, but *your* dad's name is Jim. You can get carried away, typing as fast as you can to get it all down before your train of thought gets ruined by a noise outside, or a phone call, or an instant message popping up. This is where you have to literally read your copy carefully, word-for-word, checking for errors, not to mention typos. It is important for an author to take his or her time and not just rush through the edits or blow them off. It could cost the author money! (*Really?* Yes, read on about line editing in chapter 8!)

TIME OUT FOR MOVIE BUFFS

If you love writing and enjoy seeing movies that feature fiction writers as main characters, check out some of the following movies:

Adaptation (2002)—Nicholas Cage
Dead Poets' Society (1989)—Robin Williams
Finding Forrester (2000)—Sean Connery, Rob Brown
Misery (1990)—James Caan, Kathy Bates
Shakespeare in Love (1998)—Ben Affleck, Gwyneth Paltrow
Sideways (2004)—Paul Giamatti, Thomas Haden Church
Sisterhood of the Traveling Pants (2005)—Alexis Bledel,
   Amber Tamblyn, America Ferrera, Blake Lively
Secret Window (2004)—Johnny Depp
Wonderboys (2000)—Michael Douglas, Toby McGuire

IMITATION IS THE SINCEREST FORM OF FLATTERY

Since the film industry began, movies have been remade with new twists, updating old stories to fit in current-day scenarios. The movie *Mr. Deeds Goes to Town* (1936), was updated for the new millennium by Adam Sandler. His version is titled *Mr. Deeds* (2002).

How about the way *Romeo and Juliet* (written circa 1595) was reinvented as *West Side Story* (1961)? Or *The Wizard of Oz* (1938) reworked into *The Wiz* (1978)?

Frankenstein has been filmed several times. In 1931 it was called *Frankenstein*, in 1974 it was titled *Young Frankenstein*, and in 1994 it was back to *Frankenstein* again. In 1935 a spin-off was titled *Bride of Frankenstein*.[15]

A Christmas Carol, released in 1938, was remade into a 1951 movie titled *Scrooge*. Another version, starring Bill Murray, called *Scrooged*, was released in 1988. Each version is based on the character of Ebenezer Scrooge. (You can see a list of all versions of these movies by going to www.imdb.com.)

Have you seen the movie version of Stephen King's *Lawnmower Man*, which might be viewed as a remake of *Charly*, the movie version of Daniel Keyes' *Flowers for Algernon*?[16] Intentional or not, you can't mistake the similarities. Haven't seen either movie? Do yourself a favor and rent them both. Both are great concepts: each film is about a man with very limited intelligence who is suddenly and unexpectedly given super-accelerated cognitive thinking. What is interesting is what each man does with his newfound intelligence, how he reacts, and how he fears that his ability might be taken away.

FRANKENSTEIN WAS BORN OF A TEENAGE GIRL!

It's true! Did you know that the original story of Frankenstein was published by a teen named Mary Shelley in the year 1818? She was only nineteen years old.

ONLINE INTERVIEWS

When you get a book published, it is neat to see reviews (okay, it's neat if they are *positive* reviews) of your work. But in the back of your mind, it's hard to believe someone else might actually be reading something you wrote. In fact, if it was a particularly long project, by the time it comes out you might actually find yourself reading parts as if you were reading it for the first time!

I did my first online interview just a few years ago. It was fascinating to be engaged in a discussion with readers from around the country who quoted or paraphrased parts of what I had written in order to ask questions or debate certain points.

It can be especially gratifying to learn a story you've written has changed lives or helped someone feel as if he or she wasn't so alone. Like many things you'll do in life, writing can be a thankless job at times, and you'll wonder if there is really a point to doing it, other than for your own personal satisfaction, not to mention a way to make ends meet, financially speaking. But it is necessary to promote your work and get the word out about your books.

WRITE A FAN LETTER

If you ever want to chat/email with someone you admire, try hitting the "contact me" link on his or her website. I've done it to a few people whose writing I like, and most have replied quickly. It won't work for all celebrities, but it is fun to chat with someone whose work you admire.

An online interview provides validation that there really *are* people reading your work, and it's instant gratification to have that back-and-forth exchange with someone you've never met and most likely never will. The Internet really has made the world a significantly smaller place!

TV/RADIO/NEWSPAPER INTERVIEWS

When you get interviewed the first few times, it may feel strange to have someone jotting down your words, ideas, or whatever you are saying, knowing that it will be quoted in a newspaper or magazine. Several writer friends have been interviewed on podcasts, an excellent way to get the word out about your writing. The entire world can access the interview on the Web. Plus, it's usually archived for as long as the site is active.

WRITERS WRITE, PERIOD

Writers such as J. K. Rowling, Nicholas Sparks, Stephen King, and Meg Cabot have something in common. They keep on

@@@@@@@@@@@@@@@

SIMPLICITY AT ITS FINEST

Author T. Jefferson Parker wrote a novel titled *The Fallen* in 1995.[17] After reading the first page, the writing grabbed me. It immediately gives the reader a feeling of, "I know *exactly* what you mean!"

Parker's imagery isn't flowery or poetic, but rather it is a simple narrative that anyone can relate to instantly. On page 1, the narrator, who has been knocked against a brick wall from an explosion across the street, describes himself as having his "heart pounding like a dryer with a load of sneakers."

So what? you might be thinking. *What's so great about that?* Well, it's not some cliché you hear every day like, "My heart was racing a million miles an hour!" But if you stop to think about his description, can't you instantly hear it in your head— a loud and rhythmic *bump, BUMP . . . bump, BUMP . . . bump, BUMP!* Hearing shoes in a dryer is an unmistakable sound. You don't even need to stop and think about it.

---

writing. As the saying goes, "Writers write, period." They just keep cranking out work. This is a good tip for beginning writers. Instead of writing something, submitting it for publication, then running to the mailbox every day waiting for a response, keep writing new stuff. This will pass the time more quickly and in turn may help you get published sooner by the fact of mere volume. Volume is key, after learning to write well first, of course.

CHAPTER 4 WRITING EXERCISE I: BUILDING A 3-D CHARACTER

What type of person would you imagine by simply hearing the following names:

1. William Rattner Joseph Marquis III
2. Joey Marcos Stromboleni
3. Kenny Smith

4. **Sarah Amelia Johnston**

5. **Juanita Maria Cesaras**

6. **Mikhail Juakeem Jumarez**

7. **Helen Isabella Bachleda**

After reading those names, would you ever guess that character number 1 (William) goes by the name of Rat? Probably not. How about the fact that he goes to some outlandishly expensive prep school on the East Coast? Yep, I'd buy that.

Character number 2 is a violin-playing Italian teen that covers up his insecurities by pretending his violin case holds weapons like the gangsters in old-fashioned movies. (Okay, that's a stretch, but you get where I'm going, right?)

Take the names on the previous list and create personalities and histories for two or three of the characters. Remember, while some traits might be obvious, such as, for example, character number 5 might be Latino, don't settle for the everyday stereotypes that will keep your characters one dimensional.

For example, not all prep-school kids will be honors students, on track for an Ivy League college, studying pre-law or pre-med or political science. They won't all be uppity and rude, conniving and fake, drunk all the time, or call daddy to bail them out, like most movie-of-the week dramas seem to suggest.

Go deeper. Let's look at William, character number 1, again. Is he from "old money" or "new money"? Has his entire family always been wealthy and never considered money might be an issue for others? Or perhaps his parents were immigrants who came here from another country with high hopes of the American Dream and went so far as to change their names. Maybe they work as many jobs as necessary, also applying for numerous scholarships to put their son through an expensive school in hopes that he gets every advantage possible to strive for excellence.

Even deeper: what kind of student is Rat? Does he have any learning disabilities? Is he up for the intense pressure his entire family has placed on him to succeed, perhaps being the first family member of prior generations to become a college graduate? Is he funny and charming, making friends with everyone he meets, or is he painfully shy? Does he put on airs of being snooty and selective about his relations, just to avoid conveying his *real* self?

There are countless ways you can go with a single character, creating an entire life and back story to make this person feel completely real to you. Your audience will never know one-tenth of the information you dream up about your character, as it will fall by the wayside in revisions and edits. But it will drive your storytelling, knowing *that* much about each character you introduce into your made-up world.

CHAPTER 4 WRITING EXERCISE II

Develop a character by writing a two-hundred-word entry of a person "introducing" herself to her new diary. She can describe herself through her own eyes or even say how she perceives that *others* see her. But through your character's speech, vocabulary, dialogue, and cadence you can create a real flesh-and-bones person. Remember to *show,* not *tell*.

CHAPTER 4 WRITING EXERCISE III

Pick a "first time" memory and describe how it made you feel. Remember to use all five senses—not just sight. For example, did you ever have your tonsils out? What were some of the sounds of the hospital? Was it really quiet with only machines beeping, an elevator bell heard faintly in the background, the rustle of trays of food being delivered to patients? And what did it smell like—perhaps the sting of antiseptic cleansers, or of food, or stale air from sickness with no windows open to bring in fresh air. It probably wasn't like most TV shows where everyone is running around yelling, "*Stat!*"

NOTES

1. Tami D. Cowden, Sue Viders, and Caro LaFever, *The Complete Writer's Guide to Heroes & Heroines: Sixteen Master Archetypes* (Hollywood, CA: Lone Eagle, 2000).

2. Copyright © 2004 by Loreen Leedy. Reprinted from *Look at My Book: How Kids Can Write & Illustrate Terrific Books* permission of Holiday House (New York: Scholastic, 2004), p. 7.

3. Jan Chappuis, *Six-Trait Mini-Lessons*, janchappuis@qwest .net; obtained from Megan Sloan, primary teacher and curriculum specialist, Snohomish, WA.

4. Leedy, *Look at My Book*, p. 7.

5. http://falcon.jmu.edu/~ramseyil/hinton.htm (accessed June 19, 2006).

6. StephenKing.com, www.stephenking.com (accessed January 7, 2007).

7. Stephen King, *Carrie* (Garden City, NY: Doubleday, 1974).

8. *New York Times*, June 21, 2005, The Arts, p. 1.

9. Eugene Fertelmeyer, interview with author May 2006; Stacy Chudwin, interview with author, May 2006.

10. Helen Oyeyemi, *The Icarus Girl* (New York: Nan A. Talese, 2005).

11. "Fiction by Teens," www.cplrmh.com/teenauthors.html (accessed January 18, 2008).

12. "Write Children's Books," Institute of Children's Literature, www.institutechildrenslit.com (accessed January 10, 2007).

13. Stacy Chudwin, *Sands of the Desert* (Frederick, MD: Publish America, 2003).

14. Stacy Chudwin, interview with author, May 2007.

15. "Frankstein," The Internet Movie Database, www.imdb.com/ find?s=all&q=frankenstein (accessed June 4, 2008).

16. Stephen King, *Lawnmower Man* (New York: Marvel Comics/ Bizarre Adventures, 1981); Daniel Keyes, *Flowers for Algernon* (Orlanda, FL: Harcourt Brace & Company, 1959).

17. T. Jefferson Parker, *The Fallen*, repr. (New York: Harper, 2006), 1.

5 Nonfiction Basics

FORMATTING

Since nonfiction requires diligent organization, this chapter will start with some general formatting reminders for a manuscript submission. (Tip: Copy this list and post near your computer.)

- ◎ Put title in all caps and centered on page.
- ◎ Double-space all manuscripts.
- ◎ Keep a minimum one-inch border on top, bottom, and sides.
- ◎ Use a tab of five spaces (not space bar, but Tab key) to begin each paragraph.
- ◎ For articles and early reader books, always include word count (under Tools in Microsoft Word).
- ◎ Always include a header with your last name (and first if you feel it necessary) and title of piece (as pages sometimes get separated). Also, by pressing ALT+CTRL+C at the same time, you can get a copyright symbol after your title. That, along with the date, will give you legal rights of ownership of your original work. (It is also suggested you mail yourself a copy of your manuscript and keep the envelope sealed, allowing the postmark to serve as proof of date produced and/or submitted. Remember to put the title of the piece in return address, of course.)
- ◎ Always include page number at the bottom of each page, or in your header or footer. Pages sometimes get separated on editors' or assistants' desks.
- ◎ Always use a plain font such as Times New Roman or Courier.

⊚ Always use 12-point font in *black ink only*.

⊚ At the top left corner of the first page of your manuscript, put the date, your name and contact info, age/demographics of intended audience, and word count.

OUTLINING FOR NONFICTION: A GREAT PLACE TO START!

Of course, an introduction is a great starting point when creating a book, story, or article, but for nonfiction in particular, you must really do some homework before you can even get to that point in your manuscript.

Sample Outline for Making a Nonfiction "Road Map" for Writing

I. *General research:* Find as many facts and points of view on a subject as you can. It's better to have too much information, and have to scale back, than to stretch what little information you've collected. It is always easier to cut than to fill in when you don't have enough research material.

II. *Who is your competition?*

   a. See what's already been written on a subject. Publishers hate to see, "There is absolutely *no* competition on this subject! I am the first to propose this topic." That may or may not be true. If it *is* true that no other books on a subject are in print yet, one of two scenarios may explain why:

   1. There are several publishers noticing the hole in the market, so books on the same subject are in the works at the same time and will break into the print market around the same time. That being said, other similar titles would be taking away the *umph* you hope to provide by being the "first" to have such a unique book.

   2. There isn't a need for such a book. There are *no* books out there on a subject because either the lack of information available or lack of interest, for that matter, just doesn't warrant an entire book on the subject.

III. *Ways to do research*

   a. Interview an expert.

   b. Visit a place in person.

    c. **Look through your library's archives.**

    d. **Watch an event.**

    e. **Check out books, CDs, and videos.**

    f. **Search the Internet.**

Be sure to take meticulous notes on your findings. If you are interviewing a person, ask, "Would you mind if I tape record our conversation to review it for exact quotes later?" Also, do your best to add artwork, photographs, sidebar material, quotes—any "extras" possible to enhance your findings. Remember to obtain permission to use all information gathered.

Research

Basically, "research" means to look for information. There are so many resources out there that it can be completely overwhelming. *Look at My Book* suggests the following list of places to go to find research references: videos, the Internet, almanacs, ask an expert, CDs, books, magazines, encyclopedias, newspapers.[1] (Note: Because the Internet is so vast and often overwhelming, the best place to start the search is often by "Googling" a subject at www .google.com.)

Google and other Internet search engines are great places to find a wide variety of information. In addition, try going a step further and using the information you get from the Internet. For example, go to the "contact" page of a website you find most useful. You can write a question and the webmaster will often reply with an answer. Some author sites give an e-mail address where you can ask questions directly to an author and get a personal email back. First be sure to look at any Q&A section of a website to be sure the questions you want to ask have not been answered. (You don't want to waste anyone's time just because you didn't do your homework by searching through a website thoroughly.) Come up with a list of questions for the author, and ask him or her if you can quote direct comments from his or her reply. A personal interview not only clarifies the information you have found, but quotes and more in-depth views on a subject matter can be acquired as well. If you receive a reply, you can even ask for a phone number to call to verify any facts or follow up with any last minute questions. This request may or may not be granted.

You might feel apprehensive at first about contacting an authority on a subject you might only vaguely know or understand. But if you can muster the courage to go for it and make that first contact, you might be surprised at the amount of information you will acquire. Heck, you might just get yourself mentors out of it—stranger things have happened.

MORE TRICKY (UNAVOIDABLE) TASKS

Notes

When notes appear at the bottom of the page, they are called footnotes. When they appear at the end of a chapter or at the end of the book (listed by chapter) in the back matter section, they are called endnotes. As you will see, different kinds of sources—such as an interview, a magazine article, a newspaper, a book, song lyrics, websites, or a pamphlet—are formatted differently. Your publisher's guidelines will explain how to do it.

When you cite an exact quote, paraphrased information, or certain kinds of factual information, it must be followed by a number written in superscript. Superscript, a formatting term for a smaller font, is slightly raised from the rest of the line. The notes will be numbered individually, starting with 1 at the beginning of each new chapter; the second note is 2, the third note is 3, and so on. Remember, each chapter's notes will begin with 1. Notes are a way to give proper credit to the source of information stated in your text.

Various Examples of Notes

Here are examples of notes from one of my other books:

Book

1. Melanie Apel, *Cystic Fibrosis: The Ultimate Teen Guide* (Lanham, MD: Scarecrow Press, forthcoming). [Note: Sometimes a

book you cite will not have been published yet. Put "forthcoming" instead of year of publication.]

E-mail

1. Reg Green, The Nicholas Green Foundation (www.nicholas green.org), e-mails with the author, June 2004. [Note: The date of an e-mail should be noted. When there are several back-and-forth e-mails, as with the source above, "June 2004" is sufficient.]

Encyclopedia

1. Tish Davidson, "Pancreas Transplantation," in *Gale Encyclopedia of Medicine*, vol. 4., ed. Donna Olendorf, Christine Jeryan, and Karen Boyden (Detroit, MI: Gale Group, 1999), 2149.

Magazine Article

1. Galina Espinoza, Karen Brailsford, and Frances Kinkelspiel, "Circle of Life," *People*, January 14, 2002, pp. 46–51.

Newspaper Article

1. Paul H. Johnson, "Heroes Wanted: Black Doctors Cite a Critical Shortage of Black Organ Donors," *The* [New Jersey] *Record*, March 16, 2004, p. 16.
2. Dinitia Smith, "Battling Failing Health, in Her Own Words," *New York Times*, August 5, 2002, The Arts, YNE, B1, pp. 23–24.

Pamphlet

1. *Alpha-1 Association: Alpha-1 Antitrypsin Deficiency* [pamphlet] (Minneapolis, MN: Alpha-1 Foundation, 2001). Also visit the website at www.alphaone.org (Alpha-1 Foundation).

Website

1. Gift of Hope Organ & Tissue Donor Network, www.giftof hope.org/statisticsinformation/qanda.asp (accessed June 2004). [Note: Remember to include the date you accessed the site for

information, as pages, or entire sites, are sometimes gone by the time of your book or article's publication.]

Professional Journals

1. G. K., "Hand Transplant Recipient Throws in the Towel," *Hastings Center Report* 31 (January 2001): 6. [Note: Though the author's initials are used here, first and last names are preferred when they are available.]

Interview (via phone call or in-person)

1. Joel Newman, United Network for Organ Sharing, phone interview with author, June 2004.

When a Source Is Repeated

At times, you will cite an article or some other source several times within your text. Some publishing companies want you to write "Ibid." in a note if the material is from the exact same source as in the note before (as in note 2 on p. 119). However, other companies want you to use a short note form—consisting

 GREAT SOURCES TO LEARN MORE ABOUT FORMATTING

A great resource for information about formatting your endnotes or footnotes is www.areasearchguide.com/8firstfo.html. The site has links to help with bibliographies, research guides, and quoting passages, among other formatting needs.

You can always use a list of trusty manuals, some of which should be staples on your writer's shelf:

Joseph Gibaldi, *A Manual for Writers* (Chicago: Modern Language Association of America, 2003).

William Strunk Jr. and E. B. White. *Elements of Style*, 4th ed. (Needham Heights, MA: Allyn & Bacon, 1999).

Kate L. Turabian, *A Manual for Writers of Research Papers, Theses, and Dissertations: Chicago Style for Students and Researchers*, 7th ed. (Chicago: Univeristy of Chicago Press, 2007).

University of Chicago Press Staff, *Chicago Manual of Style*, 15th ed. (Chicago: University of Chicago Press, 2003).

of the author's last name, a shortened form of the title, and the page number—each time a source is repeated, even if it is the very next note (see note 4 below for an example).

1. Toni Rizzo, "Heart Transplantation," in *Gale Encyclopedia of Medicine*, vol. 3, ed. Donna Olendorf, Christine Jeryan, and Karen Boyden (Detroit, MI: Gale Group, 1999), 1376.

2. Ibid.

3. Gift of Hope Organ & Tissue Donor Network, www.giftofhope.org/statisticsinformation/qanda.asp (accessed June 2004).

4. Rizzo, "Heart Transplantation," 1376.

Bibliographies

Writing a bibliography is a daunting task for most writers. I keep a shelf of reference books close by each time I write one. It is such an exacting task that your line editor will undoubtedly be meticulous about it. In addition to the quality of writing, when writing nonfiction, your book will be reviewed, in large part, based on the quality of your sources, which are found in the book's *back matter*. Each of the books, articles, and so on that you cite in your notes should also be included in your bibliography, with a few exceptions: personal

---

WHAT IS BACK MATTER?

Back matter, or matter that follows the main text of a book, for most nonfiction includes the following information:

- Chapter notes or endnotes (sources cited)
- Glossary
- Resources (websites, formal organizations—which should include address, phone number [often toll free], web address, and oftentimes an e-mail)
- List of people interviewed
- Suggested reading (in a bibliography format)
- Bibliography
- Index
- About the author

communications like e-mail and interviews do not need to be added to your bibliography.

Quotations/Permissions

After choosing material from a book, an interview, an e-mail, a questionnaire, or an article, make sure you send a permission form to appropriate sources you wish to quote. Include the material you wish to use. A publisher will want to know if the material cited will be used for profit or nonprofit purposes, as well as how many copies will be printed and/or circulated, the type of publication it will appear in (such as "250-page hard-cover, library-bound reference book"). When asking permission to use quotes, include a line for the signature of the person granting permission.

There might be payment involved. Permission fees range from nothing (with a request to "mention my website" or some other acknowledgment) to $4,000 or more for a single poem.

MARY WU, AUTHOR[2]

Mary Wu was first published as a teen; now she writes as a hobby.

She is a twenty-four-year-old writer who lives in a suburb just outside New York City, where she was born and raised. She works with cancer patients at Memorial Sloan Kettering Cancer Center. She is also a TransAction Council Committee member for the National Kidney Foundation and a participant in the transplant support organization in her area. With so much on her plate, one might wonder, "When does she find time to write?"

When she was eight years old, Mary Wu began journaling. Since then she's written screenplays, short stories, memoirs, and poems in the comfort of her own room. At nineteen years of age, her writing was published in the inspirational anthology *Chocolate for Teen's Spirit*, in *TeenInk* newsletters, as well as in the *TeenInk Friends and Family* anthology.[3]

These days she writes handwritten letters to people all over the world and sees writing as "just a hobby." What's wrong with that? Absolutely nothing! If you're reading this book as someone who simply enjoys writing, then great, you're in the official *club*—that of a writer. It doesn't take being published to be a "real writer"; it takes passion and love of the art form.

Mary Wu had a kidney transplant when she was only five years old, then again at age twelve. Both operations sparked her interest in "giving back" to the transplant community, as well as the National Kidney Foundation. In addition to her fiction writing, Mary is in charge of writing reviews of books for the Kidney Foundation's website.

I interviewed Mary about a variety of topics regarding writing. Here are some excerpts from that conversation:[4]

Did you attend college?

Yes, I graduated from Manhattanville College [located in Purchase, New York] with a bachelors of arts degree in January 2004.

You mentioned your love of reading. Who are some of your favorite authors?

Amy Tan, Mitch Albom, Anita Shreve, Judy Blume, Carlos Ruiz Zafón, Nicholas Sparks, and Malorie Blackman are the first ones that come to mind when thinking of my favorites.

What writer has truly mastered the writing skills you admire and would like to emulate?

Hmm, this is such a difficult question to answer because I can't choose just *one* writer, but I can narrow it down to two writers: Mitch Albom and Carlos Ruiz Zafón.

Which work or works displays the writing styles/traits you admire?

Mitch Albom wrote *The Five People You Meet in Heaven*, which, to me, really displays his exquisite writing skills. Carlos Ruiz Zafón only wrote one major, well-known book to date: *The Shadow of the Wind*. It is chock-full of beautiful and amazing inner and outer dialogue.[5]

Are there certain people, such as a teacher, mentor, or friend who got you interested in writing, or at least encouraged you to give it a try?

Two people truly provoked a writing passion in me. The first is my sister. She took her passion for writing and made it into her career as a journalist. Seeing how writing was such a release or therapy for her made me curious about this writing magic so I began to churn out simple and short stories, scripts, memoirs and journals.

The second person was my eighth-grade teacher, Mrs. Goldberg. She helped me to see that there was some sort of writer in me.

How would you describe the feeling you get when writing? What is your mood, most of the time, while you write and afterward?

Writing makes me feel like a weight has been lifted off my shoulders. It is extremely therapeutic for me to release my thoughts and feelings about everything and anything. At the same time, writing makes me also feel a bit vulnerable because I am able to reveal the *real me* and my *real* thoughts and feelings. In a way, I feel a little bit naked with my writing—like my heart, soul, and spirit are all on that paper. It is quite scary for me to be exposed that way, but it is also so fulfilling . . . like everything inside you has been cleansed.

Do you think writing might ever change over from a hobby to a career?

As much as I adore writing, I see it as a hobby. My real passion lies in the social services/human services field with direct and customer service contact with clients and patients.

Permissions from Minors

If someone you've interviewed or quoted is younger than eighteen years of age, his or her parent/legal guardian must give you written permission to publish it.

When quoting more than fifty words from someone eighteen years and older, you must obtain written permission from that person to do so. In fact, he or she has the legal right to charge you a fee to quote him or her. Make sure you obtain that person's permission, or you risk being accused of plagiarism. If you summarize, or paraphrase what was said, you must be certain to cite the source where you obtained your information. And don't forget to get permissions even when you're doing a face-to-face or phone interview.

CREATIVE NONFICTION

Creative nonfiction can be stream-of-consciousness writing that lets the writer express his or her feelings about an event, as demonstrated below in an example by Mary Wu. I have heard creative nonfiction explained as the perspective of the author, but using factually accurate narratives. If a piece is written with the opinions, memories, and point-of-view of the author while the facts remain accurate, it can also be considered creative nonfiction.

Faceless Giver[6]

On May 5, 1995, you became my faceless giver. Your family selflessly put aside their heartache, grief, pain, and turmoil to allow you to become my faceless giver to carry on and live my life to the fullest.

On May 5, 2006, I wonder: How did they do it? How did you do it? Does your family think about me after all these years? On the day I celebrate my life and living, what does your family do? If they cry and the wounds are reopened and the pain is fresh yet again, how can I celebrate? Will ever I ever meet my faceless giver's family and would they even want to see me? Why must it be that you have to die and give for me to live? It makes me see there are such amazing, generous, and genuine people and faceless givers in this world. There is so much beauty and beautiful people in this world. We take these people for granted. We take life for granted and we can't keep up now with the fast pace of technology and the power and hunger for and of money. Life goes by so quickly and we rush. We smile our smiles and say what we have to say and do what we have to do. Inside, we may feel the loneliness that eats away at us and becomes a forbidden, yet comforting, companion.

In a world where we see hatred and anger around us, there are so many beautiful faceless givers. My dear faceless giver, how will I ever repay you and your family? My answer: I will live. Yes, I will live and give back what I can to you and everyone else and, eventually, I will be the faceless giver that you are to me.

—Mary Wu, age twenty-four, New York

Online/E-mail Interviews

When interviewing subjects for this book, I posted a questionnaire on my website. I asked a variety of questions regarding writing habits, feelings, mentors, classes, favorite authors, and the strong points the respondents admire about some of their favorite authors.

Without ever meeting some of the participants, I was able to get wonderfully diverse, as well as clear, concise answers. Age certainly didn't matter when I conducted my interviews. If participants hadn't filled in their age when asked, I would never have guessed that most of them were still in their teens. I "met" (albeit "virtually" over the Internet) some truly talented writers.

TEEN VOICE[7]

The following nonfiction titles illustrate how to write with a clear voice.

Anthony Allison, *Hear These Voices: Youth at the Edge of the Millennium* (New York: Dutton Children's Books, 1999).

Marina Budhos, *Remix: Conversations with Immigrant Teens* (New York: Henry Holt, 1999).

Carol Cassidy, *Girls in America: Their Stories, Their Words* (New York: TV Books, 1999).

Al Desetta and Sybil Wolin, eds., *Struggle to Be Strong: True Stories by Teens about Overcoming Tough Times* (Minneapolis, MN: Free Spirit Publishing Inc., 2000).

Anrenee Englander, *Dear Diary I'm Pregnant: Teenagers Talk about Their Pregnancy* (Toronto: Annick Press Ltd., 1997).

Pearl Fuyo Gaskins, ed., *What Are You? Voices of Mixed Race Young People* (New York: Henry Holt, 1999).

Laurel Holliday, *Why Do They Hate Me? Young Lives Caught in War and Conflict* (New York: Simon Pulse, 1999).

Mary Motley Kalergis, *Seen and Heard: Teenagers Talk about Their Lives* (New York: Stewart Tabori and Chang, 1998).

Gayatri Patnaik and Michelle T. Shineski, eds., *The Secret Life of Teens: Young People Speak Out about Their Lives* (New York: HarperCollins, 2000).

William S. Pollack, *Real Boys' Voices* (New York: Random House, 2000).

Sara Shandler, *Ophelia Speaks: Adolescent Girls Write about Their Search for Self* (New York: HarperPerennial, 2000).

Audrey Shehyn, *Picture the Girl: Young Women Speak Their Minds* (New York: Hyperion, 2000).

The Internet makes finding facts, information, clubs, critique groups, and connecting one-on-one with people amazingly attainable. With writing such a solitary job, it's comforting to "meet" someone or "chat" even though you've never technically met. You could have a writing buddy for years and never meet face to face. It's a fascinating concept!

THE SEXY SIDE OF WRITING

Not! Many people only think of Dr. Seuss-like picture books for little kids or famous novels like Harry Potter when they think of children's literature. The fact is, librarians and teachers

A HARD LESSON LEARNED

When authors Paul and Sarah Edwards first started searching for a publisher for their first collaborative manuscript, the editor they targeted told them that they didn't write well. They decided to try a different approach than most authors do. The Edwards team hired a writer who had written more than forty books to read their manuscript. The writer had also been told by the aforementioned editor that he couldn't write. Paul and Sarah subsequently wrote an article for a major magazine whose editor told them that their writing was great. Finally, they went back to the initial publishing house, met with a new editor, and were on their way.

Paul and Sarah learned a lesson that editors' tastes can be vastly different. One person's opinion should never deter a writer from writing. If the same manuscript went to one hundred editors, unless it was completely wretched (bad punctuation, grammar, spelling errors, lame plot, and story line) a handful of editors might find the manuscript had merit.[8]

Sage Advice from Paul and Sarah Edwards

The Edwards writing team offers some excellent writing advice for young would-be writers. They talk about journaling everyday experiences, even from a young age. Also, they stress the importance of sharing your writing, even if you feel shy about it. It's a good way to see if people understand what you're trying to say.[9]

⊚ ⊚ ⊚ ⊚ ⊚ ⊚ ⊚ ⊚ ⊚ ⊚ ⊚ ⊚ ⊚ ⊚ ⊚ ⊚ ⊚ ⊚

CHECK OUT THESE NONFICTION BOOKS BY YOUNG AUTHORS![10]

Gil C. Alicea (sixteen years old), *The Air Down Here: True Tales From a South Bronx Boyhood* (San Francisco, CA: Chronicle Books, 1995).

Irwin Cait (thirteen years old), *Conquering the Beast Within: How I Fought Depression and Won and How You Can Too* (New York: Three Rivers Press, 1999).

Zack Hample (eighteen years old), *How to Snag Major League Baseballs* (New York: Aladdin, 1999).

Dave Lindsay (fifteen years old), *Dave's Quick and Easy Web Pages* (Calgary: Erin Publications, 2001).

Mark Pfetzer (seventeen years old), *Within Reach: My Everest Story* (New York: Dutton Books, 1998).

Katie Tarbox (fifteen years old), *Katie.com: My Story* (New York: Dutton Books, 2000).

Ned Vizzini (junior high), *Teen Angst? Naaah . . . A Quasi-Autobiography* (Minneapolis, MN: Free Spirit Publication, 2000).

are constantly on the lookout for more *nonfiction* books. Not only is there a huge market for nonfiction writing, but with specific topics needed, it can be a touch easier to find a publisher willing to buy your work.

You don't have to stick to boring, bland, lackluster nonfiction topics for your articles and books. I wrote an article on water towers using a photo of a gigantic ketchup bottle (water tower) I saw once! Look around your everyday surroundings for ideas that will spark children's curiosity, not to mention your own!

Of course, adult readers are intrigued by nonfiction such as how-tos, recipes, quizzes, trivia, history, and technical/professional information. Some writers find it easier to study market guides to see what publishers are looking for in terms of nonfiction needs than to write a fictional piece.

WRITING NONFICTION ARTICLES

Newspaper/Magazine/Trade Articles— Think Small!

When you write for magazines and newspapers, do you imagine a feature story with a blurb about it on the cover of *Rolling Stone*? Oh really, the *cover* article itself? Wow! Good for you. But, more often than not, you will *not* have the cover story on a magazine or newspaper each day, week, or month. It's just a mathematical fact. What you *could* be seeing in regard to your work (and paychecks) are a lot of small items you've written.

Newspapers, such as *USA Today*, literally cover all fifty states in America *each day*. That's huge! Obviously there won't be a few pages per state, although there certainly would be enough information to do so. This newspaper specializes in giving the reader a lot of little snippets from all over. It's almost like the Cliffs Notes of daily news. Cliffs Notes are the small yellow books with black stripes that summarize the classics so students don't have to read an entire novel, or so I thought when I was in high school! In truth, they are meant to complement the texts, not *replace* them. Some great benefits of Cliffs Notes are that plots, characters, themes, and so on are all laid out in a clear, succinct report, summarizing an entire novel.

What to Submit

The market for newspapers that buy small items (say, twenty-five to seventy-five words) is amazing. Sure, there will be several feature articles, but in newspapers, which use columns, there cannot be blank spaces. So unless a paper wants a ton of puny ads stuck in various areas all over the news section, it needs to use what are called "fillers." Someone has to write all of those fillers, correct? The pay for writing several fillers can really add up, so a writer can earn some good money. Plus, it is much less of a risk for an editor to give a short filler assignment to a writer new to the company than a feature story. Editors don't have much risk on their end, and if it really came down to it, worst case scenario, the editor could pound out a few last-minute fillers himself to replace ones that turned out to be unusable.

A how-to article is a great way to make a sale. Certain magazines run how-tos every month. The trick is to research which ones regularly publish them, then get the submission guidelines from the publishers you like. Check out back issues from your local library to see what the magazines' themes were for the past twelve months so you don't send them a pitch about something they've recently run. Next, request a list of upcoming themes for the next six to twelve months at each publishing house. If you're interested in a topic on a list, get the publisher your pitch as soon as possible.

How-to articles can be fun to write, but they are also a bit harder to write than you might imagine. If you're teaching people how to do something they've never tried before, and you are not there in person to help, explain, or answer questions, it takes some serious effort to write instructions readers will understand. You've only got your words—and often a limited number available (say, 50 to 250 words maximum), so you've got to be clear, concise, and get to the point quickly.

CHAPTER 5 WRITING EXERCISE I

Write an *introduction* to your *own* autobiography. Make it two hundred words or less. Use one of the starter ideas from chapter 4.

CHAPTER 5 WRITING EXERCISE II

Choose a magazine you like to read. Go to the library and check out the past twelve issues to see what topics have been covered. Next, go to the magazine's website to see if there is a list of future topics requested by editors. Pick your topic. Write a nonfiction article up to five hundred words.

NOTES

1. Loreen Leedy, *Look at My Book: How Kids Can Write & Illustrate Terrific Books* (New York: Scholastic, 2004), 7.

2. Mary Wu, e-mails to author, November 2006.

3. *Chocolate for Teen's Spirit* (New York: Fireside, 2002); *TeenInk Friends and Family* (Deerfield Beach, FL: The Young Authors Foundation, Inc., 2000).

4. Wu, e-mails.

5. Mitch Albom, *The Five People You Meet in Heaven* (New York: Hyperion, 2003). Carlos Ruiz Zafón, *The Shadow of the Wind* (New York: Penguin, 2004).

6. Wu, e-mails.

7. "Teen Voices," See YA Around: Library Programming for Teens, www.cplrmh.com/teenauthors.html (accessed January 18, 2008).

8. Diane Lyndsey Reeves, *Career Ideas for Kids Who Like Writing* (New York: Checkmark Books, 1998), 79.

9. Reeves, *Career Ideas*, 79.

10. "Non-fiction by Teens," See YA Around: Library Programming for Teens, www.cplrmh.com/teenauthors.html (accessed January 18, 2008).

6 Poetry and Songwriting Basics

Shakespeare

FORMS OF POETRY

Poetry is a wonderful way to express oneself. And there are many poetry styles to choose from.

Ode

An ode is a free form usually praising or glorifying a person, place, or thing. A classic example is the church hymn "Ode to Joy." Here is a stanza from one of the versions found on the Internet.[1]

Lyrics in English for "Ode to Joy"
("Ode An Die Freude")
Beethoven's 9th Symphony

O friends, no more these sounds!
  Let us sing more cheerful songs,
  more full of joy!
Joy, bright spark of divinity,
  Daughter of Elysium,
  Fire-inspired we tread
  Thy sanctuary.

Haiku

Next, look at a type of poetry called a haiku. It was originally a Japanese verse, typically unrhymed, but not always, made up of three lines. The first and third lines contain five syllables; the second line contains seven syllables. These poems are most often about nature. Here is an example I've written:

Snow
Heavy is your weight.
Millions of flakes on the trees.
Bending to your will.

Sonnet

William Shakespeare (1564–1616), world-renowned English poet and playwright, is especially known for his sonnets within his plays. There are several types of sonnets, two of which are the English sonnet (also known as Shakespearean sonnets) and the Italian sonnet (known as Petrarchan sonnets).

In simple terms, a sonnet is fourteen lines written in iambic pentameter, a type of meter used in poetry that describes the type of rhythm that the words establish in each line. That

Defining examples of Shakespearean sonnets can by found at shakespeare.about.com/ od/faqshakespearesworks/f/iambic.htm. Shakespeare's sonnets are written predominantly in a meter called *iambic pentameter*, a rhyme scheme in which each sonnet line consists of ten syllables. The syllables are divided into five pairs called *iambs* or *iambic feet*. An iamb is a metrical unit made up of one unstressed syllable followed by one stressed syllable. An example of an iamb would be *goodBYE*. A line of iambic pentameter flows like this:

baBOOM / baBOOM / baBOOM / baBOOM / baBOOM.

rhythm is measured in small groups of ten syllables, in the case of a sonnet; these small groups of stressed and non-stressed syllables are called "feet." The word *iambic* describes the type of foot that is used. The word pentameter indicates that a line has five of these "feet."[2]

Sonnets can follow one of several rhyme themes. An example might be a noun or adjective with a non-stressed syllable followed by a stressed syllable, such as the word beLOW. You can find a multitude of examples of sonnets in Shakespeare's works. He wrote 157 sonnets.

Perhaps the most famous of Shakespeare's sonnets is number 18. Here are a couple lines to sample from various Shakespeare poems, written in the example of stressed and non-stressed syllables.

From Sonnet 18:

Shall I / comPARE / thee TO / a SUM / mer's DAY?
Thou ART / more LOVE / ly AND / more TEM / per ATE

From Sonnet 12:

When I / do COUNT / the CLOCK / that TELLS / the TIME

From Sonnet 29:

When IN / dis GRACE / with FOR / tune AND / men's EYES
I ALL / aLONE / be WEEP / my OUT/ cast STATE

The Cinquain

The cinquain was created by an American poet named Adelaide Crapsey (1878–1914).[3] It is a poem made up of five lines (*cinq* means five in French). The format is as follows:

Format	*Example by Tina P. Schwartz*
Line one: two syllables	*my love*
Line two: four syllables	*you are so sweet*
Line three: six syllables	*your touch is my desire*

Line four: eight syllables   *I long to hold you in my arms*
Line five: two syllables   *my love*

Try your best to write a cinquain using the format above.

Limerick

The limerick, a form of poetry that is both humorous and whimsical, originated in Limerick, Ireland.[4] While seemingly fun to write, there are rules to be followed that make it more difficult to produce than one might imagine.

First, a limerick poem contains five lines. The difficult part is stressing the correct syllables. Lines 1, 2, and 5 rhyme with each other; lines 3 and 4 rhyme with each other. Therefore, limericks are built upon two separate rhyme sounds. Here is another example I've written:

la LA la la LA la la LA (rhyme a)	*There once was a boy with a kite.*
la LA la la LA la la LA (rhyme a)	*His brother and he would then fight.*
la LA la la LA (rhyme b)	*One wanted to run.*
la LA la la LA (rhyme b)	*The other had fun,*
la LA la la LA la la LA (rhyme a)	*Just watching the tail taking flight.*

Now *you* take a crack at writing a limerick!

Free Verse

Free verse is aptly named in that there aren't stringent rules like those for haiku or limericks. The poet decides the number of lines and syllables. Free verse can rhyme or not rhyme. The verse can be typed in a shape, can use a play on words such as a pun, or it can make no sense at all. Free verse is one of the easiest forms to write, because the poets can go where their thoughts take them. Free verse is also called concrete, shape, and pattern poetry.

SELF-EXPRESSION

Do you like to write poetry? Is it often about certain subjects such as misery and teen angst? Or do you get swept up with romance or even thinking up lyrics for songs? Whatever way you decide to express yourself, poetry is a wonderful

SHORT OR LONG?

Poetry can be pages long or simply a word or two. Here is a poem from a teen in love.

Untitled

To be separate from him,
is like to fly
with wings on fire.

—Stefanie, age nineteen, Illinois
(au pair from Germany)

Instant Sunshine

Sometimes things aren't always smooth sailing
My emotions tend to get the best of me
Black clouds of sorrow build up inside
Threatening to storm all over my soul
But there's one thing that drives away the clouds
A most wonderful thing called Instant Sunshine

Your Instant Sunshine turns my black heart red
Your Instant sunshine turns my black heart red
Just your smile could bring life to the dead

There are times when I feel all alone
Like I'm stranded on an island in the middle of the sea
Feeling like I'm battling the whole world alone
With nobody caring if I win or lose
But they say it's darkest before the dawn
And that's when I get a shot of Instant Sunshine

Your Instant Sunshine turns my black heart red
Your Instant sunshine turns my black heart red
Just your smile could bring life to the dead

—Boyd Herrin, written junior year of college, circa 1991

135

way to go about it. You can get across a great deal of information in a small number of words.

For some reason, more than half of the teen writers I've talked with over the years prefer to write poetry. Perhaps it's less daunting to think of writing on a smaller scale, as with a poem. However, it is quite a challenging genre to write well. Poetry

DID YOU KNOW?

Poet Langston Hughes's poems appeared in his *Cleveland Central High School Magazine*. Sylvia Plath had published many poems and stories by the time she went to college in 1950.[5] These examples reinforce the fact that age doesn't always matter when you consider publication.

Ice

I feel as if
I'm treading on ice.
Beneath my careful feet,
I see
The water creeping,
Underneath.
Step by cautious step
I go to reach the other side,
To freedom.
But, the ice is splitting,
Cracking, breaking, and so
Is my heart.
I fall
And sink beneath the ice.
My heart
Is in her bitter grip again.
I try to escape,
But every time I do,
I fall.
Treading on ice,
As if it were my heart,
Cold, frozen . . .
Broken ice.

—Shawn Wickersheim, written at age eighteen, Illinois

TEEN ANGST: HOW POETRY LETS TRUE FEELINGS OUT

So Alone

Why are people so stupid?
Why are people so mean?
They poke and prod and
Just won't stop until
They hear me scream.
Judgmental as the day is long.
Say the word; it's like a song.
They smile and nod like
They're your friends
But will they be there
'Til it ends?
I doubt it, see
'Cause this I've learned . . .
You let love in—
You will get burned.

—C. G. S., age twenty

can be quite dark, when used to get out a writer's most depressed or angry feelings, or light and airy to elevate the reader.

Feelings

With the transition to adulthood often difficult, love, hate, friendship, death, and other challenges are among the most popular subjects written about. Whether you like to share your work with others or not doesn't matter. You can keep a diary or private journal with feelings hidden. But having a healthy outlet for such feelings is a wonderful gift to give yourself.

Q&A WITH HEIDI BEE ROEMER, WRITER/TEACHER/MENTOR EXTRAORDINAIRRE![6]

Heidi Bee Roemer is a wonderful writer, a generous mentor, and an amazing teacher. Enough great things cannot be said about this woman.

Heidi, let's begin with your schooling. Do you have any advanced degrees?

I've taken college courses, but I am largely self-taught.

How long did you write and submit manuscripts before your first sale?

When my husband and I closed our decorating shops in 1992, I finally had the chance to do what I always dreamed of: writing for kids. (As a rookie writer, I had no idea how much I needed to learn!) My first sale came in 1996 when I sold an inspirational piece to a children's Sunday school paper.

How many works of yours have been published?

To date, I've sold three books and over 300 poems, stories, articles, and song lyrics to a variety of children's magazines, anthologies, and other venues.

What is your preferred genre and medium?

I'm a "fun-fact" junkie. I love to take nonfiction and present it to readers in a fresh new way. I enjoy writing nonfiction and I often take the poetry route.

How and when did you begin teaching?

It all began when SCBWI [Society of Children's Book Writers & Illustrators] friends asked me to share writers' tips. I kept adding more information and eventually developed three workshops, which included workbooks, handouts, and writing exercises. From 2000 to 2004 I taught "How to Get Published," "The ABC's of Poetry for Children's Writers," and "The Critique Workshop."

Not to embarrass you, but your reputation precedes you! I've heard several students say, "My first publication came from a poem I wrote during Heidi Roemer's class." WHAT on Earth are you teaching these students?

I believe the reason so many of my students have such great success is that most of them are gifted and highly motivated. The majority are eager to improve their skills and willing to accept input.

My approach to teaching poetry is to keep publication in mind. I instruct students to choose topics that are marketable. In order to know what is marketable, one must study the market and read currently published children's poetry. In other words, *read, read, read*!

The combination of good rhyme and strong meter is like the "skeletal structure" of a poem on which all other techniques rest. The reason many editors don't like poetry is because so much of what they receive is bad. A regular, rhythmic beat is crucial, so I teach students four basic meters.

To write truly kid-friendly poetry, one can use a variety of devices and forms. I cover mask poem, apostrophe poems, haiku, cinquain, tanka, free verse, along with devices of sound such as alliteration and assonance, and much more.

Last, I give gentle but detailed (read "nitpicky") critiques. If the poem is market-ready, I suggest a few possible publishers. If it's not ready to submit, I ask for revision. Then in time, I eagerly wait to hear what results my students have as they begin circulating their materials.

What is your favorite (published) piece that you've created? And why is it special to you?

A retelling of a Bible story called "Ready or Not," published in *Clubhouse* magazine's January 1999 issue, is one of my favorites. I enjoyed giving this old worn-out story a humorous, modern twist. Apparently, *Clubhouse* liked it too.

What are you working on in your "writing life"?

I'm awaiting the arrival of my newest book, *Whose Nest Is This?* Shortly after *What Kinds of Seeds Are These?* was published by NorthWord Press, I asked my editor if she had any topics in mind for future books. She asked if I'd like to write a book about nests in the same riddle format as my just-released *Seeds.*[7]

Currently, I'm in the process of polishing a collection of twenty-four shape poems tentatively titled *A Wiggle of Words.* Also, my good friend and talented author Laura Crawford and I are collaborating on a geometry-based ABC book called *C is for Circle.* Recently, I submitted a manuscript called *Warthogs*

Never Soak in Suds featuring thirteen endangered African animals and their outlandish grooming habits. (Fingers crossed for a sale!)

My newest venture is a blog. I teamed up with Kim Hutmacher and Laura Crawford and—just like that!—wildaboutnaturewriters.blogspot.com was created.

Did you write as a child, teen, and/or young adult? Was it usually the same genre, or always just a mishmash of various forms?

As a child, "Heidi Hallmark" crafted birthday, get well, and other cards for my family using crayons and writing original verse. In grade school, thanks to my sixth grade English teacher, Mrs. Gayle Paben, I loved writing fiction. After high school, in blissful ignorance, I submitted a collection of poems to a publisher. Though I got a rejection (and rightly so), the editor included a few words of encouragement in her letter.

What do you tell writers who are just starting to make their first submissions to publishers? That first submission is usually a big step for a person. I remember mine was addressed, stamped,

---

NATURE POEM

A tree without leaves, snow covers one side.
Cold wet sleet stuck to its hide.
It stands in the wind facing the cold,
Looking tired, sad, lone, and old,
In chaos of snow, catching the flak—
Snow is a shadow, if you switch white and black.
What used to be green is now dirty grey,
A sad pale image of a once warmer day.
Though it looks lifeless, barren and dead,
Deep underground, the cold's not broken its thread.
Under the skin, the sap will still flow—
Waiting for another warm day to grow.

—name withheld, eighteen-year-old male

TEEN POETRY

The following is a list of books of poetry by young authors:

Lee Francis, ed., *When the Rain Sings: Poems by Young Native Americans* (New York: Simon & Schuster, 1999).

Betsy Franco, ed., *You Hear Me? Poems and Writings by Teenage Boys* (Cambridge, MA: Candlewick Press, 2001).

Dave Johnson, ed., *Movin': Teen Poets Take Voice* (New York: Orchard Books, 2000).

Lydia Okutoro, ed., *Quiet Storm: Voices of Young Black Poets* (New York: Jump at the Sun, 2002).

Tupac Shakur, *The Rose That Grew from Concrete* (New York: MTV, 1999).

Esther Watson, comp., *Pain Tree and Other Teenage Angst-Ridden Poetry* (Minneapolis, MN: Tandem Library, 2001).

---

and sat on my desk for two weeks before I walked it to a mailbox. Did your "first time" go like that at all?

I held back my first submission to *Ladybug* magazine for several long, agonizing months. But I had a reason. I was a new network representative for SCBWI at the time and I had asked *Ladybug* editor, Paula Morrow, to be our guest speaker. I wanted to hear her talk before submitting my manuscript. It was also a strategic move. I was on my best (most nervous) behavior as I hoped to make a good impression in person, thinking she would recognize my name when my manuscript arrived. The story ended happily, as Paula purchased two of my poems and published them a short time later.

Do you have any words of advice to give others the strength/courage to just jump in and get something to the mailbox?

Just do it! If you think your manuscript is in its best possible form, print it up and mail it out. Getting published is such a slow, tedious project, anyway. A magazine may purchase your story but not publish it for one to five years! Why waste time? Don't let a good manuscript sit around.

Thank you for your time and a glimpse into the world of a very busy freelance writer!

LESSONS FROM A PRO

Heidi Bee Roemer once sent me a wonderful e-mail to pass on to one of my writing students. In it she summarized some key points of writing poetry.

Off-meter is one of the major reasons editors say they don't like/want rhymed manuscripts. A poem must follow a regular rhythmic beat. Once you identify which meter you're using, use it consistently throughout the poem.

There are four basic meters. (Capital letters denote stressed syllables.)

Anapest—ta ta TUM ta ta TUM ta ta TUM ta ta TUM
("'twas the NIGHT be-fore CHRIST-mas and ALL through the HOUSE . . .")
Dactyl—TUM ta ta TUM ta ta TUM ta ta TUM
("HERE at the CORN-er I SIT and I WAIT . . .")
Iambic—ta TUM ta TUM ta TUM ta TUM
("the MUSH-room WEARS a ROUND-ed CAP . . .")
Troche—TUM ta TUM ta TUM ta TUM
("SUM-mer SNOW-flake MADE of FLUFF.")

The meter is one of the most challenging aspects of writing poetry. Years ago, I used to re-type published poems, print them out, and mark the stresses in each line. I tapped the meter with my pencil. I read published poems aloud. Reading poems aloud really helps develop a good ear for meter. Read, read, read! Then try to mimic the meter patterns in your own writing. Just like anything else, the more you do it, the better you become.

Revision is a huge part of writing professionally. The poet John Ciardi had an unerring ear for good poetry and a highly developed nose for bad. "Ninety-eight percent of what writers write is rubbish," he once said. "So keep your wastebasket full."

I often tell my students the story of William J. Kennedy, author of *Ironweed*. He said it often takes him "thirty pages or more of false starts, dead-ends, and revisions" before he writes one page that meets his literary standards. He also said, "a dozen drafts are not uncommon."[8]

Mrs. Roemer's website offers tips on writing poetry and taking correspondence courses on writing. For further information, go to www.HeidiBRoemer.com.

NOT AS EASY AS IT LOOKS

What people often forget is that it is quite difficult to write poetry well. Among pace, rhythm, syllables, rhyme or no rhyme, iambic pentameter, and many other considerations, it's not as easy as it looks. Check out the sidebar on page 141 for books of poetry written by teen authors.

MATTIE STEPANEK, POET AND GOODWILL AMBASSADOR[9]

There once was a young man named Matthew Joseph Thaddeus Stepanek, but he preferred to just be called "Mattie." What you will learn will amaze you, no matter how old or young you are. If you like writing but think you are too young to ever write a "real book," remember this teen. His talent, not to mention strength and courage through adversity, allowed him to write *several hundred* poems by the time he was only *six years old*!

Left Us Too Soon

If you are not already familiar with this wonderful poet, you should know that after a life full of physical challenges, Mattie died from complications of muscular dystrophy at the age of thirteen, in June 2004. During his short life, he was able to touch *millions* of lives.

Making a Difference

Mattie once commented how lucky he was because of the great support from doctors, the Muscular Dystrophy Association, friends, and people who have written to him to tell him how his words have made a difference in their lives. "I'm so lucky that I get to see the difference. Everyone makes a difference in somebody's life. Everyone. It's just that not everyone gets the chance to realize that difference in this life. So my life is very difficult, and sometimes painful, but very full and blessed," Mattie said.[10]

Mattie's writing and philanthropic work earned him many awards and honors. In 1999, he won the Melinda A. Lawrence

143

International Book Award for most inspirational work. In 2000, he was chosen to be the Maryland State Goodwill Ambassador for the Muscular Dystrophy Association. In 2001, Ann Armstrong-Dailey and Children's Hospice International created the Mattie Stepanek Champion Award to honor Mattie's contributions to children everywhere.

In a May 24, 2002, broadcast of *American Mosaic* with Doug Johnson, Mattie said he wrote poetry to express his feelings about living with a rare illness and bringing peace to the world. His poems also told of the fun of being a child, like playing with toys and having friends. For many years, he had three wishes:

AN EXCELLENT STUDENT![11]

When Mattie Stepanek was almost eleven years old, he was homeschooled, studying a high school curriculum. He began writing when he was only three years old and by the time he died, he had written thousands of poems, penned dozens of essays and short stories, and created many illustrations.

1. To have his poems published
2. To share his message of peace on the Oprah Winfrey television show
3. To meet his hero, former president Jimmy Carter

Happily, all three wishes came true in his lifetime. Jimmy Carter and Oprah Winfrey became close, personal friends to Mattie and his mom.

Mattie had several books published, and they've become national best sellers. They are called Heartsongs (a series of titles that include the word *Heartsongs* in each one), which Mattie described as "the feeling in your heart that wants you to make yourself a better person. It wants you to help other people to do the same."[12]

What Started the Inspiration?

According to his website's "Frequently Asked Questions" section, Mattie said, "I began writing poetry when I was about three years old. My brother, Jamie, died. I loved him so much. He was my best friend. I didn't really know my other brother, Stevie, or my sister, Katie. But when Jamie died, I was angry and sad and scared and confused. A lot of my early stuff was about my feelings after Jamie died, and how I learned to cope with it."[13]

Mattie went on to explain that his mom gave him a tape recorder to make his poetry and stories if she wasn't free to write them down right away for him. When he was five, he started writing some down by hand, and he learned to use a keyboard and type when he was only eight years old.

As a teenager, Mattie wrote about many different things with pen and paper but went back to using a tape recorder because his fingers would bleed. He planned on getting a computer program that recognized his voice. . . . Someday. Anne Frank, one of Mattie's "writer heroes" wrote, "When I write, I can shake off all my cares."[14] How true, for writers everywhere!

Recommended Reading

City of One: Young Writers Speak to the World is a book with more than two hundred poems written by young people ranging in age from seven to twenty-three years old.[15] Topics covered are ambitions, holidays, culture, ancestors, metaphors, social conditions in our society, and despair among others.

In the October 2004 issue of *VOYA* (*Voice of Youth Advocates*), a reviewer says, "Despite the many topics covered, peace and social action are at the core of each section. . . . This book would be a great addition to public, school, and classroom libraries."[16]

SONG WRITING—A WONDERFUL FORM OF POETRY

To me, many song lyrics are poetic. The following three young women demonstrate examples of how music and poetry can commingle.

AVRIL LAVIGNE, SINGER-SONGWRITER[17]

Born in Napanee, Ontario, Canada, in 1984, Avril Ramona Lavigne became famous while still a teen. She has won awards as a singer and songwriter, and her first two CDs topped the charts in

ROMANCE GONE AWRY

If you watch shows like *Oprah*, *Dr. Phil*, or other daytime television, you might be led to believe there are some men who have trouble expressing emotions. But when there is a creative outlet such as writing available, many teen boys and grown men have shared their feelings and contradicted this idea. Poetry enables writers to let their emotions out. Here is a poem by a young man talking to a girl he likes.

Lift Your Head

Lift your head,
Let me dry your tears.
Please don't cry
I feel so bad when you do.
Lift your head,
Let the sun shine upon your face.
You are special to me,
You are the one I adore.
Don't look down.
Don't cry, please, don't cry.
Let me hold you
And take the burdens from your
Small shoulders,
At least for a little while.
Stand tall,
Look straight ahead.
I'll do the worrying for the both of us.
Let me be your umbrella
And shield you from the trouble
That rains down on you,
At least for a little while.
Lift your head,
Let me dry your tears.
I am here for you.

—Shawn Wickersheim, written at
age eighteen, Woodstock, Illinois

Matters of the Heart

There are moments in a man's life that sometimes seem so surreal,
But amidst the foggy darkness, there is an indescribable emptiness that he feels.
With each passing day there are so many questions and inner demons that he must face,
But through prayer and deep contemplation, he is soon humbled by grace.
Deep within his heart lies so many powerful emotions that he can barely hide,
So it comes to no surprise that he is overwhelmed by it all, like the mighty ocean's tide.
But then he remembers that his greatest strength and inner peace comes from above,
As we are reminded to love one another, because God is love.
So with newfound hope, he is ready to face another day,
But deep within his own heart he knows,
That he can't help but wonder what tomorrow will bring.

—Scott Bae, written in his early twenties, Northbrook, Illinois

several countries. By 2006, Lavigne's list of awards numbered twenty-nine, with more than seventeen nominations for a variety of awards given in countries around the globe.

Lavigne admits that as a middle child she always wanted to be the center of attention; she remembers when she was very young standing on her bed like it was a stage. She'd sing at the top of her lungs and visualize thousands of people surrounding her. She moved on from her bedroom venue to singing whenever and wherever she could, singing gospel music in church, then at festivals, on to country music at fairs and talent contests until she was discovered by Arista Records. While on a writing trip to New York City in 2000, Antonio "LA" Reid signed her to Arista at the age of sixteen. She moved to Manhattan and began work on her debut CD *Let Go*, which was released in 2002.

"I love writing," Lavigne explains. "When I get upset and really need to get it out of me I go to my guitar. Sometimes I feel like my guitar is my therapist."[18]

At first, her time in New York wasn't paying off; she wasn't inspired. But she never considered giving up. Instead, she moved to Los Angeles, which was the fresh start she needed to let the creativity flow. Soon the songs for *Let Go* began pouring out of her. She couldn't be happier with the way the album turned out, stating that she'd really grown as a writer and that her music came from her heart.

SONYA KITCHELL, SINGER-SONGWRITER[19]

Poetry can come in the form of a song. Singer-songwriter Sonya Kitchell serves as an outstanding example of a teen who has gotten her name and music out there. Interviews with Kitchell have appeared in the following media sources:

Magazines: *Marie Claire*, *People*, *Billboard*, and *Relix*
Newspapers: *Wall Street Journal* and *Los Angeles Times*
Internet/Web: National Public Radio

HER MANY LOVES . . .

On her website, seventeen-year-old Sonya Kitchell, the singer and songwriter from Massachusetts, confesses, "I love to sing. And I love to write. I write all the time, in fact. And that's pretty much what I want to do: write about everything—people, relationships, the weather, politics, and do it in a way that somehow makes a difference."[21]

By age seventeen, she had appeared on *Letterman*, performed with Herbie Hancock, and wrote every song on her debut CD, *Words Came Back to Me* (on the Velour and Starbucks "Hear Music" label), which is described as a blend of blues, jazz, folk and pop.[20]

Kitchell has been compared to Norah Jones and Joni Mitchell. She wrote her first song when she was only twelve years old. Since then, she's written more than one hundred songs!

Where Did She Come From?

In 2006, Kitchell lived with her parents on a forty-acre western Massachusetts farm where she was born. Listening to her, you might compare her to Christina Aguilera, LeAnn Rimes, or Avril

Lavigne, but she lists her influences as Ella Fitzgerald, Stevie Wonder, and the Beatles rather than contemporary performers.[22]

When Did She Start Writing/Composing?

Sonya Kitchell's earliest self-expression dates back to the afternoon of September 11, 2001, when at twelve years old, she came home from school with trouble coping with the enormity of what had happened that morning. She used her journal as a form of therapy, then a melody formed in her head, and a song was written. When she sang it for her mom and a local folk artist, they said, "People need to hear this song, Sonya." That's when music changed from being merely something she did and became her true passion. Kitchell came to see the act of songwriting "as a way of processing what I'm going through."

Sonya went on to say, "My whole life I've been a sponge for everything around me. I soak it up, and I want to take as much of it as I can and make it part of myself."[23]

Watch for Kitchell as an up-and-coming star! She's using writing in a way that you may never have thought of as a career—*song*writer.

Stranger Things Have Happened

When trying to find sources for a story, or an article, or even someone to interview for his or her point of view, you can never tell when the right person will pop into your life. Case in point: I wrote the majority of this book at a local Dunkin' Donuts, since it stays open late.

One night, I wore a Relay for Life (cancer walk) team t-shirt, and although it was 11:00 p.m., a young woman (nineteen years old) and her mom stopped in the shop. They commented on my shirt and then told me they were on their way home from a big event, similar to the relay.

It turns out the daughter is a singer, who has a CD out already! Wow, was I impressed! Even more exciting was her response when I asked if she writes her own songs. She does. I gave her my card, and she sent a press kit with a bio of herself, some photos, her CD, and publicity she had received. It turns out this woman knew how to market herself! Her name is Suzanne Firestone, and here is her story.

SUZANNE FIRESTONE, SINGER-SONGWRITER[24]

From the early age of six, nineteen-year-old singer-songwriter and Chicagoan Suzanne Firestone began her music career as a weekly soloist on a children's television show called *Lift Jesus Higher.* In 1995, an episode of the show, which featured a vocal performance by Firestone, was honored with an Angel Award.[25] (The Angel Award is an award dedicated to the promotion of quality family-oriented programming.)

Suzanne Firestone, age 19, singer/songwriter.

Suzanne's exposure on the award-winning show allowed her the opportunity to tour with the show's producer. She did television appearances and other performances. She stayed on the *Lift Jesus Higher* show until she was twelve years old.

By the time Suzanne was thirteen she was writing and performing her original works in front of large crowds. Her vocals were top notch, so much so that for two years in a row, she was invited to sing "God Bless America" at the Chicago Bulls basketball game at the United Center in Chicago.

Suzanne kept busy performing at charity events, fund-raisers, and other local venues. She was also the leader of a pop girl group. Suzanne was going full-speed ahead, pursuing her dream of becoming a musician, and by the time she was sixteen, she began receiving offers from producers to start recording professionally. She got to work on her first CD titled *Miss Perfect*, which she wrote, arranged, and recorded at age eighteen. The CD features five songs targeting the teen and preteen market.

Firestone said, "My heart goes out to young people, especially young girls who deal with low self-esteem, depression, and anxiety. I want to be a role model, influencing the younger generation in a positive way. I want to show that God is best and He is the one who makes life beautiful."[26]

She is well on her way to becoming the new voice of Christian pop/rock with the way she draws the crowd in with her positive energy. She's been said to have the "total package" by those in the industry.

CHAPTER 6 WRITING EXERCISE

Write a haiku poem. Remember, it consists of three lines total, lines one and three each have five syllables, while the second line has seven syllables. No rhyme is necessary.

NOTES

1. "Lyrics in English for 'Ode to Joy,'" www.geocities.com/camiya.geo/interests/beethoven.html (accessed February 7, 2008).

2. "Iambic Pentameter," Wikipedia, en.wikipedia.org/wiki/iambic_pentameter (accessed November 2, 2008).

3. Myra Cohn Livingston, *Poem-Making: Ways to Begin Writing Poetry* (New York: HarperCollins, 1991), 111.

4. "Limerick," Shadow Poetry.com, www.shadowpoetry.com/resources/wip/types.html (accessed February 7, 2008).

5. *VOYA*, April 2000.

6. Heidi Bee Roemer, e-mails to author, October 2006.

7. Heidi Bee Roemer, *Whose Nest Is This?* (Minnetonka, MN: NorthWord Books for Young Readers, 2009); *What Kinds of Seeds Are These?* (Minnetonka, MN: NorthWord Books for Young Readers, 2006).

8. Roemer, e-mails.

9. "Poet Heroes," My Hero, www.myhero.com/myhero/hero.asp?hero=mattieStepanek (accessed January 3, 2007).

10. "Poet Heroes."

11. MattieOnline.com, www.mattieonline.com (accessed January 3, 2007).

12. "VOA Special English Report," ManyThings.org, www.manythings.org/voa/02/020524am_t.htm (accessed September 3, 2009).

13. "Mattie's FAQs." MattieOnline.com, www.mattieonline.com (access January 3, 2007).

14. www.myhero.com/myhero/hero.asp?hero=mattieStepanek (link on bottom of first page).

15. Collette DeDonato, ed., *City of One: Young Writers Speak to the World* (San Francisco: Aunt Lute Books, 2004).

16. KaaVonia Hinton-Johnson, *VOYA*, October 2004.

17. "Avril Lavigne: Quick Fact," Biggest Stars.com, www.biggeststars.com/a/avril-lavigne-home.html (accessed June 22, 2006).

18. "Avril Lavigne," Wikipedia, en.wikipedia.org/wiki/avril_Lavigne (accessed June 22, 2006).

19. "Story," Sonya Kitchell.com, www.sonyakitchell.com/story.php (accessed June 22, 2006).

20. www.npr.org/templates/story/story.pho?storyID=5449851 (accessed June 22, 2006).

21. www.sonyakitchell.com/press.

22. www.sonyakitchell.com/press (accessed June 22, 2006)

23. "Sonya Kitchell," SXSW Music, 2008.sxsw.com/music/showcases/band/58483.html (accessed September 3, 2009).

24. Press kit from Suzanne Firestone, September 2006.

25. www.angelawards.com (accessed January 10, 2007).

26. Press kit from Suzanne Firestone, September 2006.

7 Mentors, Professional Organizations, and Critique Groups

MENTORS

Writers Connecting with Other Writers

The dictionary defines a mentor as a trusted guide or tutor or coach. A mentor is someone who has already succeeded at what you are striving to accomplish and is willing to take you under his or her wing to teach you (or at least answer your questions) how to attain your goals.

You might question that person as to how he or she achieved certain levels along the path to success. After you build a rapport with him or her, you'll be able to ask more difficult, personal, and perhaps even introspective questions that will help you push through difficult spots in your own writing. Sometimes friendships grow between mentor and novice when each cares what the other is doing and accomplishing.

CONTACT VS. MENTOR

"What separates a mentor from the average network contact is long-term commitment and a deep-seated investment in your future."

—Katharine Hansen, "Quintessential Careers: Your Job Search Starts Here"[1]

What Are Some Traits I Should Look for in a Mentor, and How Do I Approach Him or Her?

When choosing a mentor, age, gender, race, and religion shouldn't matter. The chemistry to form a friendship, or at the very least a trusting relationship with give and take, is the ultimate goal. You should be able to let down your guard and ask *anything* you need to. You shouldn't feel intimidated by the person. Also, your mentor should already have the experience you're striving for so he or she can offer helpful advice. If that person has no more experience than you, then it won't be a

FINDING FORRESTER: THE PERFECT MENTORING MOVIE FOR ALL WRITERS[2]

Sean Connery stars in the title role, playing Pulitzer Prize–winning recluse Robert Forrester. Hollywood newcomer Rob Brown costars as a young phenom writer from the intercity projects who teams up with Connery to form an unlikely pair that comes from opposite social, racial, and economic backgrounds. The film features the mentoring between the two that evolved into a memorable and lasting friendship. At first, the likelihood of such a friendship actually developing seems a bit of a stretch, but ultimately comes off as an "It could *happen*" piece of work. Viewers may find themselves rooting for both to succeed in overcoming self-inflicted hurdles (Connery living as a "shut-in" and Brown is forced to hide his intelligence and talents). *Finding Forrester* is a movie any writer looking for inspiration should add to his or her DVD collection!

⊚⊚⊚⊚⊚⊚⊚⊚⊚⊚⊚⊚⊚⊚⊚⊚⊚

MY OWN PERSONAL STORY OF FINDING A MENTOR

When receiving my first writing contract for a nonfiction book, I was incredibly happy. However, when the packet of guidelines and legal information arrived in the mail a few weeks later, it was a bulky envelope filled with *so* much information! There was my contract, formatting rules, legalities regarding "obtaining permissions," what rights were mine/which rights were the publisher's, blah, blah, blah. It then became apparent that I was completely in over my head! Seriously, the large envelope was resealed and put in a drawer for a month. Who wouldn't want to cry and call the whole thing off? I couldn't help thinking, *There's* no way *I'll figure this all out!*

I visited my local library in search of two things. One, I wanted to find books that I would like to read and therefore write. Two, I wanted to find a local author who could mentor me. One author who has written thirty-five books that my library carries lived in a city nearby. Appreciating this author's style and accomplishments, I quickly e-mailed her to ask if I could call her with some writing questions. She said sure, and since we clicked right away on the phone, I asked her to mentor me. A friendship formed, and we're still close to this day!

mentor relationship, but more of a "writing buddy." That is fine too, but it is a different role entirely, which we'll discuss in a bit.

Be bold. Research an author whom you *truly* admire and then go for it. Contact the person and flat-out ask him or her to mentor you. If the writer can't or doesn't want to do it, try not to get discouraged. Be grateful that he or she was honest with you and doesn't want to waste your time if there truly is no spare time in the writer's schedule to properly guide you. Move on to your second choice, then repeat the process until you find a mentor. Don't give up!

Have I Been, or Could I Be, a Mentor to Others?

Once you've gotten some publishing clips or other significant writing tasks accomplished, feel free to branch out and help others. You probably know a lot more than you give yourself credit for.

In my high school, there were students called *senior advisers*. You may have (or had) similar programs called *peer leaders* or *peer mentors*, for example. My school had two to four senior advisers assigned to each freshman homeroom. They were there to help with problems, concerns, fears, or merely to answer questions. Not only did I befriend my advisers, but when I was a senior three years later, I signed up to be an adviser to a freshman class as well.

It is a wonderful feeling to be able to "pay it forward." Giving back, or in this case forward, is something helpful to do that will make you feel good, too. It is a great feeling sharing what you've learned with someone who is in the same position you were, not long ago.

Writing Buddies

It is so helpful to work with a partner. Someone whose editing skills and opinions you trust is an immeasurable commodity to have. That person who can give you feedback on manuscripts or to whom you can ask important questions is a wonderful asset. You can have them point out what parts of your writing are confusing, too wordy, or otherwise unclear, and you can do the same in return. Having someone to call when you're stuck or to e-mail with a quick question can be so helpful. Writing is isolated work, so having a confidant can help you feel less alone. It's nice to be able to return the favor as well.

Mentoring/Giving Back

You don't need to have books or magazine articles published to help another aspiring writer get started. You can do lots of things to mentor other writers or would-be writers. Some examples might include

- assisting the teacher in the writing resource center at school;
- joining the editorial staff of your school's newspaper and review submissions by students;
- starting and facilitating a critique group with your peers;

FREEDOM WRITERS: BOOK MADE INTO A MAJOR MOTION PICTURE

In the fall of 1994, high school English teacher Erin Gurwell made a huge impact on her students' lives in Los Angeles. She helped them publish a book of their journaling titled *The Freedom Writers Diary: Their Story, Their Words.*[3] It was such a smash hit that it was made into a major motion picture, *Freedom Writers*, starring Hilary Swank and Patrick Dempsey.

- ◎ volunteering at your library to help younger kids learn to write; or
- ◎ mentoring a reluctant reader or remedial writing student at school.

Just an overall word or two of encouragement goes a long way as well. If you like something a peer has written, take the time to say so.

With Privilege Comes Responsibility

If you're fortunate enough to be in any sort of advanced placement program in your school, you have a distinct advantage over many kids in your community, whether they go to your school or not. You can find out if there are "high-risk" kids in your area that might be interested in writing or even attending a book club discussion. You can use the knowledge and training you have to introduce them to the wonderful world of reading and writing.

HIGH FIVE TO THAT SPECIAL TEACHER!

I asked teens if there was a special person who "turned them on" to writing, or someone they felt particularly encouraged them, someone who gave them the skills and/or confidence to begin writing. Here are some responses:

"Mrs. Strobridge—my 11th grade Lit teacher."

—Drew, age nineteen, Lake Forest, Illinois

"My mom bought me my first diary and she gave me the inspiration to write poems."

—Stefanie, age nineteen, Illinois (au pair from Germany)

"Mrs. (Gloria) Shreve—my 8th grade English Lit teacher. She was the toughest (okay, at the time I thought "meanest") teacher in all of grades one through eight! She always pushed us and was a stickler for proper grammar, punctuation, and clarity. Now I am thankful, she's partly responsible for me becoming a writer, but at the time it was awful!"

—Tina (adult), remembering Holy Cross School in Deerfield, Illinois

"My friend got me started writing. I was jealous because she had a cute diary and I didn't."

—Natalie, age fifteen, Anthem, Arizona

"My philosophy professor."

—Feride, age twenty, Illinois

"My friends are always enjoyable to be with and that makes me want to write about them."

—Lindsey, age sixteen, Buffalo Grove, Illinois

As you get older, you can continue with mentoring on many different levels. I'm in a professional worldwide organization called the Society of Children's Book Writers & Illustrators, (SCBWI). After a few years of membership, and after getting a few books published, I decided I wanted to help others get published as well. I became a network co-representative with the woman who started our local SCBWI chapter (Far North Suburban group of Illinois). Not only did I help encourage and teach others basic skills such as writing queries, pitches, and researching markets, I got many wonderful things in return. I was motivated to write more and stick to my good habits, if only to lead by example. I was able to get excited about little things, such as handwritten rejections (something that should always be celebrated whether you're making your first submission to a publisher or have a shelf of books with your own writings at the local library!).

Have you ever heard, "You get what you give"? It means that the good deeds you do will come back to you tenfold. As a writer, finding friendships and camaraderie in such an isolated field is a welcomed treasure! Oftentimes, the bond you make with someone you mentor enables you to critique them, as well as to be critiqued *by* them. Forming a "writing partnership" is a wonderful way to see your strengths and weaknesses.

PROFESSIONAL ORGANIZATIONS

The best way to find other writer buddies, mentors, critique groups, seminars, writing classes, conferences, and so on is to join a professional organization. There are many to choose from. Here are a couple of examples of organizations to demonstrate how precise or how general you can be with your writing interests.

- **American Society of Newspaper Editors (www.asne.org)—The main goal of the organization is for its members, primarily editors from around the United States, to share ideas, meet at conferences, and to better the field of journalism as a whole.**

◎ **Authors' Guild (www.authorsguild.org)—The guild began in 1912 and was then called the Authors League of America. Its primary goal is to be the nation's leading advocate for writers' interests. (Examples: effective copyright protection, fair contracts, free expression, and legal assistance, among other helpful services.)**

For a list of more groups, turn to the Websites and Professional Organizations section in the Resources.

CRITIQUE GROUPS

When looking for a critique group, try to find people who are at the same level you are in your writing. You don't want someone with less experience who will not have appropriate input to give; similarly, you don't want to have less experience than others in the group or you will not be able to offer helpful critiques either. However, in the latter situation, you might want to ask one of them to mentor you or ask if one might be willing to give you a private review of your work some time.

Similarly, if your group writes in several genres (i.e., some sci-fi writers, some novelists, some nonfiction writers, some picture book writers, and some poets), then by all means join in if you feel you are at a similar level of writing. However, if you know that there is a group for four to six people who all write horror and you want to write in the romance genre, it most likely wouldn't be a good fit. You have to be sure you at least *like* the genres that your critique group writes in, since you'll be reading a lot of the members' work!

Finding the right critique group to join is like being with friends in the same grade in school or even the same afterschool club; you know each other, you have similar interests, and you know what others are going through with every professional struggle. You can relate to and empathize with each another. When you get your first contract within months or even a year of other group members, it is the most thrilling thing! And if you're lucky enough to work with the same publishers, it's neat to compare notes and/or help each other out.

What Exactly Is a Critique Group?

You need to consider many things when looking for a critique group. A good group will become your best support. It will cheer you on with your successes, from something as small as receiving a few words of encouragement written by an editor in the "P.S." part of a rejection letter to making your first sale. Likewise, it will be there to pump you up when you decide that you stink and are wasting a bunch of paper and ink cartridges trying to pursue the unattainable.

Also, if you are in a good critique group, there will be a certain comfort level eventually, where you know each other well enough to make suggestions (and receive suggestions) that will be taken objectively, not defensively. What good is criticism if you fight each and every suggestion someone gives to you? Sure, you won't agree with everything someone says (the same will hold true when you work with an actual editor), but you need to feel the person's suggestions are in your best interest.

I've been in groups where one person never accepted edits from anyone. He had a reason for why all of our suggestions were wrong, and he believed his writing to be simply marvelous. Eventually, everyone stopped critiquing his work because we knew it was a waste of our time. All ideas would be shot down.

How Do I Join One or Start My Own? (Can I Be in One Online?)

Some people live in areas where it is difficult to get together with other writers. They might live in a very rural community, or they might work long hours in their "real" job, or they might not know a whole lot of young writers that are determined enough to want to be in a critique group.

If none of your friends are into writing, you can check your local library or coffee shop and look for a notice from other writers searching for a critique group. You could also try going to a poetry slam or open mike night, then hang out afterward and talk to others who shared work with the crowd. Approach the writers whose work you admired or appreciated, and/or who write in the same genre, and ask them if they're interested in starting up a critique group with you.

Last, you can certainly try to get a critique group together on the Internet. There are specific writing groups online, tailored to young authors, along with organizations and programs in various cities around the country (see WriteGirl profile in chapter 8) to get writers together. When I Googled "teen writing groups" in December 2007, the first three hits were

groups.yahoo.com/group/teenwritinggroup

www.elfwood.com/farp/thewriting/phoenixeyesotw /phoenixeyesotw.html (FARP stands for Fantasy Art Research Project)

www.inktank.org (InkTank's website states, "The organization officially announced its birth in January 2004 as a nonprofit organization dedicated to literacy and creative writing.")

Why Is a Critique Group Necessary?

Breaking a major rule of writing, I find a cliché necessary here. Have you heard the expression, "You can't see the forest for the trees"? Do you have any idea what that means? It means sometimes you are so close to something that you cannot properly see the big picture. In terms of being a writer, sometimes you have worked and reworked a piece so many times that it starts to make no sense to you. You need fresh eyes to actually see what you have going on. Group members can point out the good and the bad, along with the "must keeps" and the "must cuts" much easier, since they have no emotional ties to the work.

You might *love* a certain passage or a chapter you've written, remembering how you labored over each change, subtle nuance, piece of dialogue, or whatever, and even if it isn't working you may still have the hardest time giving it up. When writing fiction, I find (and other writers have backed up this sentiment) that oftentimes the entire first chapter has to go—completely cut. At the very least, it often gets moved around to much later in the book. Beginnings are hard, and it takes an objective eye that has no emotional ties to the words to be brutal with the red pen! I'm known as being quite the slasher in my critique group, but people come to me specifically when they need to really get their stories lean.

How Is a Proper and Constructive Critique Given?

When critiquing someone's work, you'll always want to start with the parts you liked best about the overall story or article. Be sure to point out specific passages and styles that work best and why you think so. Writers are putting their feelings and thoughts on the line by sharing, so you need to respect that fact first and foremost.

Next you can go over technical things like spelling, punctuation, and grammatical errors. These are facts that cannot be disputed. Either it is written correctly or not. And if not, there needs to be a good reason for it. (Say a character speaks with a certain dialect or in slang or stutters; those would be specific *reasons* not to use proper English, for example.)

Last, you'd want to end with things that need major overhauling. Of course, you want to do this as nicely as possible. You'd never begin by saying, "My gosh . . . this is complete trash! Were you sleeping when you wrote this?" or "This is the dumbest story I've ever read! It's totally unrealistic, completely boring. Just throw it out and start something new." Heck, you probably wouldn't critique a classmate you *didn't like* in that manner!

But still, sometimes teasing can hurt a person's feelings too. You can gently say something along the lines of, "Well, I see how you need to explain a bit of back story about the main character's failures, but I think that devoting fifteen pages about why it took so long for him to pass his driver's ed exam is overkill." You want to gently mention that a writer should leave the reader wanting *more*, not *less*. Even if what you're *really* thinking is something along the lines of, "*Okay* . . . we

> "Do you know what the absolute best moment is? It's when you've finished your first draft and read it, by yourself, before those assholes take something they couldn't do in a lifetime, and tear it down in a single day."
>
> —Robert Forrester (Sean Connery) in *Finding Forrester*[4]

get it! You don't need to ramble on for umpteen pages on the fact that he doesn't have his license. I quit reading after page five!"

How Do I Respond to Criticism?

Responding to criticism is a difficult lesson to learn, especially when you've put a tremendous amount of time and effort into your work. You visualize it appearing with your name in the byline of *Seventeen* or *CosmoGirl!* then are devastated when your friends/critique group all hate it. Will you figure that they are all simply wrong? They are just too dense to see the gem you've created? Perhaps you're just more mature or intellectual than your peers.

Yeah right! If *everyone* has troubles relating to your piece, I'm sorry to break it to you, but you *need* to do some major revisions! I'm not saying ditch the piece entirely, but if you show it to six friends, and perhaps a sibling and/or a parent, and they *all* are baffled and ask the same questions or point out the same "problem passage," then you've got to think that maybe they are seeing something you can't. If that's the case, you need to trust your peers and do some serious revising. (Like pulling off a bandage, do it quickly and it'll only hurt for a moment!)

Editing: The Importance of Accepting Critiques

As you may have gathered, one of the most important things a writer learns is how to accept constructive criticism. An equally important lesson to learn is judging when to take a stand and defend what one has written. Writers don't have to take *every* suggestion an editor gives them, but if they decide to forgo certain edits, they must be *sure* they can justify exactly why certain changes *shouldn't* be made. It's got to be a better reason than merely pride or the number-one sin new writers make, "I can't cut that character. It's for my mother," or "It's based on my kid, and that's what she did," or "The grandma *has* to solve everyone's problems," spoken by a writer with grandkids.

The thing writers need to understand and believe 100 percent is that the editor's job is to make the book the absolute *best* it can be. The vision of the finished piece must be shared by the author *and* the editor, so the author's intentions will not be sabotaged. Like any relationship, whether it is personal or professional, trust will come in time. You and your editor(s) will learn what buttons not to press with each other and what bad habits you won't be able to hide (i.e., forever changing tenses . . . who *me?*).

Work on thinking objectively and toughening up your skin, figuratively speaking, of course. The business of writing is competitive and not for the faint of heart. Your soul is often exposed when you share something as personal as writing, so you need to know that criticisms usually are not personal attacks. They are merely suggestions for improvement that you may or may not decide to accept.

NOTES

1. Katharine Hansen, "Quintessential Careers: Your Job Search Starts Here," QuintCareers.com, www.quintcareers.com (accessed August 25, 2006).
2. *Finding Forrester* (Columbia Pictures, 2000).
3. *The Freedom Writers Diary: Their Story, Their Words* (New York: Broadway Books, 1999).
4. *Finding Forrester*.

8 Publishing Information and Marketing Basics

GETTING STARTED IN THE BIZ

This chapter will help with the basics you need to start your own business as a freelance writer. You will learn how to submit to publishers; write queries, proposals, and synopses; target appropriate publishers; track your submissions; learn a bit about contracts and negotiations, along with pros and cons of finding an agent—or not!

BENEFITS OF WRITING

Being a writer has many benefits. Of course, I am biased. So I asked some young adults what *they* get, personally, from writing. In response to my questions—*How does writing make you feel? And do you ever rely on writing to help you feel better?*—here's what several said:

"It seems to get the feelings off my chest. It is like a therapist in some ways. I feel so much better after it's written down."
—Stefanie, age nineteen, Illinois (au pair from Germany)

"It helps me calm down when I've had a bad day."
—Meagan, age sixteen, Illinois

"I write out my frustrations sometimes when I'm mad to get it out of my system instead of fighting with someone and regretting something I might

say; or sometimes I'm so happy, I just want to get down every emotion on paper so I can have that feeling again to refer to when I'm having a horrible day."

—Lindsey, age sixteen, Buffalo Grove, Illinois

"No, I don't write to feel better, but sometimes I scribble in my sketchbook when I'm mad."

—Natalie, age fifteen, Anthem, Arizona

"Not really [I don't rely on writing to make me feel better]. But it makes me feel good after I am done [writing]! I know I expressed my thoughts in a good way!"

—Shan, age sixteen, Wheeling, Illinois

"Writing makes me feel relieved . . . confident. I have to be alone to write anything of any quality. I like it relatively quiet. I write to stay grounded to reality. I write most of the time to track progress in my life."

—Drew, age nineteen, Lake Forest, Illinois

"Writing makes me feel . . . relieved. Yes! (I rely on writing to help me feel better.) I always write letters to persons I feel negatively about; and when I am thinking about social aspects which are stressing me, I write about them. I write when I'm frustrated with people or situations or when I am inspired philosophically or emotionally. I use writing to resolve things."

—Feride, age twenty, Illinois

TRADITIONAL PUBLISHERS VS. SELF-PUBLISHING

Traditional Publishers

Traditional publishers offer a much more practical way of doing business in most cases. A publisher offers a contract for a manuscript and negotiates terms such as rights it wants to obtain versus the rights it will give to the author. A publisher will also negotiate a monetary amount for an advance (see glossary), plus the number of free copies of the book the author will receive. (You will have to pay for additional books yourself, even if you are the author—discount given, of course!)

What Traditional *Publishers Will Do at* No Cost to You

Publishers employ professional editors, layout and design departments, and graphic teams. They have access to artists all over the world, marketing teams, and so on. These companies, established for years (such as Scholastic, Random House, HarperCollins, to name a few of the bigger ones), offer an advance against royalties to the writers who sign a contract. (More about advances later.) Writers should be paid to write; it's as simple as that. Sure, there will be times that authors will do "freebies" for a cause, at their town library or children's school, but it is important to remember that writing *is* a career. If a school can't afford to pay for an author visit, some authors choose to waive their fees. But some authors have learned the hard way that if you do not value your time, work, and efforts, no one else will either. Since you will have to travel to the event and pay for any supplies you need for your presentation, it's fair to charge a minimum fee. The school's parent teacher organization could host a bake sale to cover such costs, at the very least.

Who Does What in a Publishing House?

With different sized publishers, the tasks and responsibilities will vary. Smaller houses with fewer staff have employees take on additional responsibilities compared to a larger house. A staff member in a small company might hold a few titles, taking care of several jobs by him- or herself. The following list will give you a glimpse of a few of the most important positions.

Accounting: This department might be your favorite one to receive things from. It is responsible for sending either quarterly, bi-annual, or annual royalty checks and sales figures, depending on the publisher. It handles your advance checks and other financial information you may need.

Acquisition Editor: This is the person responsible for seeking out authors/manuscripts to get under contract. This is often a person to whom you would address a query or proposal, unless another editor is specifically stated (e.g., senior editor, assistant editor, and so forth)

Art/Layout/Graphic Designer: This person handles the artwork that appears in addition to text. The designer decides size and placement of sidebars and art, as well as other things that make the overall book visually appealing. Things like fonts, amount of white space, and other design elements will fall under this category.

Content Editor: This is the person who confirms that the manuscript flows well and makes sense. In the case of nonfiction, he or she makes sure information is not repeated over and over again in various chapters. He or she also makes sure the story/information is in the right order and is easy to follow. The editor might ask authors to move sections around to different chapters, revise work, or make other requests. Often, an editor poses tons of questions to spark further thought from the author. A good editor can motivate, inspire, and improve the original content of the book tenfold! Another thing the content editor does is watch for plagiarism and ensure the proper permissions have been obtained when using quotes.

Copyeditor: The copyeditor checks substance and fine-tunes the manuscript; perhaps a story line has gotten off track and is not making sense in the big picture of the tale being told. Maybe a character's name has been spelled two different ways throughout the book and needs to be fixed to be consistent. Also, the copyeditor corrects grammar and punctuation, if necessary. For nonfiction, the copyeditor checks sources, bibliographies, quotes, permissions, and various other tasks at this point.

Indexer: This is the person who goes through books word for word and makes an index like the one in the back of this book. A good index is invaluable to reference books like those in the It Happened to Me series. Many larger houses employ their own indexers, while smaller houses will have the authors do their own, once the author receives final page proofs. Some editors feel it is best for authors to provide their own index since they know their book inside and out.

Legal Department: This department checks that permissions have been acquired when using quotes, lyrics, and other copyrighted material. It makes sure there is no libel slander, improper accusations, or plagiarism in the book. In some publishing houses, the legal department may also be responsible for acquiring the International Standard Book Number (ISBN), which is the number each book is assigned by the Library of Congress. (To sell a book in a store or online, each book must have one of these numbers. It is listed on the back of the title page, along with the author's name, copyright notice, publisher's address, and subject categories.)

Line Editor: This editor makes sure punctuation, grammar, syntax, and spelling are correct. The line editor literally goes through the manuscript line by line and word for word to check for errors. (Most books usually have at least one or two typos.) This editor also suggests ways to enhance content.

Marketing and Promotions: This is usually a team of people who will write up a press release and/or a "blurb" about the book that summarizes it quickly and succinctly. The team makes it easy for busy reviewers, librarians, or book purchasers to see what the book is about and to decide whether they want to buy it or send a review copy to them.

The marketing and promotion team also makes sure a book gets submitted to appropriate competitions. There are literally hundreds of contests for published books each year. As an author, your publisher will (or at least *should*) ask if there are certain contests where you'd like your book to be submitted. Keep that thought in the back of your mind as you are writing or revising your book.

Proofreader: The proofreader can be an in-house employee, a freelancer, or you, the author. As the proofreader, you need to check and recheck the work and make any last-minute changes after hearing back from *all* editors. Once the book makes it to the typesetter (a term still used, although many books are printed digitally, not actually "typeset" anymore; think of it as going through the art/layout/graphic design phase), you will receive a set of "first page proofs," which are your first look at the book's layout.

You will see where artwork is placed, plus where chapter headings fall. Page numbers will be in place as well. After carefully checking this version of the manuscript, you will report any necessary changes to your production editor, the editor who oversees the production process of your book. After all changes are approved and made, the author will then get "final page proofs." This is an author's final look at the manuscript before it "goes to press."

As an author, it is smart to do one's best to triple-check each and every word that's been written. With most publishers, paying for any changes past "final page proof" stage is common practice.

(Note: If you are proofreading your own manuscript, this work is merely to get it into shape for submission to publishers. Once it is acquired, your editor will take your "perfectly

ORPHANS AND WIDOWS

Have you ever heard the term *orphaned lines* or *widowed paragraphs*? These two terms refer to how a book is typeset. Orphaned lines refer to one line alone at the top of a page in a book or at the end of a chapter. Widowed paragraphs refer to a partial paragraph on the last page of a chapter. These widowed and orphaned bits of text can make stories harder to read and layouts look unbalanced.[1]

polished piece," and it'll be like a first draft all over again, as far as he or she is concerned. You two will discuss the manuscript back and forth, up and down, from each and every angle! Suggestions will be made, editing points argued and/or agreed upon, and so on. This is different than the "page proofs" mentioned above.)

Publisher: This is a person who has the final say over series, subjects, titles, and contracts offered. They hold the highest position at a publishing company as they oversee all aspects of a project, from acquisitions through "going to press," along with marketing and beyond.

Research Department: This department views the websites that are cited, to see if certain links are still active and whether information is still current. They also make sure there is no slanderous information cited or plagiarized information written.

Self-Publishing

In comparison to taking the "traditional route" by submitting to established publishers such as Random House, Penguin-Putnam, and Rowman & Littlefield, when you choose to self-publish your manuscript, not only will you (the author) have to edit and design the books yourself, but you will, more often than not, be responsible for all the marketing, promotions, advertising, public relations, and solicitations to book reviewers. Last, you are solely responsible for selling the book.

Sure, some self-publishing houses offer to list books in their catalogs and add them to their "list" of published authors, but all in all, not a whole lot is done on the author's behalf. Why should they do any more work for you, the author? The publisher has already made the majority of its money from you. (The majority of self-publishers charge an upfront fee to publish your book, and sometimes these fees can be quite costly.) Since these houses are "print on demand," they don't have a huge inventory of the books, unless authors order them.

Large sales for self-publishing are rare—with the exception of Christopher Paolini (see his biography later this chapter), the teen phenom who wrote the book *Eragon.*[2] After a large

---

EXAMPLE OF SELF-PUBLISHERS

An Offer You Can't Refuse? . . . *Perhaps*

Several websites offer *free* editorial opinions of manuscripts and give guidelines to follow. They list thorough questionnaires of what they hope to discover about you and your writing. Here are some sample questions from a few websites:

Is your manuscript complete?
Will there be photos, drawings, or other artwork included?
What is your anticipated time line?
Who is your market?
Have you sketched out a preliminary cover design, or created a
    concept for it?
Will your book be hard cover or paperback?
How many copies of the book do you want per print run?
How do you plan to sell your book?
What is your marketing focus?

One company markets itself as "Coaching and Mentoring Writers to Become Published Authors." However, you should know that ultimately it *is* a self-publishing house. If that's the route you'd like to try, since there is no investment needed to get its editorial *opinion*, then the risk to get such advice is low or nonexistent.

(Note: If you'd like a company to publish your book, fees *will be* involved, so proceed with caution and get all the facts you need to make an informed decision first.)

Beaver's Pond Press is one such publisher. According to the website, it estimates that all manuscripts will be returned within thirty days, if a SASE is enclosed.[3]

---

publisher picked it up, *Eragon* became a *New York Times'* bestseller. In fact, even more amazing, the book has been made into a major motion picture and has branched out into video games.

Hidden Fees

When someone submits a manuscript to editors at publishing companies, they may send that writer a simple form letter rejecting his or her work. However, the only cost to the writer should be the postage for mailing the manuscript and postage on a self-addressed stamped envelope (SASE). Publishing houses that charge fees for reviewing a manuscript should be avoided.

How to Find a Reputable Self-Publishing House

If you have a book that's close to your heart, as my friend Karen did, you might want your book published as soon as possible. And with the ultra-competitive "picture book" market, it could take years to find a house to produce your book. Her mother was gravely ill, and she wanted to see the book come to fruition while her mother was alive. Going the self-publishing route was the best way for her to achieve this. But how can you separate good self-publishers from bad ones?

First of all, you can check out any complaints filed against companies by going to www.anotherealm.com/prededitors/pebt.htm.

Self-Publishing Q&A

One of the first questions you need to ask yourself is whether you are going to submit your work to a traditional publisher or a self-publishing house. Let's look at the main differences between the two.

What is "self-publishing" and what does it mean? Sometimes referred to as "vanity presses," there are publishers that will take (usually) any manuscript they receive and turn it into a book. Some provide editors, for a fee, while others print up the books "as is" without any proofing or other editorial support. Many in the industry attach a stigma to "self-published" works or those published by "vanity presses."

Why not just self-publish and get your book out immediately? The catch is that the author must often pay up-front fees to have the book published, and he or she is rarely given professional, if any, editors or other staff to help shape the final content of the book. There are a myriad of people working for large publishers who each play an important role

175

in getting a book to market. They all have very specific and necessary jobs to make each book a success.

CHRISTOPHER PAOLINI, AUTHOR

Christopher Paolini was a teen phenomenon who self-published the book *Eragon*, which went on to get the attention of a traditional publisher and in turn became a best-seller. After that, *Eragon* was adapted into a Hollywood movie, premiering in December 2006. *That*, dear readers, is a lesson in successful self-publishing . . . tenfold! But who *is* Christopher Paolini, really? Christopher Paolini was a fifteen-year-old homeschooled student who wrote his first novel, *Eragon*, just for fun. He said it took one year to write the first draft, another year to edit it, then a third year to get it in proper shape with extra fine editing.[4] The family went ahead and self-published it when Christopher was eighteen, which eventually attracted the attention of Knopf (a division of Random House, a large, well-known publishing company).

ONE "BONUS" OF SELF-PUBLISHING

Not only is Christopher Paolini the author of the book *Eragon*, but he drew the interior maps and created the book's cover as well. It was only possible, Paolini said, because he chose to publish with print on demand, otherwise known as "self-publishing" or "vanity press," which gives authors more creative freedom to shape the book's "package" than a publisher would otherwise have allowed.[5]

Paolini's second book, *Eldest*, has been a best-seller as well. The hard cover version came out in 2005, and the paperback edition came out in 2007. A third book in the series, *Brisingr,* was released in 2008 and rounds out the trilogy.[6]

I Don't Like to Read!

The funny thing that Paolini admitted is that he *hated* reading as a young child. (This is not an uncommon statement coming from a writer, oddly enough.) His mom had to coax him into reading. The first book he actually chose to read was a mystery with a cover that intrigued him. That book finally turned him on to reading. It was about tomato sauce being constantly mistaken for blood. After that, Christopher was hooked. Quickly immersing himself in the written word, toys were suddenly replaced by stacks and stacks of books all over his room and under his bed.

Paolini said that it didn't stop there. He enjoyed stories so much that he went the next step and started to create some of his own. Christopher read college-level courses on the subject, teaching himself about everything from plot structure to description. He sat down and outlined the plot for a trilogy of books, struggled to figure out every detail, and then feeling ready, he began to write. Christopher credits his success to his parents' dedication and love. His mother, a former Montessori teacher and author of several children's books, instructed her children every day and played a large role in her son's pursuit of publication.

In September 2003, Paolini was interviewed by Teenreads.com.[7] In that interview, he talked about how long it takes him to make up names for all his characters. He described it as a difficult task that can take anywhere from days to weeks and sometimes even years! In fact, if Christopher can't create just the right name, he'll use

FUNNY WAY TO GET READERS

Christopher Paolini told a funny story about how he got someone to read his book. He arm-wrestled the person with the agreement that if Christopher won (which he did), his opponent would have to read his book.[8]

a "placeholder name" until he can think of a better one. Paolini wrote the glossary after completing *Eragon*, and the glossary only took a few hours to create.

Regarding his book being picked up by a huge publisher, Paolini said that he was in Seattle at an event promoting his original, self-published edition of the book. At first, he didn't really believe the news about Knopf's interest. Christopher couldn't imagine how someone at a big publisher had even heard of his book. Oddly enough, a renowned writer named Carl Hiaasen bought a copy of the book for his stepson in Montana. He loved it so much that Carl recommended it to an editor at Alfred A. Knopf, and that one incident completely changed Paolini's life. Once reality set in regarding the amount of money the publisher offered to him, along with the massive exposure his book would be getting, Christopher finally let go of his disbelief and was thrilled! He and his family screamed with excitement!

SUBMISSIONS

Query Letters

Some publishers do not allow "unsolicited submissions," which means they don't read manuscripts that they did not personally request. However, most will accept what is called a query letter. A query letter is like an advertisement for a writer's work. You (the writer) *briefly* introduce yourself, what your manuscript is about, and why you've chosen that specific publisher to target. You make it all so enticing that the editor (or editor's assistant) wants to see the entire manuscript immediately! Sounds easy, right? *Yeah, right!*

QUERY LETTER EXAMPLES

For good examples of query letters, turn to the front of *Children's Writer's & Illustrator's Market 2009* or *Book Markets for Children's Writers 2009*.[9] The books are for sale at various book stores and online. Each guide includes a variety of other "self-helps" (examples of cover letters, nonfiction lessons, and other materials) for writers.

Think of your cover letter as the preview/trailer of a movie. Before a main feature, movie audiences see quick glimpses of upcoming movies that will be released soon. You'll see the most exciting parts, in order to entice you to go see the entire movie right when it comes out. That's what your query letters should do: pique the editors' interests so they ask for entire manuscripts ASAP! Make it like a commercial for your work.

⊚ ⊚ ⊚ ⊚ ⊚ ⊚ ⊚ ⊚ ⊚ ⊚ ⊚ ⊚ ⊚ ⊚

INSPIRATION FOR ALL WRITERS: EMERGING FROM THE SLUSH PILE![10]

Author Lorijo Metz had worked for years on a middle-grade fantasy novel. Then, on a whim, she entered a contest at a local community college, though not with her novel. The contest was vague; writers simply had to "create something about a circle of light." Inspiration came to Lorijo, and from her idea came a picture book manuscript. While the manuscript did *not* win the contest, a bigger and better opportunity resulted!

Lorijo had so much fun working on the story and she did it so much faster than her novel that she wrote a query and sent it right off to publishers. After a batch of fifteen submissions all ended in rejection, she made some revisions and sent out another batch of fifteen. She immediately got a nibble. After requesting various revisions back and forth, a publisher offered her a contract. That is how she became a published picture book author. It's a Cinderella story of a writer whose query letter was plucked from the "slush pile," leading to her first published book. That book is titled *Floridius Bloom and the Planet of Gloom*.[11]

Snail Mail vs. E-mail Submissions

Some publishers specifically request e-mail queries, but for the most part, it is still a widely held practice to stick to the postal service when submitting queries, proposals, or manuscripts. So unless specifically stated, send all submissions by "snail mail" and not e-mail. You'd hate to get off on the wrong foot with a potential publisher! That being said, if a publisher *does* accept e-queries, for example, remember to keep it formal. Don't IM-speak, such as using abbreviations, bad grammar and spelling, or cutesy familiarity that you truly do not have with such a stranger.

Also, just because your query got to an office in seconds, it doesn't mean an editor will get back to *you* any quicker than if it was in the ever-growing slush pile on the floor, desk, chair,

RESEARCH AND GUTS[12]

Talk about fearless . . . a 2006 *Publisher Weekly* article reported that a twelve-year-old Chinese girl named Nancy Yi Fan researched her markets and decided to see if HarperCollins would be interested in her book. Instead of submitting a query letter, she e-mailed the CEO (Jane Friedman) directly, asking her if she'd like to read her manuscript. Although this is by no means the way to go about getting published, Friedman was intrigued and sent it on to the children's division. Her hunch was right; this young author was very special indeed and her book, *Swordbird*, was published in January 2007. Fan began writing the book in English (her *second* language) at age ten, based on a dream she had about birds fighting. The young author translated her book into a bilingual English/ Chinese edition and has since published her second book titled *Swordquest* in January 2008.[13]

armoire, and perhaps even kitchen counter. An editor's e-mail inbox may have one thousand messages to check! Don't call or e-mail again to "check in" on the status of your query. It simply annoys most editors who already don't have time to keep up with all the work they've been assigned. For a reply, wait the standard amount of time your market guide suggests waiting. If more time passes than normal for that house, *then* it is common practice to send a postcard requesting an update of your query, proposal, or manuscript, or if you choose, you can withdraw your submission altogether.

Some publishers still may not respond, or they may ask for more time. Perhaps they want to see your whole story, or if you sent the full manuscript, they may have liked your story and pitched it to their department heads, who are pitching it to their higher-ups. You never know where your work lies in the hierarchy of a publisher. It will pass through many hands before any offers are made to you, but that doesn't mean the publishers aren't still considering your submission!

Query Letter vs. Cover Letter

So how do you know if you should send a cover letter or a query letter? Are they really so different? Here's a quick checklist adapted from one of the Institute of Children's Literature market guides:[14]

Use a *query letter* when

- ◎ the publisher's guidelines specifically list it in the requirements.
- ◎ there is no attached information (such as a manuscript); the query should have specifics of what you are trying to sell the publisher, but should never exceed one page.
- ◎ you are attaching additional materials like a sample chapter or even a synopsis.

Use a *cover letter* when

- ◎ an editor requests that you send your manuscript directly to him or her; the cover letter will be a polite, professional reminder of that request.
- ◎ you've had previous contact with the editor, and he or she will know who you are; if you've written for him or her in the past, or had a conversation with him or her at a conference, perhaps he or she invited you to contact him or her and send in your manuscript(s).
- ◎ your proposal explains your book completely so a query is not necessary; however, a cover letter is still appropriate to reiterate, briefly, the nature of the work proposed.

Nonfiction Proposals

Your proposal should be tight, meaning succinct and to the point, before it is ready to go out. Your cover letter should not exceed one page. Make sure you say why *you* are the right person to write such a book, and mention any relevant experience with that topic or subject matter. If you're writing a book on dirt bikes and you've raced BMX since you were five years old, that is relevant experience. This is your time to boast about any knowledge or expertise you might have. It's not a time to be humble or understated.

Submission for Fiction

When making a submission for fiction, you'll want to follow the editor's lead. He or she might ask for an entire manuscript for a picture book; or a synopsis and one sample chapter; or an outline with three chapters of a novel; or the entire novel.

If you're sending a synopsis and a couple sample chapters, I suggest sending the *first* chapters. One author I know sent three chapters from the *middle* of her novel, which became too confusing for the editor to follow along, having no back story to reference. If your first two to three chapters aren't "top notch" and you're sending middle chapters because that's when the story "really gets good," then perhaps the story isn't ready to go out into the market after all.

Synopsis

A general rule of thumb is to keep your synopsis to just a few pages, depending on the length of your manuscript. If you can keep it to one page—great, go for it! Professional writer

---

DON'T FLAUNT "AMATEUR"—EVEN IF YOU ARE ONE

Nothing screams *rookie* more than a writer submitting a synopsis but leaving off the ending, as if you are enticing the editor to beg to read the rest of it. It's most likely not going to happen that way.[15]

No matter what tense your story is written in, the synopsis should be written in present tense (i.e., Dad *goes* to my soccer match; not Dad *went* to my soccer match).[16]

For a comprehensive list of do's and don'ts, check out a website that answers virtually every writing question you might think of: www.dailywriting tips.com.

If you start off with some basic rules, you'll avoid common faux pas that will single you out as a beginner.

Marg Gilks suggests one synopsis page for every twenty-five pages of your novel, maxing out at ten pages. If you go the whole ten pages, it had better be gripping, she says. Most editors prefer no more than five pages, and if you can keep it to one or two, that's ideal.[17]

So how do you cut your two-hundred-page novel down to eight pages, let alone five, or even two? Start the easy way: pare down your adjectives and adverbs and make sure to take out qualifying words that are unnecessary such as "very," "like," and "really." They don't advance the story; they slow it down.

Oh, I Hate It

For the amount of time people work on novels, it is baffling how so many of them blow off the synopsis. "Oh, I *hate* writing the synopsis!" Well, *duh*! Who doesn't? But for novelists, the synopsis is the most valuable tool you can use to get your (sometimes *very* long) tale summarized in a neat and tidy package. Your synopsis could almost be compared to Cliffs Notes (see glossary). Oftentimes a writer just whips off some dry generalization of what happens in the novel, thinking it doesn't matter that much, but it's quite the contrary. The writer should consider the synopsis equivalent to what a publisher might have on the jacket cover of the book. (Sometimes, the author is responsible for writing the jacket copy himself, by the way.)

GREAT RESOURCE FOR TIPS ON WRITING A GREAT SYNOPSIS

Writing-World.com includes an amazing article on writing a great synopsis.[18] If you need in-depth help writing one, start here.

Helpful hint for the day: Do yourself a favor and spend a minimum of three to four weeks writing and revising your synopsis. The time will be well spent and could potentially cut months, even years, off your submission time.

REJECTION

So you wrote a magnificent manuscript, followed the publisher's guidelines to the letter, and sent it off with visions of being interviewed on all the morning talk shows. *What? How on earth did my manuscript get rejected?* Suddenly, you're sure the idea of becoming a writer is a stupid dream you should immediately give up. Not so! Congratulations; once you get that first rejection letter, you officially have gone through the rite of passage that one gets as a *writer*. You possess something that all famous writers have dozens of, including Michael Crichton and James Patterson.

On Rejections . . .

Blogs are not only a useful tool in promoting your work, but a great place to "chat" with colleagues, friends, and family. Writing can be an isolated job, so having the support of friends to cheer you up and cheer you on is essential. On a blog, it doesn't matter if you live in separate countries or just down the street from each other. The Internet has really made the world a smaller place, where people from all over the globe can connect. The following quotes are from a blog where various writers give a friend a pep talk after she received a rejection on a manuscript for a romance novel.[19]

"Looking on the bright side, a standard rejection is the worse possible result so things can either stay the same or improve—they can't get worse!"

—Sarah, re: Sharon's online writer's blog.

"In my opinion, a first rejection letter is a HUGE rite of passage. I'm actually looking forward to mine!"

—Julie S., re: Sharon's online writers' blog.

"My commiserations Sharon—a rejection always stings—but I don't know any authors without any."

—Kate W., re: Sharon's online writers' blog.

"Thanks for the support, all. Knowing there's such a great bunch of writers out there who all care about each other makes it so much easier, doesn't it?"

—Sharon, responding to the posts on her own blog.[20]

ON MULTIPLE SUBMISSIONS . . .

Here are a couple answers to questions posted on a writer's Listserv:[21]

Is it taboo to submit more than one manuscript at a time to an editor? Author Brenda Ferber replied, "You should only submit one manuscript (ms) at a time to a publisher. If you can't decide which one to submit, why not send one ms to six publishers and the other one to six others? Then, if you get a rejection with a request to see more work, you'll have something ready to send right away."

My ms is currently at another imprint of Simon & Schuster (Atheneum), where it seems to be in a holding pattern. What is the etiquette for submitting to different imprints? It becomes very limiting when there are so many imprints under one BIG umbrella. (And I'm not sure if editors pass along mss to other imprints.) Ferber replied,

> You really aren't supposed to submit the same ms to more than one imprint at a time, so I'd send a status query to Atheneum and wait for a response before submitting to McElderry.

SIDEBARS

Sidebars are the boxes you see in the middle or side of a page in a book or magazine article. It breaks up the bigger chunks of text with some quick fact or quote and/or artwork or graphic.

If you include a sidebar that is a mini-glossary, for example, to accompany a manuscript intended for a magazine article, it might entice the publishers even more to buy it. (Not that these little extras will help sell a dodgy manuscript, but it will serve to enhance the wonderfully rich text you have written.)

The patience and the waiting are the hardest parts of the industry. And the imbalance of power doesn't always feel fair. That's why it's best to put as little mental energy as possible into that aspect, and concentrate instead on writing a manuscript (or several manuscripts) that are so unbelievably fresh, amazing, and wonderful . . . publishers will be fighting over you! Good Luck!

WHAT YOU MIGHT NOT LIKE TO WRITE, BUT HAVE TO . . .

Some authors hate writing outlines, synopses, and press releases, but if you're still in high school or college, you may be learning to do such tasks. Looking to the present, you might be agonizing over something like a term paper! Here's a quick mini-lesson to help you with "today's writing." Who knows, today's term paper could be a future article for publication!

Classroom Assignments—Term Papers

If you have to write a term paper, it's like "death and taxes." There is no way out of it. Below are some helpful hints to get through the process unscathed.[22]

Let's start at the beginning; pick *what* to write about. Choose a subject that you're interested in, since you'll be working on it for several weeks, and make sure the topic is not too broad or too narrow. After you've decided what to write about, you'll need to brainstorm the different angles you can take with your subject matter.

There are so many places from which you can gather your information: the Internet, books, newspapers, periodicals, and live interviews with people, even experts. Make sure to take meticulous notes from all the sources from which you acquire information. You can use index cards to organize your ideas and then rearrange the cards into an order that makes chronological sense.

Once you've gathered information, you *must* make sure to properly notate your sources. Make sure to cite a person's name and publishing info on any material you have quoted from another writer. If you don't give credit to another person's words, that's called plagiarism. (See glossary; also chapter 9, "Emotional and Gritty Realism.")

Once you've organized your note cards how you want them, it's time to make your outline. It will be a bit skeletal at first, but as you add sub-ideas and have a chance to go through the outline several times (thickening it up with each pass), it will start to morph into something real, on its way to becoming an article.

Next, you will take a crack at writing an actual first draft with a beginning, middle, and end; more specifically, these parts are called the *introduction*, *body*, and *conclusion*. You will tell readers what you are *going to tell* them in your piece. Then you *tell* readers what you have to say. And you end with telling readers what it is you have just *told* them. These three parts will help cement the ideas in their minds.

Limit each paragraph to *one* main idea. You can continue to prove the idea by giving examples of what you are talking about in the body of your text, if necessary, but be sure to use transition words such as *furthermore*, *in effect*, *moreover*, *specifically*, and *to demonstrate*. This will help the text flow smoothly, transitioning from one topic to the next seamlessly.

End with your conclusion, telling readers what they have read. Don't forget to restate the point, or main idea, of your paper. It's important to include footnotes or endnotes that cite all sources used. Footnotes appear at the bottom, or *foot*, of the same page, where information needs documenting. Endnotes appear on a separate page at the end of the paper/report, hence the name *end*notes. These notes are listed just before the bibliography. Since footnotes and endnotes have a variety of formats that are acceptable, check with your instructor to learn which one he or she prefers.

Next, you'll want to write a bibliography (again documenting all sources used). Of course, you'll need to revise, revise, revise, and then proofread the final draft. Last, ask a friend to look over your paper with a "fresh pair of eyes." Since you've read the thing over and over again, you will easily miss mistakes.

LEGAL INFORMATION

Q&A: "I Have My First Contract—Now What?!"

What does all that legalese mean? Don't be scared off right away. The majority of first-time contracts are standard contracts that are offered to most, if not all, new writers in a

publishing house. Unless you come out of the starting gate in a big way, like Christopher Paolini, most first-time authors don't have contracts with many complex sections. Sure, you'll want to understand what each point is, but being informed and *worrying* are two different things. It's wise to hire a lawyer if you can find an affordable one, to give the contract a quick "once over." You can find a specific lawyer who handles publishing contracts by going to an industry website that helps authors, such as www.scbwi.org. The staff at the Society of Children's Book Writers and Illustrators (SCBWI) has many professional contacts that can offer advice.

What do primary rights *and* subsidiary rights *mean?* According to www.publaw.com/subsidiary.html, *primary rights* include only those rights the publisher specifically intends to use. Usually, these rights include the right to publish the book as an original hard or soft cover edition as well as paperback reprint rights. The publisher might also want *foreign translation rights*, *serialization rights*, *book club rights*, and the *rights for special editions*. When talking about *subsidiary rights*, those refer to rights such as electronic, motion picture, television, audio book, or other forms in addition to the actual text in book format.[23]

If the publisher exercises these rights, it might put a special time frame on it, such as a clause stating "the publisher must exploit electronic rights in the literary work within three years of the publication date of the hard cover edition of the book or such electronic rights revert to the author." Motion picture, television, audio, and merchandising rights are good examples of how valuable subsidiary rights can be today.[24]

What is an "advance"? Also known as an advance against royalties, an advance refers to money given to the writer ahead of time (before a book is published or sold), as a good faith estimate of the minimum amount of money a publisher expects to profit from the book that has been contracted. (Note: to receive royalties, enough books must first be sold to recover what up front money the publisher gave, or *advanced*, to the author.)

What are royalties? Once you earn back your advance, all money earned afterward is considered a royalty, or the percentage of the profits you receive from the sale of your book. Royalties are most often paid once a year, or sometimes twice a year, depending on the publisher.

Royalties are often negotiable. However, some publishers offer a set standard royalty percentage and will not negotiate. This is often true for first-time authors.

Deductions and Expenses

When you go to pay your income tax, you can declare your writing expenses such as computer, paper, ink cartridges, Internet service, and other such expenses. You may even get a tax refund during your first few years as a professional writer! To actually show a *profit* as a writer may take a while; it takes some writers many, many years.

I don't share this information to discourage you. You need to go into freelance writing with open eyes. The more you write, the bigger advance you should earn. It all depends on who your publisher is and what books you've written—the number of copies sold. Most writers "pay their dues" in the industry before going out on their own to freelance. They intern at magazines, get jobs as assistant editors, copywriters, or a variety of other jobs mentioned in this book. While writing is tremendously gratifying, it is definitely not a get-rich-quick industry. There is real money to be earned, but it takes time, dedication, and a true love of the craft.

Legal Help

Most people, especially teens and young adults, aren't in touch with lawyers. At the very least, they do not have agents or publishing attorneys in their direct circle of friends. If this is your situation, you can go online and Google professional organization sites such as the Author's Guild and the Society of Children's Book Writers & Illustrators. Writing websites often have question and answer (Q&A) sections written by legal advisers, to help answer some basic questions that come up when dealing with the publishing industry.

Accountant

While this might be getting ahead of things, once you do finally submit work and make a few sales, you'll want to speak with some accountants. They can tell you about all sorts of tax information such as how to claim your earnings and deduct costs such as your computer, ink cartridges, paper, and other various supplies, writing courses, and even your Internet service. A portion of the money you spend on writing can be deducted from what you owe at tax time, should you make money from your writing.

Do I Need an Accountant?

Once you have a few contracts under your belt and a number of royalties coming in, you might want to consider getting yourself an accountant. Until then, you really aren't making the money to justify such a business expense. If your family has an accountant do its taxes every year anyway, then go for it. Most likely, you haven't had too many taxes to claim in your life personally, so this is going to be something to store in the back of your mind for the next few years.

AGENTS[25]

What Does a Literary Agent Actually *Do*?

Literary agents, or simply "agents," work for writers trying to sell the writer's works to publishers, as well as film and TV producers. They may work for authors, actors, athletes, musicians, and other public figures who want to be authors. By doing the marketing and business-type work such as bookkeeping, preparing tax forms, and handling appearances, agents give authors time to do their main job— the actual *writing!* It is generally believed that a membership in the Association of Authors' Representatives (AAR) signifies a legitimate agent. An author might reconsider working with an agent who isn't a member of AAR. The opening line of the

INFORMATION TO KNOW ABOUT BEING AN AGENT[26]

Courses to Take

Business, English, theater/dance

Minimum Education Level Required

High school diploma

Professional Organizations for More Information

Association of Authors' Representatives (www.aaronline.org)
Publisher's Weekly (www.publishersweekly.com)

AAR's website describes the organization as a "not-for-profit organization of independent literary and dramatic agents."[27]

What Is the Difference between an Agent and a Publicist?

SUPPLEMENT YOUR INCOME

Amazon.com has a section where you can add a link from your website and receive a percentage of all revenue generated from those customers sent to Amazon.com directly from your site. The program is called an "associates account." Go to www.amazon.com to learn more.

In the most basic of terms, the agent takes unpublished work, shops it around to various publishers, and negotiates a sale and contract for an author. Once a book is written, edited, and published, *that's* when the publicist's work begins. He or she gets the news of the author's book out to the press and various media to draw attention and create interest in the product.

ADVICE FROM A FREELANCE WRITER

Alyice Edrich is a writer whose website provides interviews with people in the publishing field. In one particular interview, she spoke with author, editor, and freelance writer Jenna Glatzer. The amount of invaluable advice given was abundant! Here are a few excerpts from their online conversation.[28]

When asked about her queries being rejected left and right, Glatzer responded,

> I had heard the advice "study our magazine" so many times before in writers' guidelines, but I never really understood what it meant. I read magazines, I thought of stories that sounded like they might fit, and I pitched them. Somewhere along the way, I learned what those editors really meant:
>
> - Study our word counts, our formats, our style.
> - Know the age group of people we profile.
> - Know who advertises with us and why.
> - Know how much disposable income our readers have and how educated they are.
>
> Assignments came much easier once I learned how to break it all down and really analyze a magazine.

Glatzer has had many articles and books published. Edrich asked what her secret was to staying on task. Glatzer responded,

> Variety and discipline. I have a strong work ethic, but I do get bored or stale-feeling if I spend all day and night on one topic. So I keep many irons in the fire at once and switch back and forth throughout the day—I may start my day by doing interviews for an article about obsessive-compulsive disorder, then research light therapy options for a query for a pregnancy magazine, then write greeting cards, then work on the latest chapter in a book.
>
> I'm always interested in what I write about; I don't take assignments if they don't interest me. So it's not hard for me to convince myself to work—I love that I get paid to learn!
>
> I have always taken my deadlines very seriously, and that's one of the reasons editors trust me. You'd be amazed by how many editors told me their biggest problem with writers is that they don't meet their deadlines.

That advice, alone, will help you build a good rapport with editors—trusting relationships where they think of you as the "go-to girl" or "go-to guy" when they need something done, and when they need it done right!

You can visit Jenna Glatzer at her website, www.jennaglatzer.com.

GENERAL PUBLISHING Q&A

What Is Work for Hire?

As discussed in chapter 2, *work for hire* is a contract where authors are paid flat fees for writing books assigned to them by a publishing house. Work for hire means you are hired to do a job and will be paid a flat fee for said job. You will not receive any further compensation, such as royalties. There are oftentimes much shorter deadlines for these types of contracts as well.

What If I Miss My Deadline?

That depends on your publisher. Some publishers say, "Send the manuscript today, or send back the portion of your advance you received so far."

Sometimes, you can't help missing a deadline. Perhaps a family emergency came up, or maybe a project took *way* longer than you anticipated. Maybe your full-time job (as many writers have at least another full- or part-time job on the side) has really been consuming your time, and you simply couldn't finish on time. If that's the case, and your editor and/or

DEADLINES ARE YOUR FRIEND

If you've talked to other writers, I'd venture to guess an almost unanimous agreement that deadlines are what get pages written. Elizabeth Curtler, a grant writer, said that it can be challenging to get started on a new project. But since she has a lot of deadlines, she often has no choice but to sit down and just write. She refers to this as being backed in a corner by a deadline.[29]

publisher has the luxury of some leeway, he or she may give you an extension. If so, do your very best to estimate *realistically* how long you will need to finish up the project. Having to ask for a second or third extension is brutal; it's not only an embarrassment, but could irritate those you work for and make you look less professional.

The best advice on the subject of missed deadlines is this: talk to your editor several weeks before your due date if you think your manuscript will be late. Like school, you may or may not get in trouble. It depends on the editor you're working with. Giving advance notice of trouble with your schedule might allow the editor to rearrange *her* schedule to work on another book or two before yours, and put yours on the back burner.

What If My Final Manuscript Gets Rejected after I Received the First Part of My Advance?

You'd have to refer back to the contract you signed with your publisher. Generally speaking, the company may give you an opportunity to resubmit and make the necessary changes that would deem it acceptable. But, legally a publisher is not bound to give you that "second chance." If the editor decides he or she just doesn't like it, and it's completely different than what was envisioned, it is his or her right (should the contract spell out the publisher's right of refusal) to turn it down and request the return of any monies given.

THE PRODUCTION PROCESS

Once the ink is dry on the contract, and it's time to get going, the writer is still forced to stare at a blinking cursor on a blank page. With six to twelve months to pound out a couple hundred pages, the math side of my brain thinks, heck, that's only three pages a week. How can I get any momentum that way?

Typically, for nonfiction, a writer could spend the first six months gathering research on the Internet, reading articles, books, and doing personal interviews. This is the "organization phase" of your job. One suggestion is to use manila file folders for each chapter, so you can file the research you gather immediately. (Organization is key for any writing, fiction or nonfiction.) Once a folder starts getting good and thick, that can be the chapter you start with.

First Draft—First Edits

Once you finish your first draft, put it aside for a few days. This is a way to "let it cool" so you can look at it with fresh eyes. It will be important to start with an open mind, especially when working on a particularly long project, as if you're reading the material for the very first time. Begin reading for content to see if there are any inconsistencies, holes, or general misplacement of information into wrong chapters. Even when writing fiction, you may want to move certain events, scenes, dialogues, or entire chapters.

Once you're sure you like the flow of the story or nonfiction layout, go back to reread it for specific word-for-word edits such as punctuation, grammar, tense agreement, spelling, and so forth. This can be hard at times, because you are so familiar with your text that your mind skims over certain mistakes easily, knowing what you *meant* to say, although it may be technically incorrect. What quirky bad habits do you have? Perhaps you are a horrific speller. Do you slip between past and present tenses? Do you write long run-on sentences or fragmented phrases? Find one bad habit you constantly repeat, and make a mental note to try and break it.

Last, you'll edit your manuscript to death and then send it to the editor in hopes that he or she sees the gem that it is and sends it right on to the typesetter. *Good luck with that!* Okay, it *might* happen, but that would be the exception to the rule, not the norm. Your editor will probably have a list of minor, or even major, changes for you to make. After the two of you go a few rounds of the editing dance, your beautiful project *will* eventually get sent on to production. Hurray!

First Pages

Now that you and your editor both agree the manuscript is "ready," it'll go to a line editor and/or a copyeditor for grammar and punctuation and content appraisal. After that, your work is turned over to the typesetter. *This* is the fun part. The production department will send you your "first pages," which is the first chance you'll get to see your book all laid out with fonts, page numbers, headings, and so on. This is where you need to meticulously check your work word for word. Make sure every footnote number is set in a superscript font. Make sure artwork or photos are included with the correct captions and sidebars are placed on the page with the corresponding text.

If there are any additions or deletions, this is the time to speak up and state your case to your editor. Make sure all the permissions are obtained and signed and all sources cited.

Page Proofs

This is your final look at the book before it "goes to press." If there are *any* changes that need to be made, speak now or forever hold your peace; actually, if you do have any changes to make, you'll probably have to *pay* for them after this point, if there is even *time* to make any changes. So take advantage of your "first pages," and scan them with a fine-tooth comb until your eyes are almost crossed, then have a friend read it through, then read it through yourself *again*! Seriously, *this is your last— absolute last—chance to make changes, so don't blow it.*

Acquiring Permissions

Magazines, newspapers, trade journals, books, encyclopedias . . . If you've used an exact quotation, you may need to acquire permission to publish it. To see if permissions are needed, you have to check the copyright. You check on the first page of the book after the title page. That page has the publisher's information, such as copyrights, Library of Congress number, author's name and year of birth, and so forth. If you're simply recapping what you've read or paraphrased something, then you need to cite the source where the information came from. This can save you plenty of time and money! Sometimes, you just can't say it any better, though, and you'll want to use an exact quote. If that's the case, you'll need to get written permission, and may have to pay a fee to the copyright holder for reprint rights.

Hot Topic: Plagiarism—Intentional or Not?

In 2006, Harvard student Kaavya Viswanathan (class of 2008) was accused of plagiarism.[30] The word *plagiarism* means taking someone's words or ideas as one's own without properly crediting the original source. Plagiarism is an illegal act. Viswanathan's book *How Opal Mehta Got Kissed, Got Wild, and Got a Life* contained several passages that were strikingly similar to two books by novelist Megan F. McCafferty, *Sloppy Firsts* (2001) and *Second Helpings* (2003).[32]

COPYRIGHT LAW: DO I NEED TO COPYRIGHT MY MATERIAL?

"Any work created in the USA after 1 Mar 1989 is automatically protected by copyright, even if there is no copyright notice attached to the work. 17 USC §§ 102, 401, and 405."—Dr. Ronald B. Standler[31]

Yes, the quotes say somewhat different things, but they start out the same—almost verbatim! If this was the only example, you could probably overlook it. However, there were dozens of similar passages that couldn't be ignored.

Viswanathan was offered a *huge* contract. It would be huge at any age, but this nineteen-year-old woman was offered an unprecedented $500,000 contract for a two-book deal while still in high school! *How did it ever get so far?*

Quotes, Paraphrasing, and Plagiarism

Dr. Ronald B. Standler, a former professor and an attorney who specializes in higher education law and copyright law, wrote an essay about plagiarism, including the difference between using an actual quote and paraphrasing work.[33] Standler says that even if a writer is not using exact,

HOW MANY WORDS MAKE UP A QUOTE?

There is a legal limit to how much you can quote from another book. For example, in my own contracts, I've been told up to fifty words can be used without obtaining permission, *but* the source must always be cited, regardless of the number of words used. Others writers have given me a figure of five hundred words, which can be an entire article. Always check the fine print of your contract or ask the publisher. However, whether it's one word or one thousand words, make sure you *always* cite your source, and to err on the side of caution, obtain *signed and dated* permissions!

verbatim quotes, he or she must still cite the source of the idea conveyed and the person who originated it.[34]

Standler also mentions when summarizing large portions of text in a simple paragraph, the writer needs to make it clear that he or she is summarizing the work of another writer, as well as cite the original source within the paragraph.[35]

For a plagiarism prevention website, check out www .turnitin.com

SEEING THE BOOK FOR FIRST TIME

Writing is fun. Writing is hard work! It is a challenge, and anyone who has written a book, especially a substantial one of many pages, will tell you at one point or another in the process, divine intervention plays a part. When you get the actual book in your hot little hands, you'll be amazed at what you're reading. The first long book I wrote, I read in amazement, crying at parts, laughing in others. My friend looked at me and said, "Geek! You wrote it! Why are you so surprised?"

Honestly, I did not remember writing half of the things in it. I felt like I was reading my book for the first time with fresh eyes! That's a real plus of the job that isn't often discussed.

MARKETING A BOOK AFTER IT'S PUBLISHED

Getting Press—It's Mostly Up to You!

Unless you're a household name whose books top the *New York Times*' best-seller list, your publisher will not have a huge amount of advertising, promotion, and/or public relations dollars set aside to promote you. In fact, aside from listing you in the catalog and sending out a few review copies, there probably won't be any budget specifically for you and your book.

"*What! How can that be?*" you ask. After all the hard work it took to write a great manuscript, find the right publisher, then spend a year in edits and rewrites, "*Where is the justice?*"

Well, believe it or not, at a 2003 SCBWI conference in New York City, a New York publisher stated that getting a picture

book to market costs approximately $100,000. Yep, that's *$100,000*! How many people in life have had such a huge amount of money invested solely in them?

Never Too Soon to Start

You may see marketing as a long way off, especially if you are simply interested in writing and have not mailed out a single manuscript. Nineteen-year-old Stacy Chudwin was published in her teens and began marketing her heart out at a young age. Her success is directly related to the efforts she put forth on the promotion side of the process.

Q&A with Published Teen Novelist, Stacy Chudwin[36]

Are there problems that you consider a negative part of the job that people who are considering writing as a profession need to know about?

I never realized before how much sheer business and marketing goes into the books that make it to the bookstores. People can be incredibly talented novelists, but if they can't write a compelling query letter or don't have engaging personalities, they may never get published. That may seem superficial and unfair, and in many ways, it is. But it's all part of the package of what it takes to be a novelist. You have to do your research, throw yourself into the industry, and hope for the best.

What can you tell the readers about marketing your own book?

You'll only be as successful as the amount of time and effort you are willing to put into it. There is no limit to the amount of publicizing you can do for a book. Also, creativity is the key. There are so many random opportunities for marketing if you look for them. You can put up flyers at a coffee shop. You can have your mom or dad brag about you to their colleagues. Word of mouth can be one of the best ways to market. Also, confidence is incredibly important. If you don't think your book is worth reading, why should anyone else?

There are exciting things you can do when marketing your book. You might enjoy these aspects, or you may choose not to partake, but here are some ideas of ways to market yourself, your writing, and earn a side income.

Travel

Some schools, bookstores, and radio stations will pay your travel to come visit them. You get to see many places you wouldn't necessarily think to visit. It's not only exciting and inspiring to be at a new location but really breaks the monotony of sitting and writing all alone, as is often done by professional writers.

Book Signings

Have you ever tried to imagine yourself at a bookstore or school with a line of people waiting to meet you and have you sign their book? C'mon, admit it, you have! It is an unbelievable feeling to have someone share a part of your book and tell what a certain passage meant to *them*, and you can clearly remember what you were feeling the day you learned that certain information, or interviewed a subject, or made a connection that just fit perfectly with what you were trying to convey. It's a great feeling to connect with readers and have people walk right up to you with compliments that basically show that they get what you are trying to say. Sometimes, they might even want to debate a point with you. It is even more thrilling to have a discussion with someone over something you both feel passionately about.

School and Library Visits

Since you are most likely still in school, it might be hard to visualize actually *being* the guest lecturer. But before you know it, you could be invited to speak at schools or libraries, locally or around the country! Whether you're hired as an "expert" on a particular subject or are there to discuss a novel you've written, visiting with students and other readers is such an inspiring, exhilarating experience. Just seeing all of the different faces and eavesdropping on conversations can give you ideas for new characters or for developing characters you've already started.

It is exciting for kids and adults alike to get to meet a real, live author so remember to respect that fact. Be prompt, be prepared, and be open to answer questions as well. You are privileged to meet people who are excited to share their thoughts on your work, so keep that in mind when you are writing and perhaps get frustrated or lonely. This is the great interaction writers crave—the give-and-take of discussing one's work. It is something to look forward to when you are writing!

Guest Lectures

When you've done extensive research and gotten something down on paper that others may never have thought about, you'll know you've hit a nerve. People will want you to come discuss your findings and share it with others. This is a real validation of your work, and you should feel proud of this accomplishment. Guest lecturing is also a lucrative way to supplement your income. Ask writers why they got into the profession, and you'll be hard-pressed to find someone who says, "For the money, of course!" (Note: Just because you are young, it doesn't mean you wouldn't make a wonderful speaker! Think about that before deciding that forensics, debate team, speech class—or whatever other opportunities to learn public speaking—is a waste of your time or for the *un*cool.)

Teaching

Whether you write fiction or nonfiction, you might have something to teach your readers on a one-on-one basis, such as giving a seminar. You can *teach* whatever interests you, whether it is technical such as building a car or fun things such as crafts. If you've written a book on eating disorders, you can

⊚ ⊚ ⊚ ⊚ ⊚ ⊚ ⊚ ⊚ ⊚ ⊚ ⊚ ⊚ ⊚ ⊚ ⊚

PAUL AND SARAH EDWARDS' BOOK:
HOME-BASED BUSINESS FOR DUMMIES[37]

Should you decide to be in business for yourself as a freelance writer, you might look at the following topics discussed in the book *Home-Based Business for Dummies*: start-up funds, marketing campaigns, taking advantage of the Internet, and setting up boundaries in your home life and writing life, among other ideas.

One of the best perks of being a writer is to be your own boss! But before you take the leap, especially if you are in your late teens or early twenties, you should research all the pros and cons about such an undertaking before even thinking of putting a plan into action!

go on author visits to discuss the topic and how your book might help someone in the audience, for example. Perhaps you truly enjoy knitting and created a book on the subject. The local library might be interested in hiring you to make a guest appearance and do a presentation highlighting the book and doing a demonstration. The possibilities are endless.

Networking

With writing primarily a solitary job, it is important to reach out to others in the field. Not only do other writers provide a sounding board for any troubles you are having, but they supply emotional support and even possible business leads, too! The remarkable thing is this—*writers in a critique group generally help each other*. They encourage each other, help critique work to make it the best possible product it can be, and often share tips and leads on editors/authors they meet to help one another get their writing published. A big part of writing, especially once your book comes out, is networking. You need to get the word out about your book to get it into peoples' hands.

As a freelance writer, building strong and trusting relationships is how you network. In sales, if you were to network and help a salesman from a competing company, it would be grounds for dismissal.

Support

As a writer, your friends and parents might be eager to read all you've written. After a while, though, especially after being published, family excitement tends to wane for most authors I've spoken to. I asked my family members why they don't read my work anymore, at least not until the actual book comes out, and they replied, "You don't need our opinions any more. You're getting contracts on your own."

"*Hmph!*" I want to say. "*That's not the point!*"

Writers get little praise and feedback during the writing and marketing process. The simple gesture of someone saying, "Ooh, can I read what you're working on right now?" might be just that speck of encouragement that gets you through the long months of writing and then trying to market an especially lengthy project.

The majority of your time working will be spent alone, with only your own thoughts, ideas, and research materials. Just meeting for a weekly coffee klatch to talk to other writers might be all the encouragement and pep talk you need to get you through the week. There are also professional groups, critique groups, poetry slam pals, and, in the case of technical problems, Apple Care and the HP support desk.

Research Appropriate Markets

There are several market guides available at bookstores and online to research fiction or nonfiction publishers. One of the most popular books among writers is the *Writers Market* guide (updated each year). In it, publishers and publications are indexed alphabetically and by genre. There are separate sections for magazine publishers and book publishers. The beginning of the book includes examples of what you need to know how to do. There are sample query letters, cover letters, synopses, writing samples, and so forth.

There are also many helpful interviews with professional writers, editors, and agents.

Market guides give all the pertinent information writers need to submit work to publishers including company names, addresses, websites, and contact names. Publishers also specify whether they accept queries or entire manuscripts, unpublished or unagented writers, agented authors, and simultaneous submissions. Publishers may note their response time as being anywhere from four to six months and whether they offer advances and royalties.

Say you've gotten a contract, written the book, gone through line edits, and had the book published. . . .

When Do I Start to Get the Word Out?

A general rule of thumb is to use the first three months before your publishing date to send a press release to all magazines, newspapers, and local press. You have a small window of opportunity to get media coverage during that three-month period before your book comes out, so it's best to give the media a heads up. The majority of publishers have semiannual lists (spring and fall), so when the "new list" comes out (with the latest books), yours will no longer be "new." Therefore, you must really prepare for your own media/ marketing blitz right out of the gate! Once the public is ready to receive the book, the first three months after publication, there should be maximum publicity, reviews, and possibly even award nomination/consideration.

Make sure your publisher knows which media you feel should get review copies, places that may have *any* kind of interest in your book. If it's a novel in which the main character has epilepsy, send a press release to the foundation that supports the disease. Many websites deal with epilepsy, so you could start right there with a market niche. Of course, the disease must have a pertinent role in the story, not just a "and by the way, he has epilepsy." Also, make a list of all the awards your book might be eligible to win, organizations that might have a personal interest, and trade magazines that have tie-ins to the story line.

Publicists Can Help with Marketing

What Is a Publicist and What Does One Do?

Publicists are hired to get your work publicity. They do all they can to arrange reviews, book signings, interviews, and feature stories for their clients; they also plan events such as a launch party. They do all the public relations work like writing press releases, gathering press clippings, and generating any kind of media excitement they can about your work and about you, the author. (Note: A publicist does not typically find agents, publishers, or distributors for the book. They may arrange radio and TV speaking engagements or coordinate travel arrangements for a book tour, however.[38])

Will a Publishing House Assign Each Author a Publicist?

A publishing house will generate as much attention as it can using its own in-house publicity department for select authors only, so authors are advised to get their own publicist to maximize the exposure they receive.[39]

What Are the Benefits of Hiring My Own Publicist?

There are many benefits to hiring a publicist.

1. A publicist has media contacts and relationships needed to secure interviews/reviews.

2. A publicist knows how to pitch your book to the media and how each journalist likes to be contacted.

3. It is a full-time job to handle a publicity campaign. That is why a publicist is hired. This allows the writer time to write.

4. When an author pitches his or her own book, it may be viewed as too self-promotional. A publicist is seen as a third party, and some journalists are more receptive to discussing a book with a publicist rather than the author. (That's not to say that journalists don't interview authors personally when doing a profile on them.)[40]

Great Articles on Publicity, Promotions, and Public Relations

There is great information on the Web about publicity, promotions, and public relations if you simply Google any of the topics. The following tips are paraphrased from Lee Toland's article "7 Vital Book Promotion Tips":[41]

1. Take "no" for an answer: don't waste your time or the media's, as you could be making a bad first impression as a pest.

2. Don't hound your publicist. It'll distract him or her from the task at hand, talking to the media. Find a time for a weekly "check in."

3. Start *now*. The most successful campaigns happen within the first six months after your book's publication date.

4. Don't pitch your *book*; pitch a concept, an idea, or a solution when you're promoting your book. It generates an interest in which the media will want to know more and ask *you* for information.

5. Create a press kit before you begin promoting your book, so it's ready to go. Ideas to include in the kit are a cover letter, press release, author bio, Q&A page, sample interview questions, and articles relevant to your topic. Your publisher should be able to provide a press release for you at the very least.

6. Know your target audience. The more focused you can be with your efforts, the better your results will be. (Tip: Authors should always start with their local media, then regional—surrounding areas and states—and finally national media.)

7. Have fun! Your enthusiasm, humor, and smile should shine through in every phone pitch, letter, and e-mail. If you're not excited about getting your work out there, then why would anyone else want to promote it?

HOW TO STAY ORGANIZED

As mentioned in an earlier chapter, tracking your submissions is of the utmost importance. If you send a manuscript to fifteen different publishers, you need to make a list of the publishing house, the contact's name and title, the date it was sent, and the name of the article/story you submitted. Next, make a space on your index card or spreadsheet to list what response, if any, was received. If your manuscript was not rejected, write down the publisher's response along with what he or she requested from you. Did the publisher offer a contract or request revisions? Be specific about the correspondence so you don't let any possible opportunities for publication slip through the cracks. Indicate the time frame the publisher wants to hear back from you.

NEXT STEP: GETTING YOUR WORK REVIEWED

Yipee, yahoo, hooray! You've been offered a contract. Once you've gotten the contract, written the book, gone through line edits and production, and have the published book, you ask yourself, *How do I get reviewers to read and recommend my book?*

You might find writing a press release challenging. Similar to writing a good query letter, a press release must entice a person to want to read your book. Although authors are often given a discount on their own books, sending out multiple copies can be expensive. Therefore, sending a press release with a picture of the book's cover (and any quotes from reviewers or professionals if available) would be a financially prudent way to promote your book versus sending out books.

Most children's book publishers send review copies to publications like *School & Library Journal* (the magazine that librarians read to decide what books to order for their library); *VOYA* (*Voice of Youth Advocates*) magazine, and other reviewing journals.

You can send a press release (which your publisher may or may not supply you with) to newspapers and television stations, especially in the town where you live since you have the "hook" of being a local writer.

WRITING REVIEWS

When customers write a review of what they've purchased on Amazon.com, the reviewers are ranked by the number of votes they received regarding the usefulness of their submissions. Anyone can submit his or her opinion at no cost. Some people have submitted over one hundred pieces! It is a form of being published, since it is posted on the Internet for everyone to see. A review can even be looked at as a form of public relations, especially if you include your website address with your name.

If you have a personal connection to a book reviewer, score! You can mention the person's name in the cover letter, "So-and-so recommended I send this book to you. Here's a bit about it. I'd love to hear your thoughts. Sincerely, . . ." Since authors usually get a set amount of free copies of their books, they must pick and choose wisely who they will send their "freebies" to. If you have an "in" with a reviewer, that is a great place to start. Otherwise, stick to sending out press releases. If interested, a reviewer will ask you for a copy of the book.

CHAPTER 8 WRITING EXERCISE

Write a query letter to a publisher about the manuscript you are finishing or have completed. Make sure your manuscript is properly formatted with proper punctuation, footnotes, or any other necessary details in case you get a positive reply asking to see the entire work! You can call the publishing house to verify the address and spelling of the person's name you are sending your manuscript to.

CHAPTER 8 MARKETING EXERCISE

Write a press release about your favorite book. Make it to the point and interesting enough to pique the reader's curiosity. Also, for fun you can include an alternative mock book cover you have designed.

NOTES

1. Jacci Howard Bear, "Save the Widows and Orphans," About .com, desktoppub.about.com/od/typelayout/a/widowsorphans.htm (accessed January 11, 2007).

2. Christopher Paolini, *Eragon* (Livingston, MT: Paolini International, 2002).

3. "Publish Your Book with a Publisher Who Puts Authors First," Beaver's Pond Press, www.beaverspondpress.com/getting-started.html (accessed April 3, 2006).

4. "Author Profile: Christopher Paolini," Teenreads.com, September 2003, www.teenreads.com/authors/au-paolini-christopher .asp (accessed April 15, 2007).

5. "Author Profile: Christopher Paolini."

6. Christopher Paolini, *Eldest* (New York: Knopf, 2005); *Brisingr* (New York: Knopf, 2008).

7. "Author Profile: Christopher Paolini."

8. "Author Profile: Christopher Paolini."

9. *Children's Writer's & Illustrator's Market 2009* (Cincinnati, OH: Writers' Digest Books, 2008) or *Book Markets for Children's Writers 2009* (West Redding, CT: Institute of Children's Literature, 2008).

10. Lorijo Metz, interview with author, November 29, 2006.

11. Lorijo Metz, *Floridius Bloom and the Planet of Gloom* (New York: Dial Books, 2007).

12. "In Brief," *Publisher's Weekly*, September 25, 2006, p. 28.

13. Nancy Yi Fan, *Swordbird* (New York: HarperCollins, 2007); *Swordquest* (New York: HarperCollins, 2008).

14. Marni McNiff, *Book Markets for Children's Writers 2006* (West Redding, CT: Writer's Institute Publications, 2005).

15. Marg Gilks, "How to Write a Synopsis," Writing-World.com, 2001, www.writing-world.com/publish/synopsis.shtml (accessed November 29, 2006).

16. Gilks, "How to Write a Synopsis."

17. Gilks, "How to Write a Synopsis."

18. Gilks, "How to Write a Synopsis."

19. "Sharon J's Writing Blog," Blogspot.com, my-novel.blogspot.com/2006/07/rejection.html (accessed September 28, 2006).

20. "Sharon J's Writing Blog."

21. SCBWI-IL Listserv (Fall 2006). Question asked by Kathy Steck; answer posted by Brenda Ferber, author of *Julia's Kitchen* (New York: Farrar Straus & Giroux, 2006); www.brendaferber.com.

22. "How to Write a Research Paper," Fact Monster, www.factmonster.com/homework/t1termpaper1.html (accessed March 22, 2006).

23. Lloyd L. Rich, "Subsidary Rights—Acquisition & Licensing," The Publishing Law Center, 1998, www.publaw.com/subsidiary.html (accessed January 15, 2007).

24. Rich, "Subsidary Rights."

25. *Career Discovery Encyclopedia*, 5th ed. (New York: Ferguson, 2003), 5:38, www.fergpubco.com.

26. *Career Discovery Encyclopedia*, 5:38.

27. Association of Authors' Representatives, www.aaronline.org (accessed August 30, 2009).

28. The Dabbling Mum, www.thedabblingmum.com (accessed November 7, 2006).

29. Diane Lyndsey Reeves, *Career Ideas for Kids Who Like Writing* (New York: Checkmark Books, 1998), 79.

30. David Zhou, "Student's Novel Faces Plagarism Controversy," *Harvard Crimson*, April 23, 2006, www.thecrimson.com/article .aspx?ref=512948 (accessed December 6, 2007).

31. Standler, "Plagarism in Colleges in USA."

32. Kaavya Viswanathan, *How Opal Mehta Got Kissed, Got Wild, and Got a Life* (New York: Little, Brown, 2006). Megan F. McCafferty, *Sloppy Firsts* (New York: Three Rivers Press, 2001); *Second Helpings* (New York: Three Rivers Press, 2003).

33. Ronald B. Standler, "Plagarism in Colleges in USA: Cases against Plagarists in College," RBS2.com, www.rbs2.com/plag .htm#anchor444444 (accessed May 29, 2008).

34. Standler, "Plagarism in Colleges in USA."

35. Standler, "Plagarism in Colleges in USA."

36. Stacy Chudwin, e-mail to author, December 12, 2006.

37. Paul and Sarah Edwards, *Home-Based Business for Dummies* (New York: For Dummies, 2007).

38. Marika Flatt, "What Is a Literary Publicist?" Write and Publish Your Book, June 27, 2006, www.writeandpublishyourbook .com/Marketing/Marketing-Your-Book/What-is-a-Literary-Publicist%3F/ (accessed January 1, 2007).

39. Tayari Jones, "Tayari's Blog: Meet Luaren Cerand, My Publicist," TayariJones.com, June 19, 2006, www.tayarijones.com/ blog/archives/2006/06/meet_lauren_cer.html (accessed January 1, 2007).

40. Flatt, "What Is a Literary Publicist?"

41. Lee Toland, "7 Vital Book Promotion Tips," Write and Publish Your Book, August 9, 2006, www.writeandpublishyourbook .com/Marketing/Book-Promotion/7-Vital-Book-Promotion-Tips/ (accessed January 1, 2007).

g Emotional and Gritty Realism

IS CLASSIC ADVICE TRUE FOR *ALL* SITUATIONS?

"Write from your heart" and "Write what you know" are pieces of advice you will hear over and over again. But is that advice still true for controversial topics such as sexual orientation, religious beliefs, highly emotional, or even gritty subject matter?

BROTHER AND SISTER TEAM WRITE A GRIM REALITY[1]

Sam Wylie, nineteen years old, and his sister Arlet, eighteen years old, spoke at an event at the American Federation of Musicians hall in New Orleans' Seventh Ward to celebrate the launch of five books, written by local high school students, about life in that ward, sometimes happy, but often turbulent. The books were written and published as part of the Neighborhood Story Project, a not-for-profit program cofounded by Abram Himelstein, who is best know for writing and self-publishing *Tales of a Punk Rock Nothing* in 1998 (which has sold more than forty thousand copies!).[2] The hope is that these books will reach beyond their neighborhood.

Siblings Sam and Arlet compiled *Between Piety and Desire*, a book of interviews, one of which features a fifteen-year-old hustler called "Avon Seller."[3] Arlet also offers an interview with her mother, a domestic abuse survivor.

After Arlet finished reading another part of the book aloud in which she interviews a young man named Antoine "Twine" Dantzler, she broke down crying, telling the audience that he was recently murdered. At the same event, eighteen-year-old Ashley Nelson proudly introduced her book, *The Combination*, about the Lafitte Housing Project. The book remains upbeat, although it ends with a visit to her mother's grave, following her death from cancer after years of drug use. "Pity is the last thing I need," Nelson revealed about her reluctance to write about her mom, and she shared that "I struggled most days I had to write, but I did it. . . . I did it!"[4]

WRITEGIRL[5]

In 2000, Keren Taylor, a former singer-songwriter, founded the nonprofit group WriteGirl out of her home. The goal to help women's voices become heard was based on the philosophy that every girl has something special to say.

The group was originally started with seven girls and thirteen of Taylor's adult friends. In October 2005, the group's fourth critically acclaimed book was released, an anthology titled *Nothing Held Back*.[6]

In 2006, the group quickly followed up with another anthology titled *Untangled: Stories & Poetry from the Women and Girls of WriteGirl*, which won the award by USA Book News for "Fiction & Literature: Anthologies in the Best Books 2006 Book Awards."[7]

Brought to You By . . .

WriteGirl is made up of fifty volunteer mentors that include authors, screenwriters, journalists, and technical writers. The group expanded in 2005 to work with thirty girls at a home for pregnant and troubled teens in South Los Angeles. The group sold several thousand of the first three anthologies on Amazon.com as well as through six independent bookstores in greater Los Angeles, Chicago, and Dallas.

The success of the group has been huge, so much so that Taylor was eventually forced to cap student enrollment at fifty; she hasn't been able to actively recruit in three years. Two of

WHAT CRITICS ARE SAYING . . .

***Untangled*, the fifth anthology from WriteGirl Publications,**

offers a fresh look into the minds of women and girls with 288 pages of honest poetry, shocking fiction, and emotional nonfiction as well as inventive tips and writing "experiments" provided by all the writers. Stephanie Almendarez, 18, muses over her coming-of-age struggles and revelations. Seventeen-year-old Shauna Herron explores the role of women in society, while Melissa Castillo conveys wisdom beyond her 15 years with vivid descriptions of her daily life, including her grandmother's intoxicating kitchen.

In *Untangled*, the girls give us a peek into their lives, almost through a magnifying glass. This book breaks the rules of what writing has to be—there is a sense of freedom in the variety of styles and subjects covered. It's like going on an adventure since every page takes you somewhere else.[8]

the greater success stories belong to two young women: Lovely Umayam, eighteen years old, and Rayline Rivera, fifteen.

At seventeen, Lovely Umayam was the organization's information ambassador and one of its fiercest advocates. She came to America from the Philippines in 1997 not knowing a single word of English. Then she realized that whatever the language happens to be, words are just words and one's voice is what matters. "That is what people can understand."[9]

During the time Lovely joined the group at age fourteen and an article about WriteGirl appeared in the October 23, 2005, issue of *The (New Jersey) Record*, her life has changed dramatically. Transforming herself from a shy girl not knowing a word of English to a confident seventeen-year-old young woman who speaks flawless English, Lovely took part in a *CNN* interview about the WriteGirl organization![10]

Lovely has been published in the first four of the WriteGirl's anthologies. Her work titled "Pieces of Me" (the title of WriteGirl's fourth book) was a finalist for the Independent Publisher Award, and she appeared at dozens of book events to read her poems, essays, and short fiction.

Many of the mentors that work with the organization have said, "Working with the girls has been, in many cases, more rewarding than [their] professional writing careers." And some have even seen their own writing styles change after working with their young protégés. The group is a success, proving to be a win-win scenario for all involved. The toughest part, according to founder Keren Taylor, is the fact that they have to turn girls away. Operating on an estimated $350,000 budget of donations and grants (circa 2005), WriteGirl cannot help all the interested parties get into the program. Taylor said, "I can't stand the thought that there will be girls we won't be able to serve. I can see how the girls have been transformed in front of our eyes." She continued, "How do you say to a girl, 'I'm sorry, I'm not going to help you. I'm not going to change your life?'"[11]

Taylor's efforts have changed so many lives for the better, already! If you'd like to contribute to the WriteGirl organization, you can go to www.WriteGirl.org for more information.

RECOMMENDED READ

Please Don't Kill the Freshman: A Memoir, originally a forty-four-page memoir published by a small press, was written by a fifteen-year-old named Zoe Trope (pseudonym).[12] It quickly caught the attention of a publisher at HarperCollins who asked her to expand it, then placed it under contract. Published in 2003, the book was recommended in the February 2004 issue of *VOYA* (*Voice of Youth Advocates*) magazine.

Not only is this book a commentary about high school, but two major themes emerge. The first tells how Trope's life is transformed by becoming a successful author, while the other deals with her relationship with her transgendered boyfriend.

The style of the book can be described as mainly stream-of-consciousness journal entries, peppered with rough language that is true-to-life. On Amazon.com, there was a wide range of reviews of the book ranging from one- to five-star ratings, with some people raving about it while others ripped it apart. The fact that people are so split about the book is intriguing . . . perhaps enough to explore further and decide for yourself?

ANOTHER GRITTY REALITY: TEENS SEXUAL ORIENTATION REVEALED

Rainbow Boys is the first in a series of young adult novels by Alex Sanchez.[13] The first book introduces readers to three vastly different teens who are from separate cliques and social groups and who attend the same high school. It is an honest look at how each character questions his own romantic preferences (sexual orientation) and comes to terms with labels, prejudice, and family reactions, not to mention self-realization.

Gay teen lit is something that provokes discussion, and some Americans are squeamish about the subject. In fact, in a few libraries and schools in New York, Texas, and Arkansas, Sanchez's book has been banned. As an assistant librarian, I chose *Rainbow Boys* as one of my "picks of the month" for reading. I wrote a review for the local paper describing the book. The publication chose not to run my review, citing the book as too controversial. *Why?* I wondered. Certainly, all can admit that teenagers are aware of their sexuality, and some are in fact gay. Why pretend homosexuality doesn't exist?

One of the most interesting techniques of Sanchez's book (from a writing standpoint) is that each chapter is told by one of the three main characters. The story's narration rotates among the three young men. This technique, while quite effective when done correctly, is extremely difficult to do well! Author Sanchez succeeds with this task because after you "meet" each of the characters, their voices become so clear, it is easy to follow who is speaking.

HOT TOPIC: SEXUALITY IN TEEN LITERATURE

Teens Interview "Boys" Author

There is a wonderful question-and-answer interview on the Young Australian Readers' Awards (YARA) website that takes place between an Australian teen and author Alex Sanchez, acclaimed author of the Rainbow series, among other popular novels. Since several of Sanchez's books are reviewed on the website, the teens who wrote the reviews were each granted an interview with the author in April 2006.[14]

219

When asked why he wrote books about gay teens, Sanchez replied that he wrote what he wanted to read: something that would have told him, "It's okay to be who you are."

When asked if people discouraged him from writing on such a topic, Sanchez replied that his biggest block was worrying about what people would say or think about him (negatively). But he also said that it was very gratifying to hear people say that his writing was realistic and that it either gave people courage to come out about being gay or inspired them to be more tolerant of those who are gay.

When asked for writing tips, he mentioned—among other things—*reading*. As we've heard before, reading is a cornerstone to becoming a great writer. Sanchez also suggested appealing to as many of the senses as possible: taste, touch, sound, sight, and so on.

Last, Sanchez mentioned not worrying about getting published or finding an agent, just sitting down and finishing your book first.

Alex Sanchez is the author of more than five books, and you can find out more about him by going to www.alexsanchez.com.

CONTROVERSIAL NEW "THERAPY"

Mainstream Americans have not embraced holistic medicines as easily as they accept prescription drugs from their doctors. Therefore, one might imagine that this popular, yet nontraditional, therapy may create a bit of turmoil.

British doctors have a new prescription for patients with mild to moderate depression: *reading*! Under a new program in the United Kingdom, patients are directed to self-help books such as *Overcoming Depression* and *How to Stop Worrying* instead of receiving prescriptions for antidepressant drugs like Prozac.[15]

Doctors say they began prescribing books due to their concern that many patients were either being medicated too hastily or going untreated, according to the *Wall Street Journal*.[16] The treatment, called "bibliotherapy," is a cost-saving measure as well. The state-run health care system in the United Kingdom can't afford one-to-one counseling for everyone, and patients can wait as long as eighteen months for an appointment. This therapy has been suggested by doctors as a good solution in the interim while waiting for an appointment.

The Site

The YARA website was created in 2002 by three year-ten (sophomore) students: Tristan, Greg, and Suzi and their teacher, Stephen. You can see their reviews by going to www .yara-online.org. Click on link "Read a Review," then click "Older Readers Reviews." The site, which now has students from across Australia (and even overseas) submitting reviews for others to read, welcomes new reviewers. Please contact YARA if you want your school to become involved, or simply e-mail your review to the website and it will be added. Send reviews to stephen@goldcreek.act.edu.au.

HOT TOPIC: AUTOBIOGRAPHY OF A CONTROVERSIAL SUICIDE ATTEMPT WITH A HOPEFUL ENDING

A Book I Couldn't Put Down

There was a book whose cover intrigued me. (Who hasn't picked a book by the cover before? Admit it!) The cover was cool looking but was such an odd perspective on a common item that I couldn't comprehend what it was at first. It was a close-up of an open book of matches photographed sideways.

The Burn Journals, by Brent Runyon, is a vivid and true account that is almost indescribable.[17] It is an autobiographical novel about a time when he was a teen, put on a bathrobe, and doused it with gasoline. He then lit himself on fire. The book briefly describes events that led up to that event but focuses mainly on his recovery. Adults might fear how suicidal teens could react when reading about the subject and the attention Runyon received. After reading *The Burn Journals*, I concluded that the author strongly advises against it, and I hope younger readers pick up on this.

Below is part of a review I posted on Amazon.com:

Amazing voice for a writer of any age
   The Burn Journals was absolutely impossible to put down. I read it in two days, even waking up in the middle of the night to read for two hours. Brent's "voice" is perfect; I feel like I know

him. I think it's a great example of how anyone can get sucked into depression, even someone who seems happy, funny, popular, etc. These are the last kids people ever seem to watch out for, but usually the ones who suffer in silence the most. I was fascinated by him and inspired by his ability to make his writing seem effortless. It felt like I was having a chat with a friend. I hope to read more about him and more by him. I hope his brother is okay, too, as the trauma seems to have affected him exponentially. I will be recommending this book to ALL friends and colleagues. Great job![18]

The review was a bit immature, perhaps. Was I gushing? Sure. But that's the beauty of writing a post on a website; as long as it's not offensive or libelous, you can go on and on about authors, actors, political figures, or whomever you admire.

I was so inspired by Brent Runyon's writing that I e-mailed him through his website. We were able to communicate, and I interviewed him for this book.

BRENT RUNYON, AUTHOR

To say that Brent Runyon had a difficult transition from youth to adulthood would be an understatement. In fact, he was quoted as saying, "The second hardest thing to do in life is to change from a child into an adult. There are so many ways to mess up . . . so many ways to get lost. It's like crossing the ocean in a rowboat."[19]

Brent was fourteen years old when he set himself on fire. His first book, *The Burn Journals*, is a memoir of his survival. It's not a book that focuses on the act he committed but on his gradual recovery and self-discovery. It's a gripping novel that stays with readers.

When interviewed about what happened, Runyon said, "I don't know if I would be a writer if I hadn't, when I was fourteen years old, set myself on fire [and lived through it]. . . . It made me an observer, and much more introspective."[20]

I interviewed Runyon by phone in 2006:[21]

It's great to meet you! I've admired your writing for some time now. Has anyone ever compared you to the "voice/attitude" of Holden Caulfield in Catcher in the Rye*?*

Yes, actually, others have noticed a similar tone between the books.

Did you actually keep journals while you were rehabilitating from your injuries?

No. The idea to do the book came after I was home and doing better physically.

Were there some gaps that you couldn't remember, since you wrote it some time after all the events occurred? If so, how did you handle the holes?

I would just skip ahead to what I *did* remember. I didn't want to just make up what I *thought* had happened from what family and friends tell me about that time. If I didn't remember something, I just didn't put anything in the book about it.

Good call, especially now, years later, seeing how other authors have fared after re-creating details from what others have reported. [James Frey wrote a book called *A Million Little Pieces* (2003),[22] and it became an Oprah Book Club selection. From Oprah's endorsement, the book was immediately catapulted onto the best-sellers' list. Oprah raved and promoted the book, and the author said it was all true, nothing fabricated. Of course, we know now that a great portion of the book was made up. Oprah Winfrey had a very public debate with James Frey regarding why he lied and the controversy his misrepresentation caused.]

How old were you when you wrote The Burn Journals*?*

I was twenty-two years old when I wrote the story. I was working for National Public Radio on a show called *This American Life*. A man named Ira Glass worked there and gave me the idea to get my story down on paper. After I started it, he read chapter 1 on the air.

Wow! That's an amazing stroke of luck to have such a huge audience with your first novel. How did it get from a one-chapter reading to a big publisher like Random House offering to buy the book?

Ira Glass was nice enough to say on-air that I was looking for a publisher at the end of the story. Nancy Siscoe, an editor at Knopf (a subsidiary of Random House), heard him say that and got in touch with me.

How long did it take for you to get a response after the radio show aired?

Three days. Actually Knopf contacted my agent, as did Simon & Schuster.

Did you have an agent before all of this happened, or did you scramble to get one in those few days?

Someone suggested I get an agent before my work was read on the radio, so when it aired and there was interest days later, I didn't have to worry about the business side of it, like negotiations, etc. It was all taken care of for me by my agent at ICM.

Do a lot of your readers try to contact you through your agent, publisher, or website? If so, do you write everyone back?

I try to answer as many as I can, but there are way too many troubled teens that I can't help out; I'm just not qualified. We have help lines and websites for further information to help with emotional problems, so sometimes giving young adults resources is a first step.

I read a lot of reviews of your book on Amazon.com and am amazed at the boldness of some reviewers. Does it get you down when someone is harsh and judgmental, or does a nice review make your day?

I try not to take the good *or* bad reviews too seriously, or I'd feel *awful* about some and unnecessarily "full of myself" from others.

Are you working on any new projects, like a new novel, right now?

All these years later, I finished a new book for Nancy (my editor at Knopf) that came out in 2006.[23]

Can you tell us the title and a little bit about the new novel?

The book is called *Maybe*. ["Brent Runyon offers a raw, wrenching novel of a boy on the edge. It's a powerful story about love and loss and death and anger and the near impossibility for a sixteen-year-old boy to both understand how he feels and to make himself heard."[24]]

You write in such an easy style that it feels like chatting with someone close to you. Was it difficult for you to get that second novel written?

My friend Christina Egloff, at the radio station, helped tremendously with the second book. She was very supportive.

Who are your favorite authors, favorite books, and what genres do you enjoy most?

E. B. White's *Charlotte's Web* is one of my favorites. I really like the style and rhythm of the book, how the story is told. *The Diving Bell and the Butterfly*, by Jean Dominique Baubielle, is wonderfully written about locked-in syndrome.[25] The genres I enjoy most are nonfiction and histories.

Do you always write for young adults?

Yes.

Do you do author visits to schools, bookstores, libraries?

Yes. I especially do visits to schools with traumas like a suicide.

Thank you so much for taking the time to speak to me and share your story with the readers. Congratulations on your success.

HOT TOPIC: EDGY BOOKS

Edgy books can pull a reader into uncomfortable worlds. The subject matter of the following three books have made some adults, and even some teens, uneasy.[26]

1. *The Curious Incident of the Dog in the Night-Time*, by Mark Haddon. This book offers a mystery with a story told by the main character, a fifteen-year-old boy with autism. It starts with him standing above a dead dog, holding a bloody fork. People want to know if/why he'd kill a neighbor's dog, but due to his disability, it's hard to get a story out of him. With the epidemic proportions of autism diagnosed in children in the new millennium, a special-needs character being so misunderstood might be considered an edgy topic.

2. *The Lovely Bones*, by Alice Sebold. This is a story of a teen who was murdered and is told from her point of view in the afterlife. The family tries to figure out who killed her and why, and she can't help them figure it out. A murdered teen giving an account of what happened at her death is beyond a parent's worst nightmare. Dealing with the grisly murder of a young person is what I'd consider emotional realism.

3. *Cut*, by Patricia McCormick. This is a story of a teenager who "cuts" (a form of self-injuring). It follows the main character through a treatment/rehab center, on the road to recovery. It's a fictional book that deals with a serious disorder that, in reality, affects three million Americans.[27]

Cathartic Poetry That Is Edgy

As many teens have conveyed to me, writing is a cathartic experience for them. By that, I mean it gets feeling out and sort of *cleanses* a writer's system of emotions that need to be purged. The following examples are poems by young adults that demonstrate this point.

Sample 1

Untitled
Black, boiling belligerence, baking in my head.
Fatal fury forging, making me see red.
Harmful heaps of hatred, eating away at me.
Sharp, shattered shards, skewering my knee.
Acid, ambient anger altering my state.
Vicious, violent vocals, the only open gate.

—name withheld, eighteen-year-old male

Sample 2

Changing Every Minute
Happy, happy, sad, sad.
This roller coaster drives me mad.
My mood is low, and then so high.
Tell me, tell me. Why? Why, why!
Medication's not my friend.
It stops the ride, I think, 'til when . . .
It starts all over, can't you see.
I'm locked inside the Hell that's me.

—C. G. S., age twenty

Sample 3

In My Mind . . .

I keep losing her–
In my mind, I see her
Walking away with someone new.
Beside me she claims
She'll always stay,
But I can't help thinking
And believing
That someday she'll leave.
What will I do?
What will I say?
I can't keep living my life this way.
Waiting.
Anticipating the moment when,
My heart will break in two
When I see her walking away
With someone new.
A glance at another,
And I go wild inside.
Is it a passing glance,
Or a pass?
I hold her hand,
Too firmly.
Will I force her away by hanging on
Too tight?
Or should I give up without putting up
A fight?
I keep losing her,
But, only in my mind.
Or am I losing my mind,
By trying to keep her?

—Shawn Wickersheim,
written at age eighteen

I'm in Control!

When asked, *How does writing make you feel?* twenty-one-year-old Adam, from Wisconsin, replied, "It makes me feel like I am doing something as opposed to searching the Internet or watching television. If I can't go outside, it's nice to sit down and write. It's relaxing and allows me to fall into my own world where *I* create the environment and run the show."[28]

How Writing Can Help Emotional Struggles

Sixteen-year-old Megan from Wheeling, Illinois, summed it up best when answering the following questions in a most candid manner.[29]

> *How did you "get into" writing?*
> I started keeping a diary in the second grade.
>
> *How does writing make you feel now, as a teen?*
> It makes me feel really good letting out my emotions. I always rely on writing to make me feel better. I have a lot of family problems, so writing down long conversations I've had or overheard in the family makes me feel better so that I will know how to avoid certain problems when I have my own family some day. I like to get the frustrations and anxiety out of my system so they aren't eating me up inside.

Emotional and gritty realism in books can push peoples' buttons. It often leads to some readers feeling the need to go to such extremes as banning books.

HOT TOPIC: CENSORSHIP AND BANNED BOOKS

Believe it or not, censorship has been recorded as far back as 450 B.C.! An author named Anaxagoras wrote his thoughts about the sun being a "white hot stone" and that the moon reflected the sun's rays. The public saw this writing as derogatory to the gods and forced him to leave Athens. In turn, the people destroyed all of his writings.[30]

A more recent period of book censorship in the United States took place in 1873. A man named Anthony Comstock founded a group called the New York Society for the Suppression of Vice, which deemed books on subjects like erotica and crime stories as something the devil would use to entice children to a life of crime and lust.[31]

Another example of censorship is Chaucer's *Canterbury Tales*, which was deemed obscene and banned for decades from the U.S. mail under the Comstock Law of 1873.[32]

Walt Whitman's famous collection of poetry *Leaves of Grass* was withdrawn from Boston in 1881 due to explicit language (according to the district attorney) but was later published in Philadelphia.[33]

Fast forward to the year 1982, when the Supreme Court decided that a balance must be struck between the school's role as an educator and the students' rights to access materials, thus making it more difficult to simply ban books based on personal preferences of individuals as to what is appropriate. This decision did not, however, stop people from challenging the content of certain books.[34]

In the 1990s through 2007, there were 6,364 challenges to books, according to data from the Office for Intellectual

WHERE TO FIND CHALLENGED BOOK LISTS

The American Library Association (ALA) cites banned and challenged books on its website: www.ala.org (type "banned books" in the search window).

On the site, there are discussions as to why books are challenged, who challenges these books, regarding the difference between a challenge and a ban, the most frequently challenged books, and frequently challenged authors, just to name a few topics.

⊚ ⊚ ⊚ ⊚ ⊚ ⊚ ⊚ ⊚ ⊚ ⊚ ⊚ ⊚ ⊚ ⊚ ⊚ ⊚

THE TEN MOST CHALLENGED BOOKS OF 2007[35]

The ALA cites the following as the most challenged books. They reflect a range of themes from sexuality to racism to religious beliefs:

1. Justin Richardson and Peter Parnell, *And Tango Makes Three* (New York: Simon Schuster, 2005).
2. Robert Cormier, *The Chocolate War* (New York: Dell Laurel-Leaf, 1974).
3. Kevin Henkes, *Olive's Ocean* (New York: HarperCollins, 2003).
4. Philip Pullman, *The Golden Compass* (New York: Ballentine Books, 1995).
5. Mark Twain, *The Adventures of Huckleberry Finn* (New York: The Penguin Group, 1884).
6. Alice Walker, *The Color Purple* (Orlando, FL: Harcourt, 1982).
7. Lauren Myracle, *TTYL* (New York: Harry N. Abrams, 2005).
8. Maya Angelou, *I Know Why the Caged Bird Sings* (New York: Random House, 1969).
9. Robie Harris, *It's Perfectly Normal* (Cambridge, MA: Candlewick Press, 1994).
10. Stephen Chbosky, *The Perks of Being a Wallflower* (New York: MTV Books/Pocket Books, 1999).

For more information on book challenges and censorship, please visit the ALA Office of Intellectual Freedom's Banned Books website at www.ala.org/bbooks.

Freedom.[36] In 2003, a school removed *The Adventures Of Huckleberry Finn*, by Mark Twain, from its approved reading list due to the use of the word *nigger*, which was perceived as damaging to students' self-esteem.[37]

Have you ever read a banned book? What did you think of it? Could you see why such a book might be challenged?

HOT TOPIC: PROS AND CONS OF REVEALING YOUR AGE (AS A MINOR)

When you are younger than eighteen years old and trying to get published, there is debate as to whether to include your age when submitting work to a publisher. Take a look at the lists of pros and cons. See if you can add more to one list or the other to help you decide whether you should include your age in a query letter.

Pros

◎ **Young writers with talent are a wonderful, and sometimes rare, commodity in a publisher's "slush pile."**

◎ **Honesty is the best policy 99.9 percent of the time in life.**

◎ **Some publishing companies love the idea of having a young writer and possible phenom.**

Cons

◎ **Prejudice might prevail, and after seeing "fifteen years old," an editor might toss out the manuscript before getting to the end of sentence three of the story.**

◎ **Legally, there could be problems for publishers if they aren't aware that an author is a minor. Your chances of working with a specific publisher might be greater if you wait a few years and keep working on your craft, so when you have some experience and seasoning, you'll make the best possible first impression, instead of looking like an amateur.**

◎ **Since rejection letters are most often form letters with no specific reason for rejection, you might not know if your age had anything to do with the publisher not accepting your work.**

Last, *never* lie about your age, or when citing a source, obtaining permissions, or any other task that must be properly documented. Such perjury will follow you throughout your career!

CHAPTER 9 WRITING EXERCISE

The ALA celebrated "Banned Book Week" in September 2009. Go to http://www.ala.org/ala/issuesadvocacy/banned/bannedbooksweek/calendarofevents/index.cfm. Choose a book from the list of banned books and read it. Then write an article about the book you read, describing if you feel controversy exists and if you agree with the author's choice of how to deal with the subject.

NOTES

1. Michael Scharf, "Looking beyond the Hood," *Publishers Weekly*, July 11, 2005, www.publishersweekly.com/article/CA624560.html?text=neighborhood+story (accessed May 29, 2008).

2. Abram Himelstein, *Tales of a Punk Rock Nothing* (New Orleans, LA: New Mouth from the Dirty South, 1998).

3. Sam Wiley and Arlet Wiley, *Between Piety and Desire* (Brooklyn, NY: Soft Skull Press/Red Rattle Books, 2005).

4. Ashley Nelson, *The Combination* (Brooklyn, NY: Soft Skull Press/Red Rattle Books, 2005).

5. Gillian Flaccus, "WriteGirl Are Winning Literary Acclaim," *The* [New Jersey] *Record*, October 23, 2005, p. F-1.

6. Flaccus, "WriteGirl Are Winning Literary Acclaim," F-1. Keren Taylor, ed., *Nothing Held Back* (Los Angeles: WriteGirl, 2005).

7. Keren Taylor, ed., *Untangled: Stories & Poetry from the Women and Girls of WriteGirl* (Los Angeles: WriteGirl, 2006); www.writegirl.org/publications.html (accessed December 28, 2006).

8. "WriteGirl Publications," WriteGirl, www.writegirl.org/publications.html (accessed December 28, 2006).

9. Flaccus, "WriteGirl Are Winning Literary Acclaim," F-1.

10. Flaccus, "WriteGirl Are Winning Literary Acclaim," F-1.

11. Flaccus, "WriteGirl Are Winning Literary Acclaim," F-1.

12. Zoe Trope, *Please Don't Kill the Freshman: A Memoir* (New York: HarperCollins, 2003).

13. Alex Sanchez, *Rainbow Boys* (New York: Simon Pulse, 2003).

14. "YARA Older Reviews," YARA, www.goldcreek.act.edu.au/yara (accessed May 24, 2006).

15. Listserv posting, Illinois SCBWI, August 17, 2005.

16. *Wall Street Journal*, July 31, 2007.

17. Brent Runyon, *The Burn Journals* (New York: Alfred A. Knopf, 2004).

18. Tina P. Schwartz, review of *The Burn Journals*, www.amazon.com, March 2, 2005.

19. "Brent Runyon: Author Spotlight," Random House, www.randomhouse.com/author/results.pperl?authorid=52604&view=full_sptlght (accessed August 11, 2006).

20. "Brent Runyon."

21. Brent Runyon, phone interview with author, August 2006.

22. James Frey, *A Million Little Pieces* (New York : N.A. Talese/ Doubleday, 2003).

23. Brent Runyon, *Maybe* (New York: Alfred A. Knopf, 2006).

24. "*Maybe*," Random House, www.randomhouse.com/catalog/ display.pperl?isbn=9780553495089 (accessed July 25, 2007).

25. E. B. White, *Charlotte's Web* (New York: HarperCollins, 1952). Jean Dominique Baubielle, *The Diving Bell and the Butterfly* (New York: Vintage International, 1998).

26. Mark Haddon, *The Curious Incident of the Dog in the Night-Time* (New York: Random House, 2003). Alice Sebold, *The Lovely Bones* (New York: Little, Brown and Co., 2002). Patricia McCormick, *Cut* (New York: Push, 2000).

27. "When Scab-Picking, Cutting Becomes Addictive," WebMD, www.webmd.com/content/article/86/99055.htm (accessed October 13, 2006).

28. Adam, e-mail to author, September 1, 2006.

29. Megan, answers to author's questionnaire, 2006.

30. Jennifer Magelky, "History of Banned Books," Washington State University, www.wsu.edu/~accessnw/resources/Bannedbooks .htm (accessed May 15, 2008).

31. Magelky, "History of Banned Books."

32. "Banned Books Online," Online Books Page, onlinebooks .library.upenn.edu/banned-books.html (accessed September 19, 2008). Geoffrey Chaucer, *The Canterbury Tales* (London: The Penguin Group, 1951).

33. "Banned Books Online." Walt Whitman, *Leaves of Grass* (Oxford, UK: Oxford Press, 1990).

34. Magelky, "History of Banned Books."

35. "Top Ten Most Frequently Challenged Books of 2007," American Library Association, www.ala.org/ala/issuesadvocacy/ banned/frequentlychallenged/21stcenturychallenged/2007/index.cfm (accessed September 3, 2009).

36. Magelky, "History of Banned Books."

37. Magelky, "History of Banned Books." Mark Twain, *The Adventures of Huckleberry Finn* (New York: The Penguin Group, 1884).

10 Contests, Awards, and Grants

TWO TOP AWARDS IN CHILDREN'S LITERATURE

The *Caldecott Medal* was named in honor of nineteenth-century English illustrator Randolph Caldecott. The American Library Association (ALA) awards it annually to the artist of the most distinguished American picture book for children.

The *Newbery Medal* was named for eighteenth-century British bookseller John Newbery. The ALA awards it annually to the author of the most distinguished contribution to American literature for children.

How Prestigious Are the Two ALA Awards?

Each award is the equivalent of the Academy Award for movies. For example, "Newbery award winner" is a label that will follow an author or illustrator forever. Whenever an author/illustrator is mentioned, he or she will be referred to as *Newbery Medal winner* Christopher Paul Curtis, or *Caldecott Medal winner* Kevin Henkes.

Many professional organizations have their own awards. The Society of Children's Book Writers & Illustrators (SCBWI) gives a prestigious award in both fiction and nonfiction categories called the Golden Kite Award. (The kite is the logo for this worldwide organization, which is highly regarded in the children's publishing field.)

TO FIND LISTS OF PUBLISHING COMPETITIONS

Since there are over one hundred competitions each year for published authors, you can start by googling "writing awards" or "awards + published in 20_ _" (fill in year of your book's publication).

It might help to research the top five or ten respected organizations for writers. Go to each organization's website to see what award it gives each year. Or you can research more specifically in your own genre/category (such as "children's" or "nonfiction" or "journalism").

CONTESTS

Are Writing Contests Really a Good Idea to Enter, or Are They All Just Scams?

Writing contests are an excellent way to break into print. You should, however, do extensive research before you submit your work. There are some contests to be aware of. Always research a company you are considering submitting work to. You can try a website such as www.anotherealm.com/prededitors/peba.htm to see if any formal complaints have been filed against a company. If you mention winning a contest that is from an unreputable company, it might backfire and actually make you look worse, not better to your (potential) editors and/or publishers.

And the Winner Is . . .

In 1992, at age sixteen, Curtis Sittenfeld won *Seventeen*'s fiction contest. Not only did she win the contest, but her prize

TOP AWARDS IN CHILDREN'S LITERATURE

You can see a list of winners and honorable mentions of the top awards in children's literature given by the American Library Association, or ALA, by going to www.ala. org and looking up Caldecott Medal and Newbery Medal. It is a good idea to see what's out there and even study how trends have changed over the years.

was a contract. The book debuted at number 15 on the *New York Times* best-seller list! The book, titled *Prep*, is described as "a Midwestern girl's trials and tribulations at an elite New England prep school."[1]

Sittenfeld, an alumna of Groton, Stanford, and the Iowa Writer's Workshop, has been featured in the *New York Times*, *Vanity Fair*, and *Elle*. She went on a seven-city tour in March 2005 to promote her book. A merchandising deal even resulted from the book. A fashion designer (Alyssa Tierney) offered a limited-edition ribbon belt modeled after the one on the cover of *Prep*.[2]

Where to Start

One of the best resources to begin your search for contests is the Writing-World website at www.writing-world.com/contests. There you'll find information regarding a variety of contests, along with some pitfalls to avoid in your entries. Here are some of the highlights from the website:

⦿ Make sure the company sponsoring the "contest" is a reputable one. Another website recommends checking each company at www.anotherealm.com/prededitors/peba.htm, also referred to as "Predators & Editors." The site lists publishing houses to avoid due to a variety of bad business practices. This is a good safety-check to ensure you're not submitting to a place that you'll regret.

◎ Make sure the judges are respected professionals in the field. Mentioning any contest wins in your own public relations could become an embarrassment if the judges are unheard of or, worse, have with shoddy reputations. Winning such a contest could become a hindrance, not a help.

◎ Find out if there is an entry fee and if it's more than $10. If so, consider two things: (1) the amount of the cash prize (if $15, why bother?); and (2), the amount the company will earn from submissions compared to the prize amount. If the prize is significantly less money than the company will earn from the entries (for example, if there is a minimum of one hundred submissions required for a prize to be granted, and the entry fee is $30 and the prize $100, the company will be profiting $2,900), it's best to send your work somewhere else entirely.

◎ Find out what the prize is. If there is no cash, royalties, and/or copies of your winning entry (most often in an anthology), then it is suspect. If, for example, you will be published on a website, this win hardly constitutes bragging rights on your résumé. You may decide to avoid these contests all together.

◎ Find out whether or not you retain the rights to your story. For a contest, you should always retain rights. Some companies actually make you sign away all rights even if you don't win!

◎ Request a list of past winners. If possible, contact them to see what, if any good, came out of their winning the contest. See if they liked working with the company and if they would do it again.

AMY PALACE, AUTHOR

Author Finds Success in Entering Contests at a Young Age

Amy Palace was a senior in high school who found success in entering writing contests.

Amy Palace, age 17, teen contest winner (2006).

At eighteen years old, her accomplishments included the following:

1. Winner in the National Council of Teachers of English (NCTE) writing contest
2. Regional winner Golden Key Award
3. Third-place winner in an essay contest about her most inspirational teacher
4. Four poems published in two years in the school's annual literary magazine, *Whispers of Immortality*

5. Essay published in the local magazine, the *Edge*
6. Submitted a general writing portfolio to the Scholastic Art and Writing Awards

In response to a 2006 questionnaire, Amy had this to say about writing:[3]

What do you like about writing?
I like the freedom to write whatever I want, whatever I feel. When I can do that [versus an essay or paper for school] then I begin to love writing and appreciate it as an art form.

THE BLOOD

A cataclysm of noise explodes through the doors and crashes into each person who ducks his head and dives into the suffocating channel of humanity. The turbulent sounds writhe and clash angrily, glancing off flat surfaces and picking up speed and intensity with every collision. Like a frenzied percussion, metal doors clink open and slam shut, books smack the hard floor, and dials grate as they turn. As each new platelet trickles in through the small entrances, it cascades among the rest in the swiftly moving current that pumps through the ever thickening artery. Clots begin to form on the edges as the platelets stop to chat with each other and get suctioned to the artery wall. Their voices buzz in the background as the turmoil of students continues to rush past them. Teachers, too, ford the blue river, carefully dancing from side to side in order to avoid contact with the clots or other debris which threaten to dam the vital flow of life. Along each side, clumps have formed into areas of distinctive social groups. One area is inhabited by jocks, another by artists, another by nerds, another by musicians. As the seconds tick away loudly on the clock overhead, the crowd continues to enlarge until an earth shattering electronic bleep pierces through the hallway. Within a minute the current reduces to a frantic trickle until finally the artery is empty. Silence cascades off the abandoned lockers, restlessly waiting for the beckon of noise once again.

—Amy Palace, age seventeen, Vernon Hills, Illinois

Was there a certain friend, teacher, or mentor perhaps that got you interested in writing?

Yes, my seventh and eighth grade writing teacher was an amazing inspiration to me and showed by example how writing doesn't have to be boring—how it can be creative, entertaining, suspenseful, emotional, and profound. She taught us to write from the ideas within ourselves and concentrated on discovering our own creative voice through free writing.

How old were you when you started writing?

In second or third grade I started a journal and still journal to this day. I started writing short stories in third and fourth grade for the school's Young Author program, and I had a pen pal at that age, too.

Do you have different journals for different aspects of your life?

I have a spiritual journal now where I basically just write to God all my emotions and struggles.

How does writing make you feel?

It makes me feel more passionate. . . . I get very excited as new thoughts occur to me and a plot unfolds before my eyes. I feel as if I am the reader, eagerly anticipating what will happen next. Of course, there are times when I have no idea where I want a story to go or I cannot figure out what to write in the next line of poetry, and it is incredibly frustrating. Sometimes, I write as an outlet for stress or anxiety, and in that case it is relieving and helps me feel calmer.

If I'm having a great day, I might write a beautiful poem or journal how great the day was. If I have a bad day, I usually write about it with great detail to vent all my frustration and cleanse it out of my mind.

Do you have a mentor?

My junior high teacher was an excellent mentor and would give me great feedback. She always encouraged me to continue writing and seek opportunities to have my work published. She was a writer herself and I would encourage her to do the same.

What's next for you? Will you go on to college, and if so where do you plan to attend?

Ode to Sleep

That wonderful addictive sleep
Engulfing from realms of the deep
Close your eyes, reality awaits
Like angels poised at gleaming gates

Dreams that swirl behind the eye
Free to dance as still you lie
Unconsciousness that grips the mind
Brings knowledge of a different kind

Sleep entices the weary head
With wishes for a cozy bed
The warm inviting pillows call
"Only tonight, forget it all!"

Throughout the day your mind cries, "more!"
Can't think when school's such a bore
You recall those nights with monsters outside
Diving under the covers to hide

Sheets pulled close up to your chin
Teddy's soft fur is now worn thin
You lie in bed and squeeze your eyes
With fleeting dreams you finally rise

—Amy Palace, age seventeen, Vernon Hills, Illinois

I now attend the University of Iowa and am an English major. I am living in the Iowa Writer's Learning Community, which is basically a floor with a bunch of other writers. I still plan to pursue some sort of writing career.[4]

How Do I Pick a Contest to Submit to, from the Hundreds of Them Out There?

Consult a market guide for contests. Each guide often has "editor's comments," which can be invaluable. Once when I was going to submit a story called "The Locket" to a publisher, I decided to read comments by editors first to get a feel for each one's personality. (It helps to have a good rapport with your editor, so if you can sense a good personality match, all the better!) My story dealt with a third grade girl's first experience with death, the death of her grandma. While reading various editors' comments, I saw one that literally ended with, "and no more 'dead grandparent' stories!" How totally embarrassing! The market guide might as well have well added, "That means *you*, Tina Schwartz!"

If you take the time to do your homework and research all you can about potential editors to whom you want to submit your work, you'll be grateful in the long run. It will save you postage and save you from making a poor first impression.

If a Contest Doesn't Offer a Cash Prize, Is It Legitimate?

Yes. Many contests don't offer money as a prize; a publication might print your work in its magazine or in an anthology and give you copies of the work. But there should be *some* sort of "prize" whether monetary or recognition in a publication.

GRANTS AND AWARDS

Where Can I Find Lists of Awards and Grants?

There are various websites that mention grants:

1. **American Grant Writer's Association (www .grantwriterassociatioin.com/pc.html)**

2. **The Institute of Children's Literature (ICL) in West Redding, Connecticut (www.institutechildrenslit.com)**
   For a complete list of contests and grants, go to *Book Markets for Children's Writers 2007*, which is a guide for children's writers published by the ICL. The contests, awards and grants are listed in the back of the book. The ICL separates book publishers from magazine publishers.

3. **The Society of Children's Book Writers & Illustrators (SCBWI) (www.scbwi.org)**
   SCBWI has the following grants available:
   Kimberly Colen Memorial Grant: This grant was established by the family of the late Kimberly Colen, along with the SCBWI, to honor Kimberly's memory by helping unpublished authors and illustrators get their first children's books published.[5]

Don Freeman Memorial Grant-in-Aid: **This grant was established by the SCBWI to enable picture book artists to further their understanding, training, and creative work in the picture book genre.**

Barbara Karlin Grant: **This grant was established to recognize and encourage the work of aspiring picture book writers.**

Martha Weston Grant: **This grant was created by the Hairston family to honor and remember Martha (Hairston) Weston. After publishing more than fifty picture books and easy readers, illustrator and author Martha published her first middle-grade novel shortly before her death. Martha always took the time to encourage others, and it's the intention of the Martha Weston Grant to carry forward her generous spirit.**

4. **Government website that features a list of grants (www .top10charts.org/index.htm)**

Other companies publish writer's market guides, often including grants, which are updated each year. Your local library and bookstore should have copies of them. These guides contain both book publishers and magazine publishers.

FARAH AHMEDI, CONTEST WINNER AND SEVENTEEN-YEAR-OLD AFGHAN REFUGEE[6]

One day, circa 1995, second grader Farah, living in Kabul, Afghanistan, was running late for school. She took a shortcut and didn't see the land mine that she was about to cross. It went off, nearly killing her. Luckily, after going to Germany for approximately twenty surgeries, she survived the loss of a leg and other injuries. She received a prosthetic leg and a whole new life. A year later, while in third grade, she was shopping at a bazaar with her mom and a Taliban rocket hit her house, killing her father and two sisters.

With such horrific events, many a person might crumble, yet Ahmedi still considers herself blessed. Years later, in 2002, she and her mother left a refugee camp in Pakistan for their new home in America. In Illinois she met her mentor, Alyce Litz, a church volunteer from Wheaton, Illinois. Litz helped Farah to set goals for herself; she also urged Farah to write her life story.

ABC's *Good Morning America* television program ran a contest inviting viewers to write their life stories. The grand prize was

Farah Ahmedi, teen contest winner.

$10,000, a ten-city tour, and publication of a story. With Litz's continued encouragement, Farah entered the ABC Memoir Contest and her story won! It was chosen from six thousand entries to become a best-selling book: *The Story of My Life: An Afghan Girl on the Other Side of the Sky.*[7] Farah was only seventeen years old when she wrote her life story in 2005!

When asked if her book had a theme, Ahmedi replied, "It's about hope, love, family and angels—about the way one person can help you turn your life around." In 2007, Ahmedi became a college student in Illinois.

Booklists and Book Awards

Each of the links listed includes information on awards, a nomination form (when available), and links to current and previous award winners or lists of titles.[8]

- Alex Awards (www.ala.org/ala/yalsa/booklistsawards/alexawards/alexawards.htm)
- Best Books for Young Adults (www.ala.org/ala/mgrps/divs/yalsa/booklistsawards/bestbooksya/bbyahome.cfm)
- Great Graphic Novels for Teens (www.ala.org/ala/yalsa/booklistsawards/greatgraphicnovelsforteens/gn.htm)

- Margaret A. Edwards Award (www.ala.org/ala/yalsa/
  booklistsawards/margaretaedwards/margaretedwards.htm)

- Michael L. Printz Award (www.ala.org/ala/mgrps/divs/yalsa/
  booklistsawards/printzaward/Printz.cfm)

- Outstanding Books for the College Bound (www.ala.org/ala/
  yalsa/booklistsawards/outstandingbooks/outstandingbooks
  .htm)

- Popular Paperbacks for Young Adults (www.ala.org/ala/yalsa/
  booklistsawards/popularpaperback/popularpaperbacks.htm)

- Quick Picks for Reluctant Young Adult Readers (www.ala.org/
  ala/mgrps/divs/yalsa/booklistsawards/quickpicks/qphome
  .cfm)

- Amazing Audiobooks (www.ala.org/ala/mgrps/divs/yalsa/
  booklistsawards/amazingaudiobooks/audiobooks.cfm)

- Selected DVDs and Videos (www.ala.org)

- Teens' Top Ten (www.ala.org/ala/yalsa/teenreading/
  teenstopten/teenstopten.htm)

If you want to link to the page containing all the awards above, use this short URL: www.ala.org/yalsa/booklists.

CHAPTER 10 WRITING EXERCISE

Look in the index of a market guide to publishers and find the section on contests. Spend a day or two sifting through all of the available contests. Remember the tips in the chapter regarding fees versus prize. Once you find contests that are worth entering, pick one and practice writing to that one's specifications. For example, you might see a contest that asks for

SCHOLARSHIPS AND GRANTS

"Free scholarship money for school. FastWeb is the nation's largest source of local, national, and college-specific scholarships." Go to the following website to fill out a form and receive information on available scholarship money: www.fastweb.com/fastweb/register/start?ref=108145-1f.[9]

a sports story for children eight to twelve years old, with a word limit of five hundred words. Do your best to write a piece according to the guidelines. Write, edit, rewrite (perhaps several times) and polish your story—then send it in!

NOTES

1. Daily Maryless, "Behind the Bestsellers: 'Prep for Success,'" *Publishers Weekly*, February 14, 2005, p. 14. Curtis Sittenfeld, *Prep* (New York: Random House, 2005).

2. Maryless, "Behind the Bestsellers," 14.

3. Amy Palace, answers to author questionnaire, summer 2006.

4. Amy Palace, e-mail to author, January 2007.

5. Marni McNiff, ed., *Book Markets for Children's Writers 2007* (West Redding, CT: Writer's Institute Publications, 2006).

6. "Picks and Pans: Books," *People*, www.people.com/people/archive/article/0,,20147490,00.html (accessed June 5, 2008).

7. Farah Ahmedi, *The Story of My Life: An Afghan Girl on the Other Side of the Sky* (New York: Simon Spotlight Entertainment, 2005).

8. "Book Awards & Booklists," American Library Association, www.ala.org/yalsa/booklists (accessed December 3, 2006).

9. "Get Matched with up to $3 Billion in Scholarships," FastWeb, www.fastweb.com/fastweb/register/start?ref=108145 (accessed July 28, 2006).

Glossary

advance (or *advance against royalties*): Money given to an author upfront, as a good-faith estimate of what the publisher feels is the minimum a book will earn back (author will not receive further royalties until the advance is earned back by the publisher)

agent (or *literary agent*): A person who represents authors and sells their works to publishing houses, negotiating the best possible rates for his or her clients

antagonist: The adversary to the main character of a story (usually the "bad guy")

anthology: A collection of literary, artistic, or musical works

autobiography: A story of one's life, where the author is the subject being written about

back story: Information given on what has happened up to the point of action being shown in a story or a film

bibliography: A list that supplies the sources where information in print or online was obtained

biography: A story about someone's life, written by a person other than the subject

blog: The abbreviation for "web log"; an interactive website anyone can create, with random thoughts, conversations, or journaling via the Internet

Cliffs Notes: A series of books that summarize the literary classics, meant to be used as a study guide or an accompaniment to the original works, *not* intended to replace reading the original text

copy: A reference to the text written in an advertisement or an article

curriculum vitae (CV): Latin word with meaning similar to résumé; summary or a set of accomplishments often supplied in a job interview

demographics: A statistical characterization of a population by means of categories such as income or age

dummy book: A mock-up of rough sketches and lines to show where text will be placed, showing how a book will be laid out

edit: To make necessary cuts, refinements, or additions to a literary piece in order to bring it to the highest quality it can achieve

first pages (or *proofs*): The first layout of a book with artwork, page numbers, sidebars, and footnotes, all laid out for the editor and/or author to read through and proof

first-person point of view: A narration style in which a main character tells the story from his or her own perspective

homophone: Words that sound the same but are spelled differently and have different meanings (example: to, too, two)

Ibid.: An abbreviation used in bibliographies to denote the source is exactly the same as the previous one cited

ISBN: The acronym for International Standard Book Number, which is a ten- or thirteen-digit (as of January 1, 2007) number that uniquely identifies books, e-books, and other book-like products internationally

kill fee: The portion of the negotiated fee that an author receives when a publisher purchases a manuscript for publication but ultimately does not publish it

Listserv: On the Internet, a group of persons all linked together via e-mail for a string of conversations, usually about an agreed-upon topic, where a "post" is sent to all people on the list to read and comment on

lyrics: The words that make up a song

manuscript: A document written and submitted with intent for publication

marketing: The process of highlighting a product's attributes; "getting the word out" about a product or service; making a product/service available for sale

media specialist: A type of teacher, usually a librarian, who works with multimedia equipment, helping to enhance class presentations and lectures

novel: A literary work of fiction made up of many pages telling a story

open mike: A venue for the public to share its own unpublished works, often held at a club, a coffee shop, or a bookstore

orphans and widows: When the end or beginning of a sentence or paragraph sits alone at the top or bottom of a column or page

outline: A list (often in chronological order) that lays out the plan for a book, article, or story

paid upon acceptance: A publisher will pay an author upon signing a contract

paid upon publication: A publisher will pay an author when the work is actually printed

paraphrase: To summarize a source rather than using direct quotes

permissions: Written approval to use already published or unpublished material from a source other than yourself

plagiarism: Using someone else's written material without citing the source, thus passing it off as one's own

plot: The main idea in a work of fiction; what a story is about

poetry slam: An open mike forum where people share their original works of poetry

point of view (POV): Who is telling the story (main character, objective observer, omniscient voice, etc.)

portfolio: A portable case that holds an artist's or illustrator's work for a potential employer to look through (similar to what writing samples or clips are for a writer)

print on demand: Also known as self-publishing or vanity press; when an author pays a printer to publish his or her book, versus seeking out a publisher to pay him or her for the right to publish the book

proposal: A presentation to promote a story or book; it may include a cover or query letter, an outline, and sample chapter or synopsis, anything to help showcase the author's idea to make a sale

quote: Saying exactly what another person said or wrote, verbatim

résumé: A list of professional accomplishments and work history

review copy: A complimentary (free) copy of a book sent to various people who may give their professional opinions about the work to the media

revise: To make changes to better your piece of writing

screenwriter: Person who writes scripts for motion pictures or television; often hired to turn popular plays or novels into screenplays

script: A story that uses dialogue, such as a television show, a motion picture, or a play

self-publishing: When an author pays a printer to publish his or her book, versus seeking out a publisher to pay him or her for the right to publish the book

setting: When and where a story takes place

sidebar: A box with text in a book or magazine article that is set apart from the regular text; it breaks up the bigger chunks of text with some quick fact or quote and/or artwork or graphic that enhances the text

songwriter: A person who writes the words and sometimes the music for songs, including songs for recordings, advertising jingles, and theatrical performances

synopsis: A summary of a book that briefly tells prospective publishers what they need to know without having to read an entire manuscript

technical writer: A writer that takes scientific and trade information and translates it into understandable "layman's terms"; he or she typically writes manuals, reports, or proposals

third-person point of view: A narration style in which someone outside the story is telling what happens

vanity press: A self-publishing house

voice: The style, tone, and other writing characteristics that are an author's own personal fingerprint on his or her writing

website: Information posted on the World Wide Web, or Internet, with an address that usually begins with "www"

work for hire: A contract for a writer to produce a manuscript for a flat fee without any further payments or royalties given

Resources and Contests

RESOURCES

Websites

Academy of American Poets (www.poets.org)

American Medical Writers Association (www.amwa.org)

American Society of Journalists and Authors (www.asja.org)

Authors League of America, Inc. (www.loc.gov/loc/cfbook/
   coborg/aut.html)

Chicago Women in Print (www.cwip.org)

Greeting Card Association (www.greetingcard.org)

National Association of Women Writers (www.naww.org)

National Black Writers & Artists Association (www.sbwaa
   .org)

National Education Writers Association (www.ewa.org)

National Writers' Association (www.nationalwriters.com)

National Writers' Union (www.nwu.org)

Romance Writers of America (www.rwanational.org)

Science-Fiction & Fantasy Writers of America, Inc. (www.sfwa
   .org)

Society of American Travel Writers (www.satw.org)

Society of Children's Book Writers & Illustrators (www.scbwi
   .org)

Writers Guild of America (www.wga.org)

Professional Organizations

Organizations for Writers

(Source: www.forwriters.com/groups.html; accessed January 10, 2007)

The American Society of Newspaper Editors, or ASNE, lists conferences for journalists and other useful information.

The Canadian Writers Association bridges the gap between a large national organization and the immediacy of local chapters.

The Horror Writers Association, or HWA, is a good place for those interested in that genre. They are the presenter of the Bram Stoker awards and have a variety of benefits for members.

The International Women's Writing Guild describes itself as being "a network for the personal and professional empowerment of women through writing."

The National Association of Science Writers is a potential resource to those engaged in writing about science. It also has a list of local chapters with local meetings.

National Writers Association is a nationwide organization with chapters from Hawaii to New York. It has a range of services available and has been in operation since 1937.

The National Writers Union is the trade union for freelance writers who publish or work in U.S. markets.

Romance Writers of America is "a non-profit professional/ educational association of 8,200 romance writers and other industry professionals." If romance is your area of specialty this may definitely be an organization to check out.

The Science Fiction & Fantasy Writers of America, Inc., is a vital resource as an organization. Among its many resources, including style guides and other sources, there is the *Warnings and Cautions for Writers*.

The *Writers Guild of America* is a tremendous resource site whether or not you are a member. There are requirements for admission and a rather large membership fee.

CONTESTS: A SELECTION

(Source: www.writing-world.com/contests; accessed July 13, 2006)

Art Deadlines List (artdeadlineslist.com)—This site has lots of art and writing contests.

Author Network Writing Contests (www.author-network .com/competition.html)—The majority of contests are for writers from the United Kingdom.

DMOZ Open Directory Project: Contests (dmoz.org/Arts/ Writers_Resources/Contests)

Freelance Writing (www.freelancewriting.com/writingcontests .php)

Google: Writers' Contests (directory.Google.com/Top/Arts/ Writers_Resources/Contests/)

Muse's Muse: Songwriting Contests (www.musesmuse.com/ contests.html)

National Press Photographer's Association Contests (www .nppa.org/competitions)—Students, professional journalists, and press photographers can enter contests featured at this site.

Poetry Machine: Awards and Contests (www.poetrymachine .com/link4.htm)

Sarah Kathryn's List of "Interesting Contests" (members .tripod.com/~SarahKat/deadlines.html)

Screenwriting Contests and Markets Online (www.moviebytes .com)—This site has links to show writing contests for screenwriters.

Screenwriting Contests Database (www.filmmakers.com/ contests/directory.htm)

Winning Writers (www.winningwriters.com)—This site offers tips and resources for writers of poetry and many other genres.

Writer's Nook News Contests Page (www.carlyphillips.com/ site/newsletter/contest-sign-up.html)—Multiple genres and categories are listed at this site.

Suggested Reading

Bauer, Marion Dane. *What's Your Story? A Young Person's Guide to Writing Fiction.* New York: Clarion Books, 1992.

Canfield, Jack, Mark Victor Hansen, and Bud Gardner. *Chicken Soup for the Writer's Soul: Stories to Open the Heart and Rekindle the Spirit of Writers.* Deerfield Beach, FL: Health Communications, Inc., 2000.

Cowden, Tami D., Caro Lafever, and Sue Viders. *The Complete Writer's Guide to Heroes & Heroines: Sixteen Master Archetypes.* Hollywood, CA: Lone Eagle Publishing Group, 2000.

Deval, Jacqueline. *Publicize Your Book! An Insiders Guide to Getting Your Book the Attention It Deserves.* New York: Berkley Publishing Group, 2003.

Frishman, Rick, and Robyn Freedman Spitzman (with Mark Steisel). *Author 101: Bestselling Book Publicity. The Insiders' Guide to Promoting Your Book—and Yourself.* Avon, MA: Adams Media, 2006.

Fulghum, Robert. *All I Really Need to Know I Learned in Kindergarten: Uncommon Thoughts on Common Things.* New York: Villard Books, 1990.

James-Enger, Kelly. *$ix Figure Freelancing: The Writer's Guide to Making More Money.* New York: Random House Reference, 2005.

Kelly, Pamela Glass. *First Time Authors: 64 Children's Writers First Published Pieces—with Author's & Editor's Comments.* West Redding, CT: Institute of Children's Literature, 2003.

Kelly, Pamela Glass, and Mary Spelman, eds. *From Inspiration to Publication: How to Succeed as a Children's Writer: Advice from 15 Award-Winning Writers*. West Redding, CT: Institute of Children's Literature, 2000.

King, Stephen. *On Writing: A Memoir of the Craft*. New York: Pocket Books, 2001.

McNiff, Marni, ed. *Book Markets for Children's Writers 2007*. West Redding, CT: Writer's Institute Publications, 2007.

O'Connor, Patricia. *Woe Is I: The Grammarphobe's Guide to Better English in Plain English*. New York: Riverhead Books, 2003.

Reeves, Diane Lindsey. *Career Ideas for Kids Who Like Writing*. New York: Checkmark Books, 1998.

Strunk, William, Jr., and E. B. White. *The Elements of Style*. 4th ed. Needham Heights, MA: Allyn & Bacon, 1999.

Truss, Lynne. *Eats, Shoots & Leaves: The Zero Tolerance Approach to Punctuation*. New York: Gotham Books, 2003.

Index

About the Author and Illustrator

Tina P. Schwartz is a freelance author from Grayslake, Illinois. Tina is a marketing consultant for eleven radio stations in the suburbs of Chicago and writes copy and voice ad, when not writing books. She is married with three children and is a self-proclaimed "tomboy" who loves babies, movies, and dogs.

Tina enjoys meeting many children during her school and library visits to promote her books, which include *Motocross Freestyle* (2004) and *Organ Transplants—A Survival Guide for the Entire Family: The Ultimate Teen Guide* (2005). She is excited to be doing teen author boot camps to accompany her new book, *Writing and Publishing: The Ultimate Teen Guide.*

C. E. Locander is a retired public relations executive whose nonfiction industrial stories have graced the pages of hundreds of periodicals. A self-taught illustrator, he is best know for his use of whimsical characters and vivid color. He has written and illustrated several children's picture books under the pen name "Professor Whimsey."

About the Author and Illustrator

A native of Chicago, Locander is a graduate in communications from the University of Illinois at Urbana. He resides in a suburb of Chicago with his wife, Mary, and their "wonder dog," Hobo, who is featured in a children's fable.